D1743770

The Transformation of a Skeptic

The Transformation of a Skeptic

A JEWISH PERSPECTIVE

Walter Orenstein

JASON ARONSON INC.
Northvale, New Jersey
Jerusalem

This book was set in 12 pt. Bell by Alpha Graphics of Pittsfield, NH, and printed and bound by Book-mart Press, Inc. of North Bergen, NJ.

10 9 8 7 6 5 4 3 2 1

Library of Congress Cataloging-in-Publication Data
Orenstein, Walter.
    The transformation of a skeptic : a Jewish perspective / by Walter
Orenstein.
       p. cm.
    Includes bibliographical references and index.
    ISBN 0-7657-6100-9
    1. Judaism. 2. Jewish way of life. I. Title.
BM561.074   1999   99-20640
                                              CIP

Printed in the United States of America on acid-free paper. For information and catalog write to Jason Aronson Inc., 230 Livingston Street, Northvale, NJ 07647-1726, or visit our website: www.aronson.com

To my dear mother,
Pauline Orenstein, of blessed memory,
who was never a skeptic.
She personified Jewish motherhood at its best.
Her love was limitless
and her encouragement inspired me
through the years
to study and to write.

Contents

Preface

Rabbi Elazar said: "Be eager to study Torah and know what answer to give to the nonbeliever."

(Ethics of the Fathers 2:19)

A prominent contemporary talmudic scholar relates that he was raised in a nontraditional home. His parents were great skeptics, and they trained him to be one as well. What they had no way of foreseeing was that he would become so great a skeptic that he grew to be skeptical of skepticism itself, which led him to embark on the road to becoming an observant Jew.

We are living in turbulent times. Society is bleeding, and no one seems to care. Concern for the feelings of others and responsibility for the welfare of one's fellow man has been relegated by many to the trash heap of discarded values. It's every man for himself today. Corruption has pervaded the highest echelons of government, and the masses, even in democracies like the United States, have become complacent. Crime is rampant the world over. From day to day new conflicts arise among neighboring countries, and the dark cloud of a catastrophic world war that would be more devastating than anything that has been witnessed by man since the beginning of civilization looms on the horizon. World peace as a goal that can be fulfilled in the foreseeable future fades with every passing day.

The masses of society plod along from one day to the next, each person absorbed in his personal routine of life. Disappointed in the failure of governments to create even a moderately content world, man has become despondent. He is overwhelmed by the situation, and he feels helpless to do anything about it, all the while knowing that he has no one but himself to blame. The moral and ethical values preached, at least venerated by previous generations as an ideal toward which to strive, have been summarily dismissed by skeptics and replaced with hedonism. But this icon of modernity has yielded only bitter fruit, for uncloseted, unhampered, and unashamed decadence prevails among the masses of today's society with virtually no outcry or protest.

In their heart of hearts, many confirmed skeptics are seeking the road that leads back home. They are ready, even anxious to reexamine the values that they and their parents and so many others of the past generation had summarily rejected. It is only necessary to approach them in the proper way to gain their listening ear.

A whole community of Jews from the former Soviet Union have come to the United States to seek a better way of life. They are well educated in their chosen professions but totally ignorant of the tenets of Judaism. They have been trained to be skeptics insofar as religion is concerned. The influx of these immigrants presents an unprecedented opportunity for Jewish outreach, and it behooves us to take advantage of this opportunity before it is too late.

Outreach is a monumental undertaking. It is difficult, frustrating, and terribly time-consuming. It demands persistence and patience. The responsibility is, indeed, an awesome one, but the reward is well worth the effort. Let us not forget the words of our sages: "Whosoever destroys a single soul of Israel, Scripture imputes guilt to him as though he had destroyed a complete world, and whosoever preserves a single soul of Israel, Scripture ascribes merit to him as though he had preserved a complete world" (Sanhedrin 37a).

I would like to express my sincerest appreciation to my wife, Nellie, who edited the manuscript and offered many helpful suggestions. Her patience and encouragement have always been a source of inspiration to me in our life together and particularly in my literary endeavors.

Introduction

I was halfway into my lecture on Jewish values in an Adult Education Lecture Series I had been giving at a prominent Manhattan synagogue when the door opened and a young man rather sheepishly entered the room. He asked if he could sit in on my lecture though he had not registered for the series. "Why not," I said, "you don't look like a heckler." Permission granted, he took a seat in the back of the room, and I continued my lecture. My guest listened intently. From time to time I would focus on him, and he would release a taunting smile as if to say, "Give me a break, Rabbi. You don't really believe this stuff, do you?" At the end of the lecture, I approached him, and the following conversation took place.

"I'm glad to see that you have an interest in learning about Judaism. Do you have any Jewish background?" I inquired.

"A smattering," he answered. "I was forced to attend religious school for a few years in preparation for my Bar Mitzvah, but nothing more. The truth of the matter is that I'm really not interested in acquiring such knowledge. Judaism is a relic of the past replete with primitive beliefs and practices. It has no place in our modern scientific world."

"I see that you are somewhat of a skeptic," I countered. "What is it that brought you to my lecture? Surely you can find a better way to spend your time."

"You're right, Rabbi. I am a skeptic, but a good friend of mine told me to come. To use his expression, he has 'found religion.' He urged me to attend one of your lectures, and listen with an open mind. Perhaps I, too, would find religion. To be honest with you Rabbi, I had little inclination to do so, but he insisted and I acquiesced. So here I am."

"And . . . ?" I inquired.

"And, with all due respect Rabbi, I really can't buy any of this religion you're trying to sell. You talk about prayer. To whom? There is no proof for the existence of God. Prayer is an exercise in futility, a waste of precious time."

"What is your name?" I asked.

"My name is Martin," he answered.

"I'm curious, Martin. What is your profession?"

"I'm a physician," he answered. "I heal the sick and I save lives. I make a very important contribution to the welfare of society, and I'm proud of it."

"Indeed, you should be," I responded. "Healing the sick is a noble calling, particularly when it is a labor of love. I'm sure that you're quite good at your work. But tell me something, how long did you study to get your degree?"

"I studied for four years in medical school," he answered, "and took a two-year residency in internal medicine, after which I took an additional residency in cardiology. Then I opened my practice."

"That's certainly a long ordeal," I said, "but then I'm sure you feel that it was worth it."

"Worth it? Unquestionably! My profession is my livelihood, and I love it," he said. "I would have studied another six years had it been required."

"Really!" I said. "You give great importance to choosing a livelihood, and rightly so. But tell me Martin, how much thought and importance have you given to choosing a *way of life?*"

Martin was puzzled by my words. "Rabbi," he said, "I don't understand what you mean."

"What I mean, Martin, is the following.

"Most decent human beings feel that they have a responsibility to contribute to the welfare of society. Many fulfill that responsibility in their chosen profession. Your contribution is being made in the field of medicine; mine is in Jewish education. You save lives, so do I. You save their bodies; I save their souls. Be that as it may, to my way of thinking there is more to life than the pursuit of a profession or a career: friendship, marriage, and raising a family. People are involved in important ethical and moral decisions every day of their lives. Wouldn't you agree that these decisions should be based on some sort of standard?"

"Yes, Rabbi, I would. But I want you to know that I have no problem making ethical and moral decisions."

"That's good to know, Martin, but tell me: do you have some standard, some objective code of ethics that guides you in these decisions?"

"No, I do not," he said. "To be perfectly honest with you, I don't think any code of ethics made by man can be truly objective. I make my own decisions. In matters of ethics, I rely on gut feelings to tell me what to do."

"I agree with you on one point, Martin. No code of ethics created by man can be truly objective. The 'ought' and 'ought not' of human behavior when left to man becomes highly subjective. You rely on gut feelings; others act on personal prejudices; some let financial considerations determine their behavior in a given situation. Behavior regarded by some to be highly unethical is considered perfectly acceptable by others. Lacking objectivity, ethics becomes an utter sham. This is one of the great dilemmas in the world. The lack of an objective ethical system is responsible for man's inhumanity toward man since the beginning of human history. It is the underlying cause of every war."

"Well, Rabbi, there is very little one can do about that. We can't change the world."

"Perhaps not, Martin; but we can change ourselves. There is an important Jewish book called *Ethics of the Fathers* in which it is written: 'In a place where there are no men strive to be a man' (2:6). Swimming with the current is no great feat; swimming against it, is an act of courage. A great sage once mused that when he was young he set out to change the world. When he got a little older he realized that changing the world was an unrealistic goal so he focused on his immediate neighborhood. Eventually he came to realize that even this was much too formidable an undertaking so he decided to concentrate on himself. He became a great teacher and rabbinic decisor. His books on Jewish law and Jewish ethics became the standard code of practice for Ashkenazic Jews. So you see, in the end he accomplished much of his original goal, for his writings have had a positive effect on millions of Jews the world over. He swam against the current and reached his destination. His name is Rabbi Israel Meir HaCohen, known to the world as the *Hafetz Hayyim.*

"Now let me repeat my question, Martin. How much time and thought have you given to your chosen way of life?"

"Quite frankly Rabbi, I guess I just went along with the way my friends and colleagues live," he answered. "I really never gave the matter any formal thought."

"What about religion? You claim that it is a relic of the past, that it is irrelevant in today's times," I countered. "Tell me how intensively you studied Jewish law and philosophy, and what it was that brought you to this conclusion?"

"To be truthful, Rabbi, I don't really know much about Judaism," he said. "I guess you could say that my Bar Mitzvah was my graduation. I never looked at a Jewish book from that day on. Nevertheless, from the little I do know about Judaism I find it to be replete with superstitions and false notions. The notion that Jews are the 'chosen people' and the blatant prejudice of Jews against Gentiles is responsible for anti-Semitism in the world. Judaism is irrational, and the rulings of the Rabbis on matters of crucial importance today are the result of whim rather than logical thinking. To be honest with you, I'm too sophisticated to accept a religion based more on magic than on reason. I reject Judaism as a life style. Besides, I can't see how any Jew today can accept God or Judaism after the Holocaust of European Jewry."

"Martin, I'm disappointed in you, and it is not because you reject Judaism. It is because you have formed opinions, or shall I say prejudices, that are based on ignorance rather than on careful investigation. This is strange behavior for a man of science. Your rather flippant approach to choosing a lifestyle is also quite disconcerting to me. How does a man of your education, intellect, and scientific training reject the way of life into which he was born without even becoming familiar with its teachings? Are you not aware of the fact that some of the most brilliant Jewish minds in today's society, men and women in every field of endeavor, believe in God and are committed to traditional Judaism? Do you know that there is an organization called the 'Orthodox Jewish Scientists,' some of whose members are world renowned in their field of expertise? Do you believe that all these men and women are deluding themselves? Surely you owe it to yourself to investigate the doctrines of Judaism before rejecting them? Doesn't something as important as a lifestyle demand more careful consideration?

"Isn't Judaism entitled to be heard? Should it not be given a fair trial before you sentence it to death? Perhaps it is merely a relic of the past, a primitive set of beliefs and superstitions to be relegated to the trash basket of discarded notions, as you say. On the other hand, it might have something of value to offer. Surely you would agree that the only way this can be determined is through careful study and investigation."

"Well, to be completely honest with you, Rabbi, I don't really have the time or the inclination to study Judaism," he answered. "I'm happy with my present lifestyle. I believe that for all intents and purposes I'm a good person. I love my fellow man, and I'm honest and fair in the way I treat people. I love and respect my parents. I'm married to a loving wife whom I cherish, and I have a wonderful family. True, I don't practice Judaism, and perhaps you would not consider me a Jew, but what's wrong with my lifestyle?"

"You are making a common mistake, Martin. You are as much a Jew as I am. Every person born of a Jewish mother is a Jew. What's more, whether you are willing to acknowledge it or not, you are a practicing Jew. From what you have just told me, I know that there are at least a dozen *mitzvot* (commandments) that you are fulfilling by your lifestyle without even being aware of it, and I'm sure that there are many more."

Martin looked a bit puzzled. My last statement startled him. He paused for a moment, but then got up and walked toward the door. His hand on the doorknob, he paused again and turned to me.

"This is too much for me, Rabbi. I really don't want to think about it. Glad to have made your acquaintance." He turned away again and left.

"Well, at least I made the effort," I said to myself. I gathered my papers together and prepared to leave when the door opened. It was Martin.

"I really don't want to take up your time, Rabbi," he said, "but your last statement intrigued me. I can't get it out of my mind. What has my integrity, my marriage, and the love of my children to do with Judaism?"

"A great deal, Martin," I said. "As I told you, these values that you have committed yourself to and hold so dear are Jewish values. Many of the commandments found in the Torah have been adopted by society as part of its code of ethics, at least in theory. You have been exposed to some of these values, and you have chosen to incorporate them into your lifestyle. What you do not realize is that society has been conditioned by the Jewish religion. Be that as it may Martin, I don't want to bore you with ancient notions. My best wishes to you for a successful future as a physician. Perhaps some day we will meet again, when you have more time, and we will discuss these matters at length."

"Just one minute, Rabbi, are you implying that I have been conditioned by religion? I have no religion. I have freely chosen the ethics by which I live. If I have been influenced by anything it is the secular society."

"Yes, Martin, it is the secular society that has influenced you. But what has influenced the secular society? In 1972 a very important book was published in England called *The Disputation*. For personal reasons the author wished to remain anonymous. I strongly recommend that you read it one day when you have some time. But to answer your question, let me quote one passage from the book:

> The fact that there are to be found agnostics and atheists of high moral life does not invalidate the claim of religion. One might just as well argue that work is not essential to the production of wealth because there are people who have wealth without ever having done any work. We live after all in a world that has been fructified for thousands of years by religious ideas, and in such a world the fruits of religion are sufficiently rich and attractive to be shared by people who have neither worked nor done anything to contribute directly to their growth. Whether morality could exist independently of all religious influences has yet to be discovered. The religious impetus of hundreds of generations may carry people along the path of moral life for some time, even as the train glides along after the steam is shut off; but without the driving force of religion stoppage is inevitable, and with that stoppage end the moral and spiritual values of life. [p. 55]

"In essence, Martin, the ethics and morality of religion have shaped the secular society, and as you yourself have admitted, it is the secular society that has molded your value system."

"All right, Rabbi, you win," he said. "You have aroused my curiosity. If you can spare the time and are willing to teach me, I would like to meet with you for six months on a regular basis to study the principles of Judaism. But I must warn you from the start, it is curiosity alone that motivates me. I'm not at all interested in becoming a practicing Jew. Judaism is just not for me, so don't try to convert me."

"Agreed, Martin, agreed," I said. "Now tell me, what is your Hebrew name?"

"Moshe," he said unhesitantly. "But why do you ask?"

"No special reason," I answered. "Perhaps it's mere curiosity. Call me next week, Moshe, and we'll set a time and place for our learning sessions."

I met with Moshe twice a week for six months. There were times when we studied together until late hours of the night, but it was a labor of love. In our "give and take" sessions, we touched on many of the essential principles of Judaism. The material that follows has been taken from these sessions.

Session I
The Jewish
Understanding
of God

I am certain that you will fully agree with me, Moshe, that the construction of an edifice begins by laying the foundation. The foundation enables one to build upward. We shall do the same with the construction of the edifice of Judaism. We will begin with the foundation. There is unanimity among the sages that nothing is more basic to Judaism than the principle of the existence of God. Without God there is no revelation. Without revelation there is no Torah, and without Torah there is no Judaism. Maimonides, the twelfth-century talmudist, philosopher, and physician, was a prolific writer. The *Mishneh Torah*, his *magnum opus* on Jewish law, begins with the words:

> The foundation of foundations and the firmest pillar of all wisdom is to know that there is a First Being who brought every existing thing to be and that all existing things from heaven and earth and from between them, could not be but for the truth of His own Being.

Proofs for the Existence of God

It is interesting to note that in another of Maimonides' works, *Sefer ha-Mitzvot*, where he lists and briefly explains all of the 613 commandments of Judaism, he speaks of "believing" in the existence of God rather than "knowing." Now it has been well established that Maimonides was never redundant in his works; his language was precise. As one would expect in a book of law, every word was relevant to the law or philosophical principle he was discussing. Why then does he differ in his reference to the principle of God's existence from one book to the other? Perhaps what Maimonides had in mind is that one must believe in the existence of God with the same certainty with which one accepts factual information, truths that can be verified at will. The argument of the nonbeliever is well-known: If there really were a God, He would see to it that people would have no doubts on the matter. A true God would have made Himself known to humanity in no uncertain terms rather than rely on so-called miracles to establish His existence, for miracles have not convinced those who did not experience them. Considering that this has not happened, how can we believe that there is a God?

I am sure that you are aware that philosophers throughout the ages have attempted to prove the existence of God by reason. Yes, through the generations, many so-called "proofs" have been offered. Let me briefly outline the most common among them.

The Cosmological Proof

This proof argues that an analysis of the nature of things reveals that everything has a cause. When I see a table, I know that it was caused by a carpenter who made it. When I observe the trees in the forest, I know that they were caused by the interaction of seeds with the earth in which they were planted. When I see a child, I know that the child was brought into the world by its parents. This means that all existing things are dependent on other existing things. This being the case, there must be a first cause that is not itself caused and has set this pattern of nature into motion, for a thing that is dependent on others cannot be a first cause. This first or original cause is called "God."

The Ontological Proof

This proof asserts that the definition of God, by all who use that term, is "the being greater than which nothing can be conceived." As such, it is argued, God must exist. For were He not to exist, one could logically conceive of a more perfect being, namely, a God Who has the quality of existence.

The Teleological Proof

Lastly, there is what is commonly referred to as "The Argument from Design." This is perhaps the oldest but certainly the most widely quoted proof and the one that has met with the least resistance among the philosophers. Indeed, even the renowned German philosopher Immanuel Kant considered it with respect. It purports the following: Study of the universe leads to the conclusion that there is order in nature, a design or pattern in operation. Philo, the first-century Alexandrian philosopher, put it very beautifully:

> Who can look upon statues or paintings without thinking at once of a sculptor or painter? Who can see clothes or ships or houses without getting the idea of a weaver and a shipwright and a house builder? And when one enters a well-ordered city in which the arrangements for civil life are very admirably managed, what else will he suppose but that this city is directed by good rulers? So then he who comes to . . . this world, and beholds hills and plains teeming with animals and plants, the rivers spring-fed or winter torrents, streaming along, the seas with their expanses, the air with its happily tempered phases, the yearly seasons passing into each other . . . must he not naturally or rather necessarily gain the conception of the Maker, Father, and Ruler also . . . in this way we have the conception of the existence of God.[1]

There is a purposive mind that has created, designed, and set the universe into motion, so goes the theory; this purposive mind we call God.

In past generations, the contention of orderliness in nature was based simply on observation; today our observation has been infinitely enhanced by sophisticated technology. With the advent of instruments such as spectroscopes, radio telescopes, and microwave communication, order in the universe is a given. Astronomers now tell us that our solar system is just one among a hundred billion in a galaxy that is one of several hundred billion in the universe. Their observations confirm that the universe is a very highly ordered system, much more highly ordered than could possibly be expected from a mere chance "big bang."[2]

It is no secret that in the past, science and religion have disagreed on the matter of the origin of the universe. In recent years, however, there has been a distinct change in the thinking of many prominent physicists.[3] They are coming to the conclusion that matter was probably created *ex nihilo* (from nothing) in less than a second's time. This is not to say that they accept the notion of a Creator. Nevertheless, when other developments in theoretical physics are also taken into account, the argument for an intelligent and providential Creator becomes even stronger. In point of fact, forty percent of American scientists today believe in a God to Whom they can pray.[4] Of course, creation *ex nihilo* is a fundamental principle in Judaism.

The Statistical Arguments

Now we should also consider several statistical arguments that the world did not come into existence by chance. Let us begin with a simple illustration. Take ten pieces of paper, number them from one to ten, put them in a box, and shuffle them. If you were then to draw them out one by one, we know mathematically that the chance of drawing number one first is one in ten; of drawing one and two in succession is one in a hundred; one, two, and three in succession, one in a thousand. The chances of drawing all ten in succession are one in ten billion.

Now think of the planet earth. So many conditions are necessary for the formation of life on this planet that there is not one chance in billions that it could have happened by accident. Consider this: the earth rotates on its axis one thousand miles per hour. If it were to rotate at only one hundred miles per hour our days and nights would be ten times longer, in which case the sun would in all likelihood burn up our crops, and anything left would freeze at night. If the crust of the earth were ten feet thicker, we would have no oxygen and we would die. There are many other scientific examples of the precision of nature in the world. Viewed from a purely mathematical perspective, life on our planet could not possibly have originated by chance.

Needless to say, none of these proofs or arguments are definitive, but they certainly offer "food for thought." In point of fact, there is no definitive proof known to man for the existence of God. We will later address the matter of whether it would be in any way beneficial to man were he able to construct such a proof.

Be that as it may, given that there is no definitive proof known to man for the existence of God, on what basis should he accept it as a fact? Even more important, how can we build a whole lifestyle on the assumption that God exists, that He is concerned with man, and that He has revealed the Torah for man's benefit when we are not even sure that He exists?

Essentially, we can do so on the basis of Jewish tradition. By Jewish tradition, we mean the faithful transmission of doctrines from one generation to the next. These doctrines date back to biblical times. They were revealed by God to Moses, our teacher, who taught them to the people of his generation. Subsequently, they were transmitted by parents to children and by teachers to students from generation to generation. We accept these doctrines as absolute truths, for we firmly believe that on matters that constitute the essence of life a parent will not lie to his child nor a teacher to his students.

God's Concern for Man

Admittedly, man has failed to produce a definitive proof for the existence of God. Yet even if it could be established definitively that God exists, this fact alone would have little impact on our way of thinking and the choices we make in life unless it could likewise be established that God is the Creator and Master of the world, that He is concerned with its destiny and the destiny of its inhabitants, and that He has at some point in history revealed that concern to man. In a word . . . providence! Reason is merely man's faculty of understanding. Proof that God exists cannot in and of itself induce obedience to God and to His Law. The late Eliezer Berkovits, one of the most outstanding Orthodox Jewish thinkers of our generation, writes:

> Reason may tell the difference between right and wrong; perhaps even the difference between good and evil. It cannot, however, provide the obligation for doing good and eschewing evil. The source of all obligation is will, and the motivation of a will is desire. . . . Reason may describe what is: it cannot prescribe what ought to be, except hypothetically.[5]

Quite frankly, were it not for providence, it would not and could not make an iota of difference to man whether or not God exists.

In Maimonides' *Thirteen Principles of the Jewish Faith*, both creation and providence are included. In a creed that was subsequently formulated to be recited by Jews daily, we find:

> I believe with perfect faith that the Creator, blessed be His Name, is the Author and Guide of everything that has been created, and that He alone has made, does make, and will make all things.

> I believe with perfect faith that the Creator, blessed be His Name, rewards those that keep His commandments, and punishes those that transgress them.

Miracles Past and Present

By providence, we mean God's concern for the welfare and the preservation of humanity. How do we know of His concern? Are there witnesses to God's "hand" in history in ancient or in modern times? Most certainly there are! We have documents, primary sources, that reveal that God is concerned with man and that He demonstrated that concern by communicating with our patriarchs Abraham, Isaac, and Jacob; with Moses and Joshua, King David and King Solomon, as well as with the prophets of later years.

I believe that it is important at this point to identify the primary sources of which we are speaking. The Bible consists of twenty-four books in which are depicted events in history, commencing with Creation until the early part of the Second Commonwealth, a span of almost 3,500 years. In Hebrew, the Bible is called *Tenakh*, an acronym for *Torah, Neviim, Ketuvim*, which are its three components, that is, Torah, Prophets, and Writings. The Torah, which was revealed by God to Moses and consists of five books, ranks highest in authority; the Prophets, consisting of eight books, rank second; and the Writings, consisting of eleven books, rank third.

A mere perusal of these sources reveals that God performed miracles for the people of Israel: He brought plagues upon the Egyptians and redeemed the Israelites from slavery. He split the Red Sea and revealed the Law on Mount Sinai. These are but a few manifestations of God's concern for man.

You say that these things happened in the ancient past, that we can only be sure about things that happen in the present. Then let us speak of the present. Look at a map of the countries in the Mideast. Trace the vast lands of Saudi Arabia, Egypt, Syria, Iraq, and Iran, and take note of their size. One cannot help but be impressed. Can you find the country of Israel on the coastline of the Mediterranean Sea? Compared to these countries, it is a mere speck on the map. This little country, smaller than the state of New Jersey, has stood up against the vast armies of the Mideast in three major wars and has emerged victorious.

It was the first day of the war in 1967. I recall vividly what some of the most respected authorities on war strategy in the United States were saying: Israel is outnumbered in both armies and equipment. Their technology is light-years behind that of the Arab nations. It is a hopeless situation. There is not a chance in a million that this small country will survive the war. Victory? It would take nothing short of a miracle. We were all devastated. What would happen to our brethren who had chosen to live in this beautiful land and defend it against its enemies? What would happen to the dream we held through two thousand years of exile? As we all know, in six days the war was over. The vast Arab armies were defeated, Israel emerged victorious. How? Why? Only a prejudiced mind would fail to recognize this as providence, the intervention of God in the historical process.

For half a century, the Arabs have threatened the annihilation of the State of Israel and have gathered support for their cause from almost every country in the world. Meanwhile, Israel grows stronger and ever more prosperous. In point of fact, for two thousand years the world has been trying to annihilate the Jewish people but has failed to do so. Why? Are we not one of the smallest nations in the world? How have we been able to escape when mighty nations like Greece and Rome have virtually vanished from civilization? Is this not evidence of a providential God Who is concerned for His people Israel, who have dedicated their lives to bringing His message to the world?

Not to be passed over or underrated is testimony from personal experience. Some of us have experienced God's intervention in our lives in ways that defy any other reasonable explanation: being the sole survivor in an accident; spontaneous reversal and cure from a disease that was supposedly terminal. Many who were inmates in the death camps during World War II tell stories of how they survived, a series of events that defy rational explanation and must be classified as acts of Divine providence. For these individuals no further proof for the existence of God is necessary. In point of fact, for such individuals proofs are irrelevant.

The Credibility of the Sources

Let us now return to our discussion on the credibility of the Bible, for it is the primary source upon which our tradition is based. Given that Jewish tradition has been faithfully transmitted, how does one know that the primary sources upon which these traditions are based are credible? Could the Bible not be the work of wise men with good intentions, good imaginations, and a gift for writing rather than the revealed word of God?

Perhaps the best answer to this question is given by Eliezer Berkovits.[6] An event may be considered within the realm of possibility, says Berkovits, if it is neither a logical contradiction nor a practical impossibility. An encounter between God and man is not a logical impossibility for there is nothing in the term *God* or the term *man* that would contradict the concept of such an encounter, and it is not self-contradictory. Is the encounter a practical impossibility? Here Berkovits explains:

> There is nothing in our experience to justify a statement that an event, never observed by us—especially when it purports to be different in kind from all other occurrences of our experience—could never have taken place. Experience, by its very nature, may only reveal what is, but not what has to be or cannot be.[7]

One must admit, however, that there is a wide gap between accepting the possibility that an event has happened and accepting as fact that it did actually happen. We must therefore address the matter of credibility more directly.

The Bible is history, and as we know, history is based on eyewitness accounts. The trustworthiness of the record of historical events is determined by the trustworthiness of the witnesses. The higher their ethical and moral stature, the more reliable their written word. Who were the eyewitnesses to biblical history? They were the prophets from Abraham to Malachi. They were the wisest men of Israel, yet they did not seek position or power. Only because the charge to speak in God's

Name was thrust upon them did they consent to do so, and when they spoke the word of God—quite often a message of impending doom— they feared neither the people nor the kings. Their wisdom and their insight, which are revealed in their writings, marked them as men and women of the highest ethical and moral fiber. Their ethical doctrines are unequaled by anything written to this day.

These were the witnesses of biblical history. Their integrity is impeccable; their trust in God and their unqualified obedience to His word are unparalleled in human history. But what is perhaps most important to keep in mind is that they spoke in the name of God. Indeed, the encounter with God is the *conditio sine qua non* of all prophecy, but can we trust them? Can we rely on their written testimony to God's concern for man? Put eloquently by Berkovits:

> If these men were misleading their people knowingly, there is no honesty on earth. But if they were themselves deluded, then we have to conclude that the condition of man in general must be one of essential delusion and one may not trust one's own eyes.[8]

Ample consideration in this regard must be given to what is perhaps the greatest event in human history, namely, the revelation of the Law on Mount Sinai. Whatever reservations skeptics may have concerning the credibility of an individual prophet's encounter with God, such concerns are irrelevant when the event was witnessed by more than six hundred thousand men plus women and children. The late Rabbi Dr. Isidore Epstein confirms this important point:

> But if an individual, however exalted and perfect, might be the victim of delusions and hallucinations, and believe that God had spoken to him, it is another thing to say that the collective consciousness of a whole people should fall victim to the same self-delusion and hallucination.[9]

The authenticity of the Torah we possess today and its immutability are listed as the eighth and ninth principles in Maimonides' "Thirteen Principles of the Jewish Faith."

> I believe with perfect faith that the whole Torah, now in our possession, is the same that was given to Moses our teacher, peace be unto him.

> I believe with perfect faith that the Torah will not be changed, and that there will never be any other law from the Creator, blessed be His Name.

The agnostic would say that since neither God's existence nor the notion that He revealed His word to man can be proved definitively, we should suspend judgment on the matter and assume a position of neutrality. From a practical standpoint, however, neutrality is meaningless. Suspension of judgment means suspension of action, and suspension of action means rejection. Judaism is first and foremost a religion of action; beliefs must be complemented by behavior that conforms with those beliefs, otherwise they are of little significance. In short, neutrality is tantamount to rejection.

The Danger of Relative Ethics

When we last spoke, Moshe, you told me that you are an ethical and moral person, and that you do not need an objective code or standard to guide you in determining what action to take in a given situation. You said that you leave it to your gut feelings to make the proper judgment. I then told you that many people live by that rule, and that living by one's "gut feelings" is the root of all evil in the world. Let us develop this point a bit more fully.

Every human being has his conception of reality. Some of what he believes is based on what he has been taught, some on what he has learned from books, and some is based on personal experience. We all live in accordance with our perception of things. If we believe in a providential God Whose concern for man has manifested itself in the revelation of the Torah, a system of absolute ethics by which man can live a dignified life, at peace with himself and in harmony with his fellow man, then self-preservation, if nothing else, will motivate us to live by that system. If, on the other hand, we do not believe in God or providence and posit that the world exists and operates purely by chance, without morality and without purpose, then with very few exceptions, people will ultimately live selfishly, even brutally. The point is made succinctly by our sages. Hananya ben Kinai said: "It is written: 'When a person sins and commit a trespass against the Lord by dealing deceitfully with his fellow man . . .' (Leviticus 5:21). No man deals falsely with his neighbor until he denies first the Root [God]."[10] N. Berdyaev writes: "When a man denies and effaces the Divine image in himself, he cannot long preserve the human image, and the animal then predominates in him. By losing the support of God he submits himself to the unstable elements of the world, which must sooner or later submerge him."[11]

One need look no further than Nazi Germany from 1939 to 1945, the years of the Holocaust, to see where disbelief or the distortion of beliefs can lead. At the time, Germany was considered to be among the most civilized and intellectually sophisticated countries in the world. The German people were highly skilled and highly educated as well. They were not savages; they only behaved like savages. It was their distorted immoral philosophy that led them to commit the most barbaric acts of torture and murder known to man. Man, the most intelligent and the most sophisticated of God's creations, can be more dangerous to himself and do more harm to others than the most vicious beasts of the jungle. The lesson of Nazi Germany must be engraved in the mind of every civilized human being for all time, never to be forgotten.

You believe that you are free to make ethical and moral judgments. Correct! You are truly free to make choices. Now you say that gut feelings are your guide. Be honest with yourself. Are you always objective in your judgment? Are your gut feelings based on fact or fiction, on ethics or prejudice, on magnanimity or selfishness? Can you be sure in any given situation that self-interest has not affected your judgment?

Consider this: If you have the right to make decisions on the basis of gut feelings, so must every other human being have that right. Now even if one were to assume that your judgment in the ethical situations with which you have been faced in life has consistently been proper, that is, it was neither harmful to yourself nor to anyone else involved in those situations, can such an assumption be made of everyone else in society? Of course not! How then can we leave ethics and morality to gut feelings?

History has taught us that when a society has formulated and accepted a moral standard or a constitution, most members of that society will maintain at least a semblance of morality even if the standard has been violated by many, so long as times are good and everyone is more or less content with his lot in life. Should the tides turn, however, and discontent set in, morality will slowly fall by the wayside and hatred and cruelty will take over. Furthermore, Eliezer Berkovits writes:

If there is no possibility for a transcendental value reference . . . and man alone is the creator of values, who is to determine what the values are going to be? . . . Man of course. But which man? Man as such, in the abstract, as a norm, does not exist. . . . There are only people . . . with different temperaments, varied desires, and manifold self-created goals which set them at cross purposes with each other. . . . Some like to side with the persecuted; others enjoy cherry pie, while others again find meaning in an otherwise absurd universe by feeding the crematoria with human bodies. In a universe in which all values are based on human choice and decision, anything may become such a value.[12]

Belief in God and morality have always gone hand in hand in Judaism. Even before the revelation of the Torah, when Abraham was asked by Avimelekh why he had insisted that Sarah was his sister, he responded, "For I thought surely the fear of God is not in this place, and they will slay me for my wife's sake."[13] On these words Rabbi Samson Raphael Hirsch writes:

You have the same laws and rules and order as everywhere else. Only, I could not assume that here, more than everywhere else, the fear of God prevails . . . which forbids me voluntarily to dishonor and which should forbid you to touch the wife of a stranger or to kill him should he dare to offer resistance to your immoral customs.[14]

The Rationale for Absolute Ethics

What is the reason for the close association between belief in God and morality?

The observant Jew accepts God as the Supreme Being of the universe, "the sheltering Rock perfect in all His works," Who is concerned with the world. He also accepts the principle that God is concerned with the world, that He has manifested His concern by revealing the Torah, a code of ethics and morality that, by nature of the fact that it is God's creation, is flawless and eternal. The Jew's commitment to the Torah comes out of a sense of awe and reverence for God, to be sure, but also out of a sense of responsibility to create the best possible society. For he knows that adherence to *mitzvot* will bring peace and harmony to the world.

The Talmud teaches: "All commands left to the heart are adjoined [in the Torah] to the words 'You shall fear your God.'"[15] What the sages meant by "commands left to the heart" is, of course, the ethics and morality of the Torah. The words "You shall fear your God" can be taken in two ways: the lower level of fear of God is in reality fear of punishment from God; the higher level is awe of God and reverence. In *Ethics of the Fathers*, the talmudic treatise on ethics, we find the principle: "Reflect upon three things and you will not come within the power of sin: know what is above you, a seeing eye and a hearing ear, and all your deeds written in a book."[16]

In a world where power politics rule, where from a practical standpoint self-interest, rather than honesty, is the best policy, any man-made system of ethics is suspect. Altruism is indeed a noble virtue, but it is seldom the sole motivating force behind man's behavior. Consciously or subconsciously, the old cliché "What's in it for me?" plays a prominent role in most of the decisions people make. Belief in a providential God Who monitors man's behavior and rewards and punishes him accordingly can be a strong deterrent to immorality. Most of us need a policeman to keep us in line. True, fear is not the ideal way to induce obedience, but it does usually work.

In conclusion: We have established that there is no definitive proof for the existence of God, but there are several good arguments from both the philosophical and the scientific perspectives that present a formidable challenge to the atheist and the agnostic. In order for God to be relevant to man, however, He must be a providential God Who is concerned with man. Providence is a fundamental principle of the Jewish religion. The objective student of Jewish history must admit that from time to time God has manifested His concern for the Jewish people by intervening in the process of history on their behalf. At times, what was involved was their very survival. But He has also shown His concern by revealing His word to the prophets of old. The revelation sine qua non took place in biblical times on Mount Sinai before more than a million people.

All of this is recorded in the Bible, which is composed of the Torah, the Prophets, and the Writings. Like all historical works, the credibility of the Bible is based on the credibility of its authors. There is no doubt that the prophets were individuals of the highest ethical and moral character. They profess to have spoken in the name of God, and we have no reason to doubt or even to question the truth of their testimony.

Be that as it may, there is a more practical reason for accepting the existence of a providential God Who revealed the Torah to the people of Israel. Acceptance inspires commitment. Commitment to the ethical and moral principles of the Torah are a strong inducement for personal morality. History will testify to the fact that man-made ethical systems have not been very effective. For despite man's professed concern for his fellow man, in the final analysis the quest for personal gain prevails. Selfishness prevails over altruism, with most people, and malevolence overrides mercy and kindness.

There is an exception to what we have designated as the rule in society, and it is statistically verifiable. Although the observant Jewish community is not free from crimes of an ethical and moral nature committed against society—every human being has his or her weakness—on a day-to-day basis there are less crimes of this sort among observant Jews than in any other segment of society. This variance must be attributed at least to some extent to the fear of Divine retribution.

When we first met, Moshe, you said that you felt that decisions on Jewish law were made by the rabbis rather arbitrarily. Although this didn't really make any difference to you since you are not committed to Judaism, you gave me the impression that you were bothered by it, nonetheless. Knowing your academic and cultural background, I feel that this may have played a major role in your decision not to commit to Judaism, so I decided to devote our next session to a discussion on how decisions in Jewish law are made.

Session II
Adventures in
Rabbinic Reasoning

The first time we met, Moshe, you told me that religion is based on superstition and false notions, that its tenets are irrational, and decisions in Jewish law are made on whim rather than on reason. Nothing could be further from the truth, and I would like to take you on an adventure in rabbinic reasoning today to prove my point.

The Oral and Written Law

Let us begin by understanding the significance of the terms "Oral" and "Written" Law. As we have already indicated, there are two parts to the "Law" that was communicated by God to Moses: the Written Law and the Oral Law. When Moses was about to depart from this world, he wrote the Written Law on scrolls and gave copies of it to the twelve tribes of Israel. One copy was put in the Holy Ark to be kept for posterity. The Oral Law, as its name indicates, was to remain in oral form. It consists of interpretations of the Written Law. Often very general and at times even ambiguous, the Written Law would be unintelligible to us were it not for the interpretations that are part of the Oral Law.

Considering this, for one to approach the Written Law without a thorough background in the Oral Law and its methods would be, to say the least, shoddy scholarship.

An interesting statement is found in the Talmud on the importance of the Oral Law: "Words were given orally and words were given in writing, and we do not know which of the two sets is more valuable. However, from the verse 'According to these words have I made a covenant with you'(Exodus 34:27), we learn that those that were transmitted orally are the more valuable."[1]

One of the great rabbinic decisors of the nineteenth century, Rabbi Zevi Hirsch Chayes, made the following comment on the significance of the Oral Law:

> Allegiance to the authority of the said rabbinic tradition is binding upon all the sons of Israel, since these explanations and interpretations have come down to us by word of mouth from generation to generation right from the time of Moses. They have been transmitted to us precise, correct, and unadulterated, and he who does not adhere to the unwritten law and the rabbinic tradition has no right to share the heritage of Israel.[2]

And again:

> These precise interpretations were already known as ancient traditions transmitted orally from Sinai, for how otherwise could such a law as taking "the fruit of a goodly tree" at the Feast of Ingathering have been given to Moses in general terms without instructing him in detail regarding the nature of the fruit. . . . Such explanatory details, therefore, must have been given clearly to Moses in connection with every precept, and this in spite of the fact that the rabbis endeavored to deduce them from the Torah by means of the exegetical rules.[3]

Through the ages various enactments and decrees were issued by the sages and rabbinic authorities: the enactments called *takkanot* applied to the positive commandments and were instituted to reinforce the moral teachings of the Torah and to promote religious observance; the decrees called *gezerot* applied to the negative commandments and were instituted to protect the people from violating biblical law.

Four Fundamental Principles

The following principles were always adhered to by the rabbinic authorities in their decisions:

1. Majority rules. This principle derives from the Torah. When there is a difference of opinion among the sages of the Talmud on a particular matter, authority lies with the majority. This principle has been honored in the subsequent codes of Jewish law and in the responsa literature to the present day with rare exceptions.

2. When there is a difference of opinion among the sages as to what the proper ruling would be on a particular issue—some taking a stringent position, others a lenient one—when biblical law is involved, the stringent opinion is followed; when the laws involved are of a rabbinic nature, the lenient opinion is followed.

3. Financial loss is always taken into consideration when determining the law in a given situation. This means that when great financial loss is involved, the rabbinic authority may choose to follow a lenient minority opinion.

4. Human life is sacred. The laws of the Torah were given to man that he live by them, not die by them.[4] The laws of *Shabbat* and virtually all biblical and rabbinic laws may be set aside in order to save even a single human life.[5]

Two Practical Questions

Having defined the Oral and Written Law and having introduced you to some fundamental principles of Jewish law, let us now pose two interesting practical questions.

1. Would it be permissible for an observant Jew to invite a nonobservant Jew to his home for a *Shabbat* meal, knowing full well that in order for him to get there he would have to travel on *Shabbat,* which is clearly in violation of the law?

2. Would it be permissible for a Jewish waiter working in a nonkosher restaurant to serve nonkosher food to a fellow Jew? Would it

make any difference if the person being served was the owner of the restaurant?

We will begin with an important caveat. The conclusions we come to in our discussions here are purely academic; they are not meant to be halakhic rulings. Every situation is unique and demands careful analysis by a qualified rabbinic authority. Jewish law is not rigid; it is flexible. When we are concerned with people, there are very few situations in which the law is black or white. Now let us proceed with our analysis.

If a rabbi were to answer the first question by whim or gut feeling, he might say, "Yes, by all means invite the nonobservant Jew to participate in a *Shabbat* meal!" He might argue that participation in a *Shabbat* meal might very well awaken that spark of Jewishness that exists in every Jew. It might inspire such a person to seriously consider making a commitment to observe at least some of the laws of *Shabbat.* Who knows? Such an initial commitment might eventually lead to a total commitment to *mitzvot.* The second question might elicit a positive response as well. Why should the waiter risk his job? The customer is obviously not at all concerned with the laws of *kashrut* for, if he were, he wouldn't be in the restaurant to begin with.

These and other such issues that present themselves in daily living, but are not specifically addressed in the Code of Jewish Law, are of serious concern to observant Jews. Financial matters, medical issues, business ethics, social interaction, and family problems, to name just a few, have continually been addressed by rabbinic authorities. Hundreds of volumes of responsa literature have been written through the centuries by rabbinic decisors expertly trained in Jewish law and in decision-making policy to handle these issues. Although some of this literature has been lost through the ages, much is presently available to rabbinic authorities for consultation. No! Jewish law is not decided by whim. Quite the contrary. Reason and due deliberation are the hallmark of rabbinic decision making.

Let us begin our inquiry into the issues we have raised with Leviticus 19:14. "You shall not curse a deaf man, and before a blind man you shall not place a stumbling block. You shall fear your God: I am the Lord."

If the words *before a blind man you shall not place a stumbling block* are meant to be taken at face value, one wonders why it would be neces-

sary to enumerate it among the 613 *mitzvot*. Surely no normal person
would consider such a thing. Why would it be mandated? It would not
at all be presumptuous to assume that something more than the literal
meaning must be implied in these words. In the *Sifra*, a legal commentary on the book of Leviticus written in about the third century, we
find the following explanation.

> Before one who is [intellectually] blind concerning a particular matter.
> If one comes and asks you: "The daughter of so and so, is she qualified to
> marry a priest?" Do not answer, "Qualified!" when she is disqualified. If
> one comes to you for advice, do not give him improper advice . . . Lest
> you say, "I have given him good advice," know that in matters of the
> heart it is said, "You shall fear your God: I am the Lord."

The *Sifra* indicates that the verse is not simply to be taken literally.
It refers to intellectual, not visual, blindness. One who knowingly gives
false advice to another person transgresses this biblical commandment.
According to Rabbi Meir Leibush Malbim, the renowned Bible scholar
of the nineteenth century, the choice of the term *n'tinah* rather than
simah, both of which mean "to place," confirms the interpretation of the
Sifra. In biblical usage, placing an object before someone of which he is
unaware, such as placing a stumbling block before the blind, would call
for the term *simah*.[6]

Now it is of the utmost importance to delineate the parameters of
this *mitzvah*. The Talmud teaches the following:

> How do we know that one should not stretch forth his hand with a
> cup of wine to a Nazirite or a limb from a living animal to an Noahide?
> From Scripture which says, *Before a blind man you shall not put a stum-
> bling block. . . .* Of what case are we speaking? Where the two persons
> are on opposite sides of a river. You can prove it by the use of the words
> "one should not *stretch forth*"; it does not say "one should not *give*." This
> proves it![7]

Let us understand the meaning and the implications of this talmudic
discussion. A Nazirite is a person who has taken a vow not to drink
wine for a given period of time. A Noahide (non-Jew) is forbidden by
Jewish law to eat a limb from a living animal. One who offers wine to
a Nazirite or a limb from a living animal to a Noahide becomes an accessory to the transgression of a biblical commandment. The param-

eters of this law are precise: it only applies in a situation where the
Nazirite or the Noahide are unable to transgress the law without the
aid of the accessory.[8] Their being on opposite sides of the river, the
Nazirite cannot reach the wine unless the accessory stretches forth his
hand and gets it to him from across the river. The same is true regarding the Noahide. Does this mean that being an accessory under those
conditions would be permissible? Absolutely not. Although under such
conditions there would be no biblical transgression, it is prohibited by
rabbinic law as a preventative measure.[9]

Let us consider another example. Jewish law mandates washing one's
hands before eating a meal. The law also teaches:

> One who feeds another person need not wash his hands, but the one who
> is eating must do so even though the food is being put directly into his
> mouth, and he never touches it. The law that mandates washing of the
> hands would likewise apply to one who eats with a fork.[10]

Appended to this ruling is the following statement by Rama (Rabbi
Moshe Isserles): "It is forbidden to feed one who has not washed his
hands because of the prohibition of putting a stumbling block before
the blind."

Feeding someone who is mandated to wash his hands and chooses
not to do so is being an accessory to that person's transgression of the
law, and is it biblically prohibited, assuming, of course, that the recipient cannot feed himself. However, when the food belongs to the recipient and he is able to feed himself, the biblical law would not apply. Being
an accessory would be prohibited by rabbinic law, however, as a preventative measure.[11]

We now have the background to approach the questions we posed
at the beginning of this session intelligently.

To invite a guest to one's home for a *Shabbat* meal, knowing full well
that he lives a great distance away and he must travel in order to get
there, would be a violation of the biblical prohibition of putting a stumbling block before the blind, for he would not be traveling to your home
on *Shabbat* had he not been invited, and traveling on *Shabbat* is prohibited. Even if the guest were to come before *Shabbat*, stay for the meal,
but travel home before *Shabbat* has ended, inviting him would still be
biblically prohibited. The fact that he would probably be traveling on

Shabbat anyway is irrelevant. The solution to the problem would be, of course, to invite him for the entire *Shabbat*.

Every Jew is obligated to observe Jewish law. The laws of kosher food are of biblical origin. Any Jew who eats nonkosher food transgresses the law. Here again, the fact that a particular person has chosen not to be at all observant of the laws is irrelevant. To serve nonkosher food to a Jew, therefore, is to be an accessory and in violation of putting a stumbling block before the blind. Now you will recall that the biblical prohibition applies only in a situation where the person being served cannot obtain this food himself. If the person being served is the owner of the restaurant, he can take the food himself any time he chooses to do so. Consequently, the biblical prohibition of being an accessory would not apply. To serve him would be prohibited by rabbinic law, however, as a preventative measure. On the other hand, if the food is of a type that is only prohibited by rabbinic law as a preventative measure, one might rule more leniently because of the principle that one does not institute a preventative measure in order to prevent the violation of another preventative measure.

Vivisection in Jewish Law

In previous generations society's concern for the welfare of animals was minimal. Experimentation with animals for the benefit of mankind was rarely if ever given a second thought. Today, however, the pendulum has swung to the opposite extreme: the welfare of animals has become a serious concern in the minds of a significant segment of society. There is no doubt that there are good psychological and sociological reasons for this change of heart—we are a society that has witnessed the Holocaust, the most horrendous manifestation of man's inhumanity to man in history—but that is not our concern here. Considering where society stands on this issue, it is no wonder that the practice of vivisection to perfect the treatment of human illness and disease has come under attack by the Friends of Animals and other such animal rights groups.

Let us pose the following question: What is the attitude of Jewish law toward animals and where does it stand on the matter of vivisection first and foremost for the benefit of man?

It is quite clear from biblical as well as rabbinic sources that Judaism preaches kindness to animals. The Bible teaches us that God provides for all his creatures. In Psalms 145:9 we find: "The Lord is good to all, and His compassion is over all His works," and again in Psalms 145:16, "You open Your hand and satisfy the desire of every living thing." Last, "[God] Who gives the beast its food, the young ravens that after which they cry." Numerous *mitzvot* are concerned with kindness to animals. Although we have been given permission to use animals for food, it is forbidden for both Jews and Gentiles to remove a limb from a living animal and eat it. An animal must be put to death by slaughter, a method that has been scientifically established as the most humane.

Maimonides writes:

> The commandment concerning the slaughter of animals is necessary because the natural food of man consists only of vegetables and of the flesh of animals. . . . Since, therefore, the desire of procuring good food necessitates the slaying of animals, the Law enjoins that the death of the animal be the easiest.[12]

We are permitted to eat certain birds and their eggs, but in doing so the feelings of the mother bird must be considered. Thus in Deuteronomy 22:6,7 we read: "If, along the road you chance upon a bird's nest, in any tree or on the ground, with the fledglings, and the mother sitting over the fledglings or on the eggs, do not take the mother together with her young. Let the mother go and take only the young, in order that you may fare well and have a long life." In Leviticus 22:28 we read, "And no animal from the herd or from the flock shall be slaughtered on the same day with its young." Maimonides explains the reasons for these laws as follows:

> It is also prohibited to slaughter an animal and its young on the same day, in order to avoid slaughtering the young animal in front of its mother; for in these cases, animals feel great pain. There is no difference in this case between the pain of man and the pain of other living beings, since the love and tenderness of the mother for her young ones is not produced by reasoning but by imagination and this faculty exists not only in man but in most living beings . . . . This is also the reason for the law that mandates letting the mother go from the nest when we take

the young. For in general, the eggs over which the bird has sat and the young that need their mother are not fit to be eaten. If then, the mother is let go and escapes of her own accord, she will not be pained by seeing that the young are taken away.[13]

Rebecca, the second matriarch of the Jewish people, showed exceptional kindness to Abraham's servant Eliezer, but she was found to be a suitable wife for Isaac because she showed kindness toward his camels as well.[14]

The major biblical source for kindness to animals is Exodus 23:5, which reads, "When you see the donkey of your enemy prostrate under its burden and would refrain from lifting it, you must nevertheless lift it with him." The law applies to all people, friend or enemy, Jew and non-Jew alike. It shows not only the charitable attitude one should have toward one's fellow man when he is in difficult straits, even toward one's enemy, but also the humanitarian attitude of the law toward animals.

Now it is important to understand the rationale behind the law that mandates kindness to animals. It is clearly not for the sake of the animal *alone* that the Torah enjoins us to be kind to them. Maimonides makes this clear.

> As for the decree of the sages to avoid causing suffering to the animal . . . it is set down with a view to perfecting us so that we should not acquire moral habits of cruelty and should not uselessly cause pain to others; that we should be prepared to be kind and merciful to all living creatures except when necessity demands the contrary in case of need [for food] . . . for we must not kill out of cruelty or for sport.[15]

All this notwithstanding, it must be made perfectly clear that as important as kindness to animals may be in Jewish law, it does not take preference over human welfare. Parenthetically, the saving of a human life, even momentary life, takes preference over the laws of *Shabbat* and almost all the *mitzvot* of the Torah.[16] No such consideration is given to animals. Now let us understand to what extent vivisection has contributed to the extension of human life.

Because of the physiological similarities between the animal and the human body, man has been involved in vivisection since ancient times. Through the years, he has gained tremendous insight into the working of the human body from animal experimentation. The discovery and identification of hormones and the use of antibiotics and vitamins would have been impossible were it not for our ability to test scientific theories on animals. The treatment and cure of diseases that have attacked both man and animal would never have been possible were it not for our ability to experiment on animals. When the issue is seen from this perspective, we must decide where our priorities lie, and there can be only one answer—with man.

Rabbi Yehiel Weinberg, the noted twentieth-century talmudic scholar and rabbinic decisor, points out that the prohibition of cruelty to animals applies only where the welfare of the general population is not involved. He makes the following comment: If one may violate almost all the *mitzvot* of the Torah to save the life of a single human being, by what right might one assume that the *mitzvah* that prohibits cruelty to animals may not be violated? As such, says Rabbi Weinberg, experimentation with animals in order to discover better methods for treatment of illness and disease is certainly permissible.[17]

We must conclude that vivisection is clearly permissible according to Jewish law, perhaps in some situations even obligatory. Nevertheless, consideration must be extended to the animal as well. One of our contemporary decisors on Jewish law, Rabbi J. D. Bleich, qualifies the permissibility to experiment with animals by insisting that "pain may be inflicted upon the animal only to the degree absolutely necessary in order to obtain the required information. Otherwise the pain does not serve to satisfy a legitimate need and is prohibited. ... the benefits must be practical in nature and not just the satisfaction of intellectual curiosity."[18]

The Jewish Attitude to Cryogenics

Let us now raise an issue that at the present time is for the most part theoretical, albeit with the tremendous strides that science and technology have made in the last century it may very soon become a practical one.

With the knowledge we now have in the area of cryogenics, that is, the study of the effect of very low temperatures on matter, serious attention has been given by a number of scientists to the feasibility of freezing the human body immediately after death and reviving it at some time in the future. The rationale for such a procedure is that people who die from incurable diseases could be preserved in a vault at very low temperatures to prevent the body from decaying appreciably, and they could be revived when a cure is found for the disease that afflicted them. At present, the technology for revival is still in its primitive stages.

Assuming that science and technology have progressed to the point where revival of a frozen body is possible, would freezing the human body after death be permissible according to Jewish law?

Several practical questions can be raised: What would be a person's status in the frozen state? Would he be considered dead or alive? What would be his relationship to the family he had when he was alive? When revived, would he resume those relationships?

The process of refrigeration and resuscitation itself would raise several halakhic questions: Would the refrigeration of a body after death be a violation of the law that calls for immediate burial? If the process demands that the body be frozen immediately before the onset of death, would this be permissible according to Jewish law? Would the laws of mourning apply to a person who is refrigerated after death? Would it be permissible for the wife of such a person to remarry?

With regard to the status of a person who is refrigerated after death, there is an incident recorded in the Bible and discussed in the Talmud that significantly influences this matter. In 2 Kings, Chapter 2, we are told that the prophet Elisha revived a young boy who had suffered head pain and had died. The *Midrash* makes the following comment:

> One who touches a corpse is [ritually] unclean, but the son of the Shunamite woman [brought back to life by Elisha] was not unclean . . . when he died everything in the house became unclean . . . when he came to life again he was clean, but then he touched things that were in the house and that made him unclean.[19]

A dead body is considered ritually unclean, but a living person is not.[20] It is clear from the *Midrash* that the boy was dead; otherwise, the statement that everything in the house became unclean would be erroneous. When he was revived by Elisha, however, the boy became clean again.

With regard to the marital status of a person during the period in which he is frozen, assuming that he can be revived, all rabbinic authorities would agree that his living status in all its ramifications would remain intact. Were this not so, a person who dies on the operating table and is subsequently revived—a common occurrence today—would lose all status, causing great complications for him in life.

Let us now consider our original question: If a person dies today, is it permissible to freeze him, anticipating that a cure for his condition will some day be found, at which time he would be revived and treated? Let us also consider what would the ruling be if the person is still alive but has been designated by his physician as terminally ill?

In 1 Kings 17:21 we are told that the prophet Elijah, who was the teacher of Elisha, also revived a dead child. Now Elijah was a *kohen* ("priest"). Jewish law forbids a *kohen* from defiling himself by touching a dead body or even entering a cemetery. The Talmud records that Rabbah bar Abuha encountered Elijah standing in a non-Jewish cemetery. When he questioned him, Elijah, explained that a non-Jewish cemetery does not cause ritual defilement.[21] The later sages asked: "How did he revive the widow's son if he was a *kohen*?" "One can answer," they said, "that he was certain that he would be able to bring him back to life. It was permitted because of the law of saving a life."[22]

Now we have already pointed out that the law of saving a life takes precedence over almost all the laws of the Torah. As such, Elijah was able to handle the dead body despite the law that prohibits a priest from defiling himself. Even more is implied by this comment. Where there exists a possibility that life can be restored, the law of saving a life applies even after death. This being the case, some argue that it should be permissible for a dead person to be frozen until a cure is found for his illness, when there is good reason to believe that he could then be revived and cured. Just as the law of saving a life overrides the law of defilement, it should override the law that demands immediate burial of the dead as well.

With regard to the matter of whether it is permissible to freeze a person who has not yet died but is on the verge of death, there is a responsum that bears directly on this issue as well. Human life takes the highest priority in Jewish law, even ephemeral life. We have already learned that one may violate the *Shabbat* in order to save a person's life, even if he is not expected to live for more than a few moments. Consider the following: A person is mortally ill. In the opinion of his doctors, he is not expected to live for more than a brief period. The only hope is a drug that will either cure him or kill him. May such a drug be administered?

Initially, it would seem to be better to do nothing. Since we are concerned with ephemeral life, perhaps the patient should be allowed to live out his allotted time in this world rather than risk immediate death. This would be a "gut" reaction, in point of fact contrary to Jewish law. Ephemeral life is certainly an important consideration. Where we are dealing with an experimental drug, and a request is made to administer it to a patient mortally ill in order to test its effect on humans, with no prospect for cure, it would be prohibited because of our concern for ephemeral life. But if it is possible that the recipient will be cured, our concern for ephemeral life is overridden by the prospect of a cure.[23]

Kipah: Male Head Covering

One of the most obvious identifying characteristics of the traditional Jew in our society is the *kipah* or *yarmulka.* We will conclude our adventures in rabbinic reasoning with an analysis of the sources relevant to the following questions.

From what source does the practice of wearing a *kipah* derive? Is it a *mitzvah,* a rabbinic decree, or merely a custom? What is the rationale for this practice and what are the parameters?

In the Talmud we find the following statements: "R. Huna the son of R. Joshua did not walk four cubits bareheaded. He said: 'The Presence [of God] is above my head.'"[24] R. Huna the son of R. Joshua said: "I should be rewarded for not walking four cubits bareheaded."[25]

It is clear from these statements that R. Huna considered keeping his head covered at all times to be exemplary behavior. Had this been obligatory, he would not have merited special reward. The rationale "God's Presence is above my head," can be understood either as a sign of his humility or his modesty. Maimonides writes:

> We do not sit, move, and occupy ourselves when we are alone and at home, in the same manner as we do when we are in the presence of a great king . . . . to be truly men of God we must . . . bear in mind that the great King that is over us . . . is greater than any earthly king. . . . When the perfect bear this in mind, they will be filled with fear of

God, humility and piety. . . . The great men among our sages would not bare their heads because they believed that God's Glory was round them and over them.[26]

Clearly, Maimonides considers covering one's head to be an expression of modesty, perhaps humility as well. In another work Maimonides adds, "Extreme modesty is cultivated by scholars. They will not do anything that might expose them to contempt. They will not bare their head or body."[27] In contradistinction, Rabbi J. M. Epstein, the nineteenth-century halakhic authority, focused on humility. He writes:

> The rationale for this is that the head, which contains the brain, is the source of wisdom and awe of God. One should not expose it before God Whose Glory fills the earth, just as one should not stand in a holy place bareheaded. One who does not abide by this practice invites impudence to take control over him.[28]

As admirable as the gesture may be, none of the early sources designate the practice of covering one's head to be obligatory. A somewhat stronger position is taken in the *Code of Jewish Law* where we read: "One should not walk four cubits bareheaded," but this seems more like advice than obligation. Were it not for the fact that an entirely different point is raised by a major halakhic authority, covering the head for men would have remained in the realm of exemplary but not obligatory behavior.

In his commentary on the *Code of Jewish Law*, Rabbi David HaLevi, the seventeenth-century rabbinic decisor, focuses on the *mitzvah* that prohibits a Jew from mimicking the Gentiles and makes the following point: since it is customary among Gentiles to remove their hats when they are seated in a house or assembly hall, for a Jew to do so would come under the biblical prohibition of "You shall not walk in their ways" (Leviticus 18:3).[29]

This puts an entirely different perspective on wearing a *kipah*. We are no longer dealing merely with expressions of humility or modesty, but rather a biblical prohibition. Indeed, to his way of thinking, wearing a *kipah* is not a matter of exemplary behavior; it is obligatory. The position of Rabbi David HaLevi is the accepted ruling today.[30] It is to be understood, of course, that this stringency would only apply in those countries where uncovering one's head is an expression of respect, such as Europe and the United States, as opposed to the countries in the Mideast.[31] Finally, it is important to note that none of our discussion applies to the recitations of blessings or prayer, at which times donning a *kipah* is obligatory for all Jews the world over.[32]

We have demonstrated the halakhic method, and we have shown quite vividly the sophisticated rabbinic reasoning involved in determining Jewish law. The method has not changed from talmudic times to the present. We will employ this method from time to time in our discussions of issues in Jewish law.

In our session on the credibility of the Torah, we took it for granted that the Torah is of Divine origin, that it was revealed to Moses at Sinai. We never concerned ourselves with what is termed in secular scholarly circles "higher and lower biblical criticism." As traditional Jews, we reject the suppositions and conclusions of biblical criticism. Now I know that if you become interested in Judaism, sooner or later you will become aware of this school of thought. To prevent you from becoming confused, even worse, misled by this approach to the Bible, I would like to give you some background on the origin of biblical criticism and at the same time acquaint you with the approach of some of the traditional Jewish Bible scholars to the questions raised by this school of thought. We will devote the next session to this topic.

Session III
Faith and the
Pursuit of Scholarship

At our first session we stated quite emphatically that the Torah derives from God, word for word and letter for letter. Its tenets are absolute truth; its credibility, beyond question. The Torah was revealed to Moses, the greatest of all prophets, by the Almighty Himself. To the secular scholar, however, the Torah is considered the literary endeavor of a number of different authors who lived years, perhaps generations apart. This fundamental difference in approach has rendered the principles of biblical criticism patently unacceptable to the traditional Jewish scholar.

There are two approaches to dealing with this phenomenon: one can designate it as being the conjecture of nonbelievers, and disregard it, as many reputable Torah authorities have done, or one can face up to the challenge, study the traditional biblical literature, and develop an approach to handle the difficulties posed by this school of thought. Let me state unequivocally at the outset that both approaches are valid. It is to those of us who prefer to take the second approach, however, that this session will be devoted. We will begin by examining the historic development of the school of biblical criticism.

The History of Biblical Criticism

In the middle of the seventeenth century, Thomas Hobbes in England and Isaac de la Peyrere in France inaugurated a critical method of biblical analysis that, with some changes and refinements, has become the accepted approach of modern nontraditional biblical scholarship. In his book *Leviathan*, Hobbes cited many biblical verses that he claimed could not have been written by Moses. He maintained that the whole Torah is a compilation of different documents that were edited and put in final form in Babylon by Ezra and Nehemiah in the fifth century. Four years later, Isaac de la Peyrere published some of his own ideas, claiming, among other things, that there were men who lived on the Earth before Adam, and that the miracles in the Bible, such as the regression of the sun dial in the time of King Ahaz and the interruption of the sun's normal course in the time of Joshua, were natural rather than supernatural events.

At about the same time, a well-known philosopher by the name of Baruch Spinoza wrote a book called *Tractate on Theology and Politics*, in which he put forth some of the theories of Thomas Hobbes and Isaac de la Peyrere, which he claimed to be his own. Spinoza, a born Jew, did not accept the tradition that the Torah is the word of God nor would he admit that it was revealed to Moses, who subsequently committed it to writing. In point of fact, he contended that there were several hands in the composition of the Torah. It should be noted that Spinoza's ideas about God are contrary to Jewish belief as well. Eventually, Spinoza totally separated himself from the Jewish community, which in turn declared him a heretic and excommunicated him.

About a century later, a Roman Catholic physician by the name of Jean Astruc suggested that the appearance of two names for God in the book of Genesis meant that there were two independent documents that Moses made use of in composing the book. Astruc published his theory, which was further developed by others and became known as the "higher criticism." It is important to differentiate between the higher criticism, which attempts to establish authorship by speculating on the biblical text, and the lower criticism, which attempts to establish the most authentic version of the biblical text.

In what is known as "The Documentary Hypothesis," the school of biblical criticism challenges the Mosaic authorship of the Torah. It purports that the Torah is composed of four basic documents. The oldest document of Genesis is identified by its use of the *Tetragrammaton* (this is the four-letter name of God, which is not to be vocalized and is referred to as *Hashem*, meaning "the Name") as the name of God; it is called the "J" document. The second oldest document is identified by its use of *E-lohim* as the name of God, and called the "E" document. The "J" and "E" documents were combined and edited in the ninth and eighth centuries B.C.E. Toward the end of the seventh century B.C.E. the book of Deuteronomy, called the "D" document, was composed. It is suggested that this document was a reworking of the "JE" document. Finally, in the sixth to fifth centuries B.C.E. the book of Leviticus, called the "P" document, was composed.

In 1875, Julius Wellhausen, a German professor of history, published a book entitled *Prolegomena to the History of Ancient Israel*, in which he attacked the entire Bible from Genesis to Chronicles. Had the book been written three hundred years earlier, it would probably have been dismissed as the ravings of a heretic, but in the nineteenth century evolution was in the air, and the Bible was open for attack. George Hegel, the renowned German philosopher, promulgated the theory that all history had developed from lower, more primitive stages in Asia and Greece to higher stages in other areas of the world, reaching the pinnacle of development in the Western Europe of his day.

Wellhausen felt that what applied to nature and history could be applied to the Bible as well. Since monotheism is the highest stage of religion, argued Wellhausen, the religion of the early Hebrews, which was far removed from nineteenth-century Western Europe in both time and geographic location, had to have been polytheistic. Only later in history, in the days of the prophets, could the Israelite religion have evolved to monotheism. The Torah, which clearly bears the stamp of monotheism, could not possibly have been written in the time of Moses, he argued. It had to have been written in the time of the prophets.

Wellhausen went on to claim that the history of Israel did not begin with Abraham but rather with the Exodus of the Israelites from Egypt. In the fifth century, under the aegis of Ezra the scribe, the various documents were combined and edited by the priests to give the impression that the Torah was one homogeneous work written by Moses. In the Torah narratives that depict the lives of the patriarchs, these editors infused ideas that betray the thinking and the level of cultural and economic sophistication that existed in their own time, the sixth and fifth centuries B.C.E. For all intents and purposes, Wellhausen's contentions implied that the Torah as it appears today is simply a forgery.

Wellhausen's method was rather interesting. He became obsessed with dissection. He perused the Bible from beginning to end, and whenever he found a verse that contradicted his theory, he claimed that the verse was not part of the original text, that it was interpolated by a later author. The more he and his adherents studied the text, the more documents they found. At times they claimed to have found traces of as many as five or six different authors in a single verse. Considering that there were virtually hundreds of such verses, his hypothesis should have been summarily dismissed by every objective scholar and thinker. In point of fact, however, the Wellhausen hypothesis remained pretty much in vogue until the early twentieth century.

In 1887, the Tel Amarna letters were discovered. These cuneiform tablets revealed correspondence between Egyptian, Babylonian, and Palestinian diplomats, showing a well-developed culture as early as the fourteenth century B.C.E. Later, in the early twentieth century, archaeologists made an interesting discovery in their investigation of the Mesopotamian region, specifically, the towns of Nuzi and Mari, which were located in Northwest Mesopotamia. They found thousands of clay tablets, comprising public and private archives on which the social and business activities of the leading citizens of the town of Nuzi were recorded. These tablets dated from about the eighteenth century B.C.E., the time of Abraham. Parenthetically, they enlighten us concerning several practices of the patriarchs that are recorded in the Torah, and serve to authenticate the biblical record. Let me cite one example.

The tablets speak of the institution of marriage and reveal that when a husband wanted to put his marriage on the highest level, he would give his wife the status of a sister and refer to her as his wife or sister interchangeably. Haran, the city where Abraham lived, and Nuzi, were both part of an integrated ethnic and cultural area, so that what applied to Nuzi applied to Haran as well. When the Torah tells us that Abraham and Isaac referred to their wives as sisters, it is telling us, among other things, that they were honoring them in the eyes of the people of Haran.

The truth of the matter is that style is not the sole determinant of authorship. One can find a little of the style of one author in the writings of another and a little of both their styles in the writings of a third author. Now while this might indicate that one author copied the style of another, it is not necessarily indicative of multiple authorship. Of course, none of the suppositions or contentions of literary criticism are relevant to the Torah, whose text Moses received from the Almighty, word for word.

Let me conclude this brief summary of the development of biblical criticism with the words of Rabbi Adin Steinsaltz, a contemporary Bible and Talmud scholar, who made the following comment on the trustworthiness of biblical criticism in light of the knowledge we have today.

> From the very beginning up to our times you can see a continuous line of mistakes. For instance, one of the minor results of the discovery of the Dead Sea Scrolls was that a whole set of theories, from dating biblical books to finding the authenticity of what is called the masoretic text, was instantly eradicated. And yet, in many universities, people are still teaching Bible according to these erroneous disproved principles.[1]

The Jewish Approach: Three Principles

How does traditional Judaism handle the contentions of biblical criticism concerning the authorship of the Torah?

The position of traditional Judaism is based on three unimpeachable principles: the Torah is of Divine origin, and every word of the Torah was revealed to Moses at Sinai; the masoretic text of the Torah is the only authentic text and as such the only acceptable one; and the only interpretations of the Torah that are acceptable are those that are based on the Oral Law.

The Talmud states unequivocally that with the exception of the last eight verses of Deuteronomy, which according to one opinion were written by Joshua, Moses wrote the entire Torah.[2] There is a difference of opinion among the sages, however, as to whether the Torah was revealed to Moses all at once or in parts during the forty-year journey in the wilderness.[3]

The Torah is the most sacred object of the Jewish people. Its text has been meticulously preserved through the ages. Mere perusal of the laws of writing a Torah scroll makes this quite evident. We firmly believe that the text of the Torah is the one given by God to Moses at Sinai. Maimonides made this the eighth of his *Thirteen Principles* of the Jewish faith. In the abstract of his work it reads: "I believe with perfect faith that the whole Torah now in our possession is the same as was given to Moses our teacher, peace be unto him."

In the *Mishneh Torah*, his monumental halakhic work, Maimonides writes that one who claims that Moses wrote one word or even one letter on his own is considered a heretic.[4] This unequivocal position taken by the sages through the generations is not only a matter of faith in the integrity of the sages, it is of crucial importance to our understanding of the development of Jewish law. For Jewish law is based on the precise wording of the biblical text.

An interesting point is made by the renowned Bible and Talmud scholar of the twentieth century Rabbi David Tzvi Hoffmann, in his Torah commentary.[5] In his introduction to Leviticus, Rabbi Hoffmann observes most insightfully that even if one were to admit the possibility of an obscure passage being corrupt, a text that was revealed to Moses through prophecy cannot be restored no matter how well grounded the suggested emendation is, historically. Although there are some variants of the Torah text found in the Talmud, says Rabbi Hoffmann, these are insignificant and pose no theological or halakhic problems.

In this regard it is important to note that great care was taken by the sages to preserve the authentic Torah text. In the tractate *Soferim*[6] we are told that there were three Torah scrolls in the Temple in Jerusalem. One was called *M'onah*; the second, *Zatute*; the third simply *He*. The names indicated word variants. Based on these scrolls, the sages constructed what they considered to be the authentic Torah text, which was called *Sefer HaAzarah*. This name is mentioned in the *Mishnah*.[7] *Sefer HaAzarah* served as the official authoritative text of the Torah, which meant that newly written scrolls were copied from it. The scrolls used by the kings of Israel were copied from *Sefer HaAzarah* as well.

The third principle posits that the only acceptable interpretations of the Torah are those that do not conflict with the Oral Law. It is important to fully comprehend the significance of this principle. As we have already noted in our previous session, the Oral Law was revealed to Moses together with the Written Law. Both derive from the Almighty. The Oral Law was meant to give us the proper understanding of the Written Law. Should one discover what appears to be a contradiction between that which is stated clearly in the Written Law and that which has been handed down as a tradition in the Oral Law, it is treated in the same way the sages treated conflicting biblical passages, namely, according to what is known as "The Thirteen Principles of Biblical Interpretation."[8] The last of these principles states: "When two biblical texts contradict each other, the meaning can be determined only when a third text is found which harmonizes them."[9]

It is important to note that the binding authority of the interpretations of the sages on the Torah text applies only to the *Halakhah*, namely, those biblical verses that prescribe a norm; it does not apply to their commentaries on the narrative material in the Torah. These commentaries were written by men of the highest ethical, moral, intellectual, and spiritual qualifications, to be sure, and they are of great value in understanding the text, but they are not binding.[10]

With regard to the contention of Wellhausen and others that the Torah was written during the prophetic era, Dr. Yehezkel Kaufmann, a contemporary Bible scholar (not at all a defender of traditional Judaism) has shown most convincingly that even from a critical literary perspective, it could not have been written that late. The religious and the moral are given equal emphasis in the Torah, says Kaufmann, while in the prophetic writings, the moral is given primacy.[11] The Torah stresses the covenant made between God and the patriarchs, which guarantees God's eternal grace manifest upon Israel; in the prophetic writings, the covenant with the people, which will be renewed in "the end of days," is emphasized. In the Torah the national enemy of the Israelites is Amalek whereas in the prophetic era, Amalek was but one of the enemies of the nation of Israel. Last, the fact that the destruction of Jerusalem and the Temple, a common theme of the prophets, is not even alluded to in the Torah clearly testifies to its antiquity.[12]

Among the matters with which the Bible critics are concerned is the fact that the creation of man appears in both Genesis 1 and Genesis 2, and that there are substantial differences between the two versions. It is their contention that these are two documents, two versions of creation, each written by a different author, each using a different name for God. Of course insofar as traditional Judaism is concerned, this position is untenable, and we shall offer an explanation of the discrepancy. Let us first note, however, that the Bible scholars were certainly not the first to notice the repetition of the creation story in Genesis 2. Rashi (an acronym for Rabbi Solomon Izhaki), the eleventh-century French commentator on the Talmud and the Bible, made the point quite succinctly. On Genesis 2:8 he comments:

> I have seen in the *Beraita* of Rabbi Eliezer son of Rabbi Yose the Galilean dealing with the thirty-two rules of interpretation according to which the Torah can be interpreted ... [that] when a general statement of action is followed by a detailed account of it, the latter is a particularization of the former. "And He [God] created man" (Genesis 1:27) is a general statement, but it does not explicitly state when he was created and what God did to him. Now [in chapter 2] it repeats and explains these things: "And the Lord God formed man," and He made grow for him the garden of Eden and He caused a great sleep to fall upon him. He who hears this might think that it is a different account entirely, whereas it is nothing else but the details of the former general statement.

What the sages are telling us here is that the second chapter of Genesis is not a new story of creation at all; it is simply the same story retold, but from a different perspective. The emphasis being on man, we are given a much more detailed description of his creation. In the first version, man is given just five verses; in the retelling, he is given almost two complete chapters. In the first chapter we are merely told that the female was created; in the second chapter we are told why and how she was created. In point of fact, if one were to study the book of Genesis carefully, one would find that the technique of going from the general to the particular is a common occurrence.[13] The fact that man is the focus of creation and perhaps the raison d'etre of the world is noted quite succinctly in the Talmud.

> And God saw all that He had made and behold it was very good. And it was evening and it was morning *the* sixth day. (Genesis 1:31)

> What is the purpose of the article *the*? It teaches us that the Holy One, blessed be He, stipulated with the works of creation and said to them, "If Israel accepts the Torah, you shall exist, but if not, I will turn you back into emptiness and formlessness."[14]

Man in Genesis 1 and 2

There is another approach to the problem. In a brilliant philosophical discourse on the creation of man, what he calls the Adam 1 and Adam 2 personalities, the late Rabbi Joseph B. Soloveitchik (the Rav, as he is referred to affectionately by his students) offers a novel approach to the discrepancies in the first two chapters of Genesis. The Torah records the following:

> And God created man in His image, in the image of God He created him; male and female He created them. God blessed them and said to them, "Be fruitful and multiply, fill the earth and master it; and rule the fish of the sea, the birds of the sky, and all the living things that creep on the earth." (Genesis 1:27–28)

> The Lord God formed man from the dust of the earth, and He breathed into his nostrils the breath of life; and man became a living being. . . . The Lord took the man and placed him in the garden of Eden, to till and to tend it. (Genesis 2:7, 15)

The account of the creation of man that appears in Genesis 2 differs from that which appears in Genesis 1 on four points. In Genesis 1 man is created in the image of God, and nothing is told of his body; in Genesis 2 man is created from dust of the earth and the Almighty breathes into his nostrils the breath of life. In Genesis 1 man is charged to be fruitful and multiply, to fill the earth, and to master it; in Genesis 2 he is charged to till and to tend the garden. In Genesis 1 the man and woman are created concurrently; in Genesis 2 the man is created first. Not until later (verse 22) do we read that the woman was created. Lastly, Genesis 1 refers to God as *E-lohim* (trans. "God") while Genesis 2 refers to Him as *Hashem E-lohim* (trans. "Lord God"). What is the reason for these discrepancies? The Rav writes:

> We all know that the Bible offers two accounts of the creation of man. We also are aware of the theory suggested by Bible critics attributing these two accounts to two different traditions and sources. . . . It is of course true that the two accounts of the creation of man differ considerably. However, the answer lies not in an alleged dual tradition but in a dual man, not in an imaginary contradiction between two versions but in a real contradiction in the nature of man. The two accounts deal with

two Adams, two men, two fathers of mankind, two types, two representatives of humanity, and it is no wonder that they are not identical.[15]

Adam 1

The Adam 1 personality of which Genesis 1 speaks is created in the image of God, which the Rav calls "man's inner charismatic endowment as
a creative being." He resembles God in that he has the potential to become a creator. As such he is commanded to master all that he is capable
of knowing about the world. (It is almost as if God said to him, "Just as I
am a creator of worlds, so must you be one.") By commanding man to
master his environment, God directed him to the functional and practical aspects of his intellect. To be "human" for Adam 1 means to live a
dignified life. Dignity is attained through glory, which the Rav understands to be man's ability to dominate his environment. It is through
mastery of the world that Adam 1 attains dignity, his ultimate goal in
life. The Adam 1 personality is never encouraged to delve into the metaphysical realm, for such inquiry would in no way affect his ability to master
his environment. The success of science technology, says the Rav, is due
to the fact that it has "sacrificed qualitative metaphysical speculation for
the functional duplication of reality."

The pursuit of dignity means that Adam 1 must find answers to the
question, "How does the cosmos function?" Completely utilitarian in
his quest, the goal of Adam 1 is to harness the power of nature and put
it at his disposal. But a dignified life must be one that embraces responsibility. There is no dignity without responsibility, and responsibility
cannot be realized until man masters his environment. Adam 1 is ag-
gressive and bold; he is a creative being engaged in *imitatio Dei*. The
mathematician and the scientist personify the Adam 1 personality. The
history of Adam 1, is in the Rav's words:

> The great saga of freedom of man-slave who gradually transforms him-
> self into man-master . . . Adam 1 transcends the limits of the reason-
> able and probable and ventures into the open space of a boundless uni-
> verse. . . . Man reaching for the distant stars is acting in harmony with
> his nature which was created, willed and directed by his Maker.[16]

Dignity is a two-step process: Adam 1 must actualize his potential,
and he must communicate his accomplishments to others, for dignity is

linked with fame. "There is no dignity in anonymity," says the Rav. Adam 1 is a social being; he belongs in society. He needs to be with others because his success is dependent upon the joint effort, the social contract. Alone, he cannot possibly fulfill the charge to master the world given to him by the Almighty. That is why Adam 1 is created male and female concurrently. He is given a partner, which leads to a family, eventually to a community. Last and most significant, the drive Adam 1 has for the discovery of nature and the mastery of his environment is legitimate and in perfect harmony with the potential with which he was endowed by the Almighty. It is made perfectly clear by the Rav that the pursuit of all facets of knowledge of the universe with which Adam 1 identifies is a manifestation of obedience to God. By no means should this pursuit be misconstrued as rebellion.

Adam 2

Adam 2 is also intrigued by the cosmos, but in an entirely different way. He is not at all interested in *how* the cosmos functions. Neither his Maker nor his psyche demands that he master his environment. Adam 2 wants to know *why* the world came into being, why things are as they are, and where his place is in the Divine scheme of things. While Adam 1 is bent on mastery, creative and dynamic, Adam 2 is contemplative and receptive, discovering the image of God in His works in nature: he is awe-stricken at the majestic mountain, the towering oak, the beautiful red rose, and the simple blade of grass. Adam 2 is, indeed, preoccupied with God. This is alluded to, says the Rav, in the biblical phrase, "And He [God] breathed into his nostrils the breath of life."

Adam 1 and Adam 2 have the same goal: to fulfill the Divine imperative, that is, to fulfill the Divine imperative to actualize their potential as human beings. How the Divine imperative applies to them as individuals depends on their personality, the intellectual, emotional, and spiritual bent with which they were endowed. Adam 1 seeks dignity; Adam 2 seeks redemption. "An existence might be replete with dignity and mastery, and yet remain unredeemed," says the Rav. How does one experience redemption?

A redeemed existence is experienced in the privacy of one's own personality. It needs no community, for it does not have to be acted out vis à vis the outside world. One can live a redeemed life on a desert island. Who is a redeemed person? Someone who experiences his life as legitimate and worthwhile, for it is anchored in something greater than himself. Redemption is attained when man humbles himself before God. Again, in the words of the Rav:

> Cathartic redemptiveness, in contrast with dignity, cannot be attained through man's acquisition of control of his environment, but through man's exercise of control over himself. . . . God summoned Adam the first to advance steadily, Adam the second to retreat. Adam the first He told to exercise mastery and to "fill the earth and subdue it," Adam the second to serve. He was placed in the Garden of Eden to cultivate it and to keep it.[17]

Adam 2 is lonely; he is the lonely man of faith. He needs a companion, but only if he acquires this companion through the surrender of part of himself will it be meaningful to him. So the Almighty casts a deep sleep upon Adam 2, and he is overcome. In defeat, he sacrifices part of himself. Eve comes into being.

In conclusion: Rabbi Soloveitchik contends that the differences between the two accounts of the creation of man are not due to dual authorship and/or dual traditions, but to dual personalities. The Torah wants to portray two prototypes of man, each with his own particular approach to life and the Divine imperative. Though fundamentally different from each other in focus and in goal, they are both in conformity with the Divine Will.

The Multiple Names of God

Let us now proceed to the matter of the multiple names of God. In what is termed the "higher criticism," the Bible critics contend that the use of different names of God in the Torah text is indicative of multiple authorship.[18] This contention is termed "The Documentary Hypothesis." In point of fact, this hypothesis is not only contrary to a principle that we have already indicated has been accepted and designated by the sages as *fundamental*, namely, the Mosaic authorship of the Torah, it is also a rather simplistic rationale for the appearance of these names in the biblical text.

The sages of the Talmud and *Midrash* have clearly indicated that the context in which the various names of God appear reveals the significance of these names. Each name represents a different Divine attribute. Rashi, for example, contends that the name *E-lohim* connotes the attribute of strict justice while the *Tetragrammaton* connotes Divine mercy.[19] It is not multiple authorship, but rather multiple attributes, that is implied by the different names of God. The late Professor Umberto Cassuto, a contemporary Bible scholar, wrote a fine critique of the major suppositions and contentions of the higher criticism that is well worth considering on this matter.[20]

Both the scholar and the layman are impressed by what seems to be random use of the *Tetragrammaton* and *E-lohim* in the Torah, says Cassuto. In the first chapter of Genesis the name *E-lohim* appears exclusively, but in Genesis 2:4 the *Tetragrammaton* is adjoined to *E-lohim*. It is impossible to believe that the Torah, which is so precise and exacting in spelling out its demands on man's ethical and moral behavior and the way God must be worshiped, would be indiscriminate on so important a matter as the names of God. To posit that the Torah was written by several authors, each with his own name for God, is illogical and totally out of character, says Cassuto. How, then, do we understand the significance of the various names of God?

The name *E-lohim* is generic, a common noun meaning "deity," says Cassuto. At times it refers to the God of Israel, but it can also refer to the idols of the nations. The *Tetragrammaton*, on the other hand, is a proper noun referring exclusively to the God of Israel. In the halakhic portions of the Torah and in the writings of the prophets—with the exception of a few verses in Isaiah—the only name that appears is the *Tetragrammaton*. In what is known as the "wisdom literature," namely, the poetic portions of the books of Job, Ecclesiastes, and Proverbs, the *Tetragrammaton* appears exclusively. In those chapters of the book of Psalms where the author means to praise God not only as the God of Israel but as the Master of the universe, and he invites the nations of the world to worship together with Israel, the names *E-l* and *E-lohim* are found most frequently. The principle is quite clear, says Cassuto. Whenever the theme in the Bible relates to the nation of Israel exclusively, such as in the prophetic and poetic literature and the halakhic portions of the Torah, the *Tetragrammaton* appears. When the theme is of a general ethical nature, and it relates to other nations as well as Israel, the name *E-lohim* appears.

In the Torah narrative, the *Tetragrammaton* appears when what is depicted is the personal nature of God as He relates to Jewish tradition, the nation of Israel as a whole, and to individuals, says Cassuto. The name *E-lohim* appears when the transcendental nature of God or His relationship with other nations or other traditions is depicted. In the story of Creation in Genesis 1, the name *E-lohim* appears exclusively because God is portrayed as the transcendent Being Who created all things by His word alone. True, the creation story concludes with *Shabbat*, an institution given exclusively to Israel and one might have expected the *Tetragrammaton* to be used, but we must recognize that the reason given here for *Shabbat* is of a cosmic nature, says Cassuto, to remind us that God created heaven and earth. This universal idea applies to all mankind. It is for this reason that the name *E-lohim* appears even with regard to *Shabbat*. Moreover, says Cassuto, the fourth commandment reads, "Remember the *Shabbat* day to keep it holy . . . " It does not read, "Know that there is a *Shabbat* day." The institution of *Shabbat* was already known to the world when it was given to Israel.[21]

The story of the Garden of Eden depicts God as the Master and Teacher of ethics. As a precursor and indicative of the commandments He would in the future give to the nation of Israel, God demands of Adam that he be responsible for his actions and charges him not to eat from the tree of knowledge. As such, the *Tetragrammaton* is the appropriate name. Since this is the first time it appears in the biblical text, it is adjoined to the name *E-lohim* in order to teach the important principle that God, the Teacher of ethics, is also the Creator of the universe.[22]

In the final analysis, we must recognize that what is really behind the disagreement between tradition and scholarship is the fundamental premise with which each begins. The critics begin with the assumption that the Bible was written by man. As a literary endeavor, it is subject to language and style considerations no different than any other literary work. The traditional Jewish commentators, on the other hand, begin with the fundamental belief that it has been handed down father to son and teacher to student from the time of Moses, that the entire Torah is the word of God. The recipient of this document that derives from God, word for word and letter for letter, was none other than Moses. It is as simple as that. Must God conform to a homogeneous style for it to be recognized that the Torah derived from Him? Must

He conform to what was known of history and language by the Israelites in ancient times in order for the Torah to be considered authentic?
When one assumes the Divine authorship of the Torah, all linguistic
and stylistic considerations become moot.

Let me close today's session with the words of Rabbi Samson Raphael
Hirsch:

> Before we open it [the Torah], let us consider how we shall read it. Not
> for the purpose of making philological and antiquarian investigations,
> nor to find support and corroboration for antediluvian or geological
> hypotheses, nor either in expectation of unveiling supermundane mys-
> teries, but as Jews we must read it—that is to say, looking upon it as a
> book given to us that we may learn from it to know ourselves—what
> we are and what we should be in this our earthly existence.[23]

At our next session, I intend to introduce you to Jewish ethics. Many
people labor under the misconception that Judaism is only concerned
with ritual and synagogue worship; they are totally unaware of the fact
that ethics plays a major role both in Jewish philosophy and in *Halakhah*.
We must always keep in mind that the Ten Commandments—to which
all 613 *mitzvot* can be traced—are divided into two parts: five concern
man's relationship with God; the other five are concerned with man's
relationship with his fellow man. Both derive from God, and both are
of paramount importance.

Session IV
The Role of Ethics
in Jewish Thinking

When we met for the first time, Moshe, you were surprised when I told you that many of the ethical principles to which you are presently committed are found in the Torah. I would like to spend today's session illustrating this point.

In Deuteronomy 28:9 we read: "The Lord will establish you as His holy people, as He swore to you if you keep the commandments of the Lord your God and walk in His ways." It teaches us an important principle in life: to walk in the ways of God. This means that just as we experience God's compassion, so must we be compassionate; just as we experience His forbearance, so must we be forbearing; just as we experience His abundant kindness and truth, so must we be abundant in kindness and truth. We must contemplate God's ways in the world, His benevolence toward man, and incorporate His ways into our personality so that benevolence becomes the hallmark of man's behavior toward his fellow man.

A substantial group of laws that relate to the relationship between man and his fellow man begins with Leviticus 19:1, which reads: "The Lord spoke to Moses saying: Speak to the whole Israelite community and say to them: You shall be holy, for I, the Lord your God, am holy." Here again the Torah charges us to imitate God; to do so is defined as holiness. But how is holiness defined? The term *kadosh* is most often translated as "holy," but what it really means is "unique" or "separate." Just as God is unique or "totally other" from all things that exist in the universe, so must the Jewish people be separate from all the nations of the world in their way of life, namely, their ethical and moral behavior. Let us now discuss some of these laws.

Love Your Neighbor

Perhaps the most commonly known biblical verse is Leviticus 19:18, which reads: "You shall not take vengeance or bear a grudge against your kinsfolk. Love your neighbor as yourself: I am the Lord." This injunction is one of the 613 *mitzvot* given to the people of Israel. Did you know that the original source of this principle to which you say you are committed is the Torah? Let us examine some of the ramifications of this law and its philosophy.

Taken literally, this *mitzvah* is perplexing. As magnanimous as one might be toward one's fellow man, it would be virtually impossible to love any other human being as oneself, let alone every human being. Here is an example of where the Oral Law resolves the difficulty. Our sages explain that in this context what is meant by love is consideration, fair and amicable treatment. While it may be impossible to love every human being as we love ourselves, it is certainly within the realm of possibility to treat all other people fairly and with compassion, the way we would want to be treated by others. The Talmud makes this point in a well-known anecdote:

> It happened that a certain heathen came before Shammai and said to him, "Make me a proselyte, on condition that you teach me the whole Torah while I stand on one foot." Thereupon he repulsed him with a builder's cubit which was in his hand. When he went before Hillel, he said to him, "What is hateful to yourself, do not to your neighbor: that is the whole Torah, the rest is commentary. Go and learn it!"[1]

Considering that this law appears in the Torah as a positive commandment, what motivated Hillel to formulate it in the negative? It is because "Love your neighbor as yourself," when taken in its broadest sense, would be an impossible demand upon man and, indeed, a foolish one, for one should not love everyone. It pertains only to the first part of the biblical verse. We are forbidden to take revenge or bear a grudge against our fellow man or harm him in any way that would be hateful to ourselves. To behave in this way toward our fellow man would be a manifestation of love.[2]

Nevertheless, it is important to note that this commandment has positive implications as well. In his commentary on the Torah, Rabbi Samson Raphael Hirsch writes:

> We are to assist him [our fellow man] in everything that furthers his well-being and happiness as if we were working for ourselves. . . . This is something which does lie within our possibilities and is something which is required of us even towards someone whose personality may be actually highly antipathetic to us. For the demand of this love is something which lies quite outside the sphere of the personality of our neighbor and is not based on any of his qualities.[3]

We are charged to be compassionate to our fellow man. A person who loves his fellow man as himself will not steal from him or commit adultery or deal dishonestly with him in business. When one speaks about one's fellow man, one must be respectful and ponder carefully before the fact what one will say and what one will choose to omit. In *Ethics of the Fathers* 4:23, we read: "Do not appease your friend while he is angry, and do not comfort him while his dead lies before him, and do not question him when he vows, and do not strive to see him when he is disgraced." One who honors one's fellow man in this way honors God as well. Isaiah 49:3 tells us that the Almighty says of him: "You are My servant Israel in whom I glory." One who dishonors one's fellow man in these matters, on the other hand, has violated a positive command.[4]

Isn't it interesting to note that Rabbi Isaac Ashkenazy, the renowned sixteenth-century talmudist and mystic known as the "Ari" (an acronym for Ashkenazy Rabbi Isaac), advised that the *mitzvah* to love one's fellow man be taken upon oneself anew every day before commencing with the Morning Service.[5]

Taking Revenge and Bearing a Grudge

Let us now focus on the first part of the biblical verse, that is, revenge and bearing a grudge. The sages point out that there is a difference between these two human weaknesses. Take the following example. David needs a lawn mower. He tries to borrow one from Joseph, who refuses to lend it to him. Some time later, Joseph comes to David to borrow his electric saw. Now David refuses. He might take revenge by saying, "Just as you refused to lend me your lawn mower, I refuse to lend you my electric saw." On the other hand he might say, "You refused to lend me your lawn mower, but I'm not like you; I will lend you my saw." That would be considered bearing a grudge. In the first instance, David acts on his animosity toward Joseph and refuses Joseph's request; in the second, he demonstrates his ethical superiority to Joseph by granting his request. Both are forbidden by the Torah. What is interesting to note is that while the Torah prohibits us from taking revenge for something done to us personally, it does not prohibit avenging wrong done to others.[6]

It is biblically prohibited to harbor ill feelings toward our fellow man even if those feelings do not lead to taking revenge or bearing a grudge. In Leviticus 19:17 we read: "You shall not hate your brother in your heart; reprove your neighbor but incur no guilt because of him." Hate is a powerful emotion. When translated into action, it can cause the recipient a great deal of harm. However, the Torah forbids hate even when it is merely maintained in one's heart for one never knows where it may lead. One who feels that he has been wronged by another person should confront him and make a sincere effort to resolve the matter instead of withdrawing and harboring hatred in his heart.

Unprovoked Hatred and Reproval

The Talmud tells us that the Second Temple in Jerusalem was destroyed because of *sin'at hinom* (unprovoked hatred).[7] In the time of the great Rabbi Akiva, twenty-four thousand of his students died because of this sin. *Sin'at hinom* is a plague that has taken a heavy toll in the Jewish community in every generation. Most often motivated by jealousy, it leads to resentment and finally to hatred. Ironically, it is usually due to misinformation. Under no circumstances should such unprovoked hatred be tolerated. It is the responsibility of the rabbinic authorities in every generation to bring such hatred out into the open and dispel it. Every human being is a descendant of Adam and Eve. However distant, we are all related to each other. When we interact, we should treat each other with fairness and compassion and keep in mind that before God, all human beings stand together, one community of mankind, one people.

To recognize all people as "the community of mankind" means to be responsible for the well-being of our fellow man. (It also bears with it the responsibility of society as a whole, and we will discuss this more fully later.) Should we become aware of a particular person's unethical or immoral behavior, we are charged by the Torah to reprove him in the hope of effecting a change in his ways. The source for this *mitzvah* is Leviticus 19:17, which reads: "You shall not hate your kinsman in your heart. You shall surely rebuke your friend, but incur no guilt because of him." Reproval must be motivated by love, not hatred. As we read in the book of Proverbs, "He whom God loves He reproves, even as a father the son in whom he delights" (3:12).

Nevertheless, like every *mitzvah*, reproval has its parameters. Reprove once, twice, three times, until it becomes evident that the sinner will not listen no matter how many times he is told.[8] Beyond this point, reproval is no longer obligatory for it can be dangerous to both parties. This means that with regard to a secular Jew who transgresses the laws of Judaism blatantly and often displays impatience, even contempt for those who observe the laws, and upon whom reproval will have no effect, not only does the obligation to reprove fall away, it becomes forbidden. For our sages point out that just as it is praiseworthy for one to say that which will be received graciously, so is it praiseworthy for one not to say that which will not be received graciously.[9]

As we have indicated, the Torah ordains reproval only when it is motivated by love and concern for the recipient and the desire to set him back on the right path of life. But even then, care must be taken not to humiliate him, for with most people humiliation would be counterproductive: it would tend to alienate the recipient, and thus be contrary to the meaning and purpose of the *mitzvah*. This is what is implied in the words "incur no guilt because of him." It is no wonder that the sages require that rebuke be done in private.

In many situations, the success or failure of reproval is as much dependent upon where it comes from as it is on how it is given. Many adults are not very much impressed or affected by reproval from their peers. They disregard it and continue in their ways. A strong expression of disapproval by a rabbi or some other highly respected member of the community, on the other hand, would not be taken lightly. In all likelihood, it would motivate them to seriously reflect upon their behavior, and this might lead them to change their ways.[10] A teenager would tend to react much differently to reproval. If it came from an adult, even a respected member of the community, it would not have as much impact as reproval from a peer.

A teacher of mine once mused, "I don't know why we are born, and I don't know why we must die, but I do know that while we are alive, we'd better hold tightly to one another." The ethical and moral laws of the Torah certainly reflect this feeling.

Misleading the Blind

Let us look at another example of Jewish ethics. In Leviticus 19:14 we read: "You shall not curse the deaf, nor put a stumbling block before the blind, but you shall fear your God: I am the Lord." Taken on face value, who would argue with such a *mitzvah?* One might wonder why it is even necessary for such a *mitzvah* to have been included in the Torah.

In point of fact, there is a great deal more to this *mitzvah* than would be demanded if it were taken literally. For visual blindness is not the only kind of sightlessness, and stones are not the only kind of stumbling blocks. The law teaches man that he is prohibited from dispensing misinformation to people who are ignorant, that is, intellectually blind. If a person comes to us for advice on a particular matter, we are forbidden from intentionally advising him improperly. Do not tell a person to go out on a journey early in the morning, say the sages, when you know that if he does so he will surely be accosted by thieves.[11]

On first blush the concluding words of Leviticus 19:14, "but you shall fear your God," seem superfluous. What do they add to the *mitzvah?* Rashi, in his biblical, commentary makes an important clarification.

> Because in this case it is not given to human beings to know whether the intention of this man was for the advantage or disadvantage of the person whom he advised and he thus might be able to evade the responsibility by saying, "I meant it for the best," Scripture states with reference to him, "but you shall fear your God." He is cognizant of your secret thoughts.[12]

The ramifications of this law are almost boundless in their concern for the welfare of society. One is prohibited from being an accessory to an individual who is intent on committing a forbidden act. For example, an accountant is prohibited from falsifying a tax form in order to save his client from paying money he owes in taxes. A physician is prohibited from falsifying a medical insurance form to enable his patient to get back money that is not rightfully due to him.[13]

Assault and Battery

We have not yet spoken of the prohibition against inflicting physical harm upon one's fellow man, but this should be self-evident. In Exodus 21:18 the Torah teaches: "When men quarrel and one strikes the other with stone or fist, and he does not die but must take to his bed, if he then gets up and walks outdoors on his cane, the assailant shall go unpunished, except that he must pay for his loss of time and for his cure."

A person who inflicts injury upon his fellow man is responsible whether the damage he caused was intentional or unintentional. The injured person is entitled to compensation. In assessing the compensation, the following must be taken into consideration: the kind of disability that resulted, if any did at all; the pain suffered; medical bills; loss of time and earning power; and the embarrassment and indignity suffered by the injured party because of the injury. With regard to the last point, the age and the position in the community of the injured party must be taken into consideration. In addition, the person who inflicted the injury must seek forgiveness from the injured party.[14]

Property Damage and Theft

Jewish law teaches respect and high regard for the wealth and property of our fellow man as well as his person. Leviticus 19:11 reads: "You shall not steal; neither deny, neither deal deceitfully with one another." The Talmud adds: "Let the property of your friend be as dear to you as your own."[15] Were these words meant to be taken literally? Surely it would be unrealistic to expect people to consider the property of others as dear to them as their own. I believe that what the Talmud means is that we must treat the possessions of others with the same regard as we would want others to treat ours. An investment broker, for example, should be as careful, as honest, and as resourceful in advising his clients on how to handle their investments as he would be about his own. Just as he would be alert to the dangers that might threaten his own holdings, so must he alert his clients with regard to theirs. But this is the limit of his responsibility. If his clients choose to act contrary to his advice, he cannot be held responsible or even faulted.

It makes no difference whether the amount is substantial or negligible, whether it concerns a corporation, a small business or an individual, the act of stealing is forbidden. It should be noted that Jewish law has extended this prohibition to include using another person's property without his permission.[16] To be sure, swindling, false advertising, and any other questionable business practices are included in this prohibition. Rabbi Samson Raphael Hirsch adds:

> In business as in social intercourse, everybody must be able to demand the truth from us, and even if it is to our disadvantage must be able to depend on our admission of the truth. . . . Flatterers who steal from their fellow man the most important truth, the truth of knowing oneself, and hypocrites who pass the whole of themselves as a false coin, belong to the most objectionable characters which are to be banished from Jewish social life.[17]

Taking something that belongs to another person, even if the object is taken merely as a practical joke with the intent of returning it, is clearly forbidden. To purchase stolen property, even an object that is merely suspected of having been stolen, is likewise forbidden. Taking undue advantage of someone by withholding that which is rightly due him, such as paying a worker less than he deserves simply because he is in desperate need of a job, is equally forbidden. A day laborer must be paid at the end of the day when he completes his work. To postpone paying him until the following day is unfair and prohibited by the Torah as well. For in Leviticus 19:13 we read: "You shall not retain that which is due to your neighbor. You shall not commit robbery. The wages of a laborer shall not remain with you until morning."[18]

Bribery: A Serious Crime

In the American system of justice an individual is presumed innocent until proven guilty. Jewish law goes far beyond the democratic system here. In Leviticus 19:15 we read: "You shall not render an unfair decision: do not favor the poor or show deference to the rich; judge your neighbor fairly." What is the meaning of the term *fairly?* Our sages explain that the Torah demands that there be total objectivity in a Jewish court of law. The reputation, moral character, or previous record of the litigants must carry no weight at all in the eyes of the court. The judge must base his ruling only on the case that is before him. If the evidence clearly exonerates a reputed scoundrel, the judge must find him completely innocent. On the other hand, a person of sterling character must be judged guilty if the evidence clearly points in that direction.

Bribery is a serious crime; it perverts the court. Perverting justice in a court of law by engaging in bribery is a serious offense forbidden by Jewish law, whether the bribe is monetary or otherwise. In Exodus 23:6–8 we are taught: "You shall not subvert the rights of the needy in their disputes. Keep far from a false charge: do not bring death on the innocent and the righteous, for I will not acquit the wrongdoer. Do not take bribes, for bribes blind the clear-sighted and upset the pleas of the just."

This law applies to Gentiles as well. In the category of establishing a system of justice, it is one of the seven Noahide commandments.

On first reading, one might conclude that the law that prohibits bribery applies only to judges, since almost identical words appear in Deuteronomy 16:19 where it is written: "for bribes blind the eyes of the discerning and upset the plea of the just," where it is clearly addressed to judges. The consensus of opinion in the Talmud, however, rejects this conclusion and posits that the law applies to all public officials.[19]

An arbitrator may not accept a bribe even if it comes from both parties and is meant to ensure that judgment will be deliberate and justice will prevail, so as to protect the innocent and convict the guilty. The rationale for this ruling is quite obvious: if both parties give him something, the arbitrator might feel obligated to both of them and suggest a compromise even in a situation where one of the parties is clearly in the right.

Judgment of our fellow man outside the court is an entirely different matter. As Rabbi Samson Raphael Hirsch explains:

> Judgment in a court of justice and social judgment do not serve the same purpose. The former has to test the action solely as to whether it is in accordance with the dictates of justice or not, quite apart from any consideration of the individual circumstances or conditions and without regard to the motives. An action, although it may not be legal, can be entirely excusable and yet at the forum of justice must be judged as punishable. And an action judged by its motive can be stamped as highly vicious and yet legally be within the law and unpunishable. But society, on the other hand, above all, the personality, the character, in its eye, and every action is, to it, only a symptom by which to judge the integrity or the reverse of it members.[20]

In contradistinction from the courts, in social life we should not be too hasty in judging our fellow man. Who knows what we might have done in the same situation? "Do not judge your fellow man until you have been in his position," said the sages.[21] We should always look for an excuse, not to justify wrongful behavior but to understand it, and based on our understanding to try to forgive rather than condemn. Put quite succinctly, "Judge all men favorably."[22]

The Priority of a Human Life

It is stated in Sanhedrin 37b: "Whosoever preserves a single soul of Israel, Scripture ascribes merit to him as if he preserved a complete world." Judaism puts the highest possible priority on human life, perhaps more so than any other religion. It is common knowledge that with the exception of murder, idolatry, and forbidden sexual relations, any and every law of the Torah may be violated in order to save one human life, even if that person is not expected to live more than a few moments longer. In Leviticus 19:16 we read: "You shall not go about as a talebearer among your people; neither shall you stand idly by the blood of your neighbor." Rashi explains: "Do not stand idly by and witness his death when you can save him."

The Talmud spells it out clearly. If a person sees his neighbor drowning or attacked by robbers, he is obligated to take action and help him. Where he is physically incapable of doing so, he is obligated to secure someone to do it for him.[23] A physician must do what he can if he is present in an emergency medical situation; he is forbidden to turn away. A person who has evidence that enables him to testify in a court of law on behalf of his fellow man is obligated to do so.

What are the parameters of the *mitzvah* of saving a life? Must I put my own life in danger to save the life of another person? Maimonides explains that Jewish law demands my concern, my particular talent or training, and at times, even expenditure of my own funds, to save the life of my fellow man. However, I am not obligated to put my own life in danger.[24] To do so is simply foolish piety.[25]

Charity or Righteousness

Our final example of man's responsibility for the welfare of his fellow man concerns the needy and the poor. In American society helping the poor is referred to as charity, which by definition means "that which is bestowed gratuitously on the poor for their relief." This clearly implies that giving charity is an act of magnanimity. The Jewish approach to helping the poor is fundamentally different. Funds for the poor are commonly referred to as *tsedakah*, which literally means "righteousness." One who gives to the poor fulfills a commandment and as such performs an act of righteousness. Deuteronomy 15:7 teaches: "If there is a needy person among you, one of your kinsmen in any of your settlements in the land that the Lord your God is giving you, do not harden your heart and shut your hand against your needy kinsman. Rather you must open your hand and lend him sufficient for whatever he needs."

Wealth is a blessing from God; it must be handled judiciously. A person who believes that his accumulation of wealth is due entirely to his own initiative, which in turn gives him the right to keep it all for himself, is making a profound error in judgment. The Torah warns

> When you have eaten your fill, and have built fine houses to live in
> . . . and your silver and gold have increased, and everything you own
> has prospered, beware lest your heart grow haughty and you forget
> the Lord your God . . . and you say to yourselves, "My power and the
> might of my own hand have won this wealth for me." Remember that
> it is the Lord your God who gives you the power to get wealth, in ful-
> fillment of the covenant that He made on oath with your fathers, as is
> still the case.[26]

It is interesting to note that although we are not obligated to enrich the poor, Jewish law ordains that when we give *tsedakah*, we consider the position of the impoverished person to whom it is being given. If one has the means, one should try to restore the needy person's dignity and self-esteem by providing him with some of the luxuries he once enjoyed. With one person it might be fine clothing; with another, a decent apartment in which to live.[27] Interestingly, the *Halakhah* ordains that a needy relative takes precedence in this instance over all other needy individuals, and the needy of the city in which one lives take precedence over the needy of other cities.[28] The responsibility to support the poor and provide for all their needs makes it necessary for every Jewish community to create a special fund-raising project or organization for this purpose. It is simply too much of a responsibility to leave to the individual alone.

Of course, the highest degree of *tsedakah* is giving a needy person a loan of money. In Exodus 22:24 we are taught: "If you lend money to My people, to the poor who is in your power, do not act toward him as a creditor: exact no interest from him." It is sufficiently clear from this verse that when lending money to a fellow Jew, it is prohibited to take interest for that loan. This is the basis for an organization called "The Hebrew Free Loan Society," found in most large cities.

Finally, in Exodus 23:2, 3 a special charge is given to the judges of Israel: "Do not side with the mighty and do wrong . . . nor must you show deference to a poor man in his dispute." Despite the emphasis of Jewish law on helping the needy and the obligation that falls on society to restore their dignity, a needy person who comes before a judge in a lawsuit must not be given special treatment. He must be treated fairly, but he must not be favored in judgment simply because of his financial condition. This is true justice.

We have spoken thus far about the obligation of society to be concerned with the individual. Let us now focus on the obligation of the individual to society at large.

The poet and clergyman John Donne wrote, "No man is an island entire of itself . . . any man's death diminishes me, for I am involved in mankind."[29] These simple heartfelt words express the poet's philosophy of life and his feeling of responsibility for the welfare of society. The Torah, with which, being a clergyman, Mr. Donne was most assuredly familiar, preaches this as well.

Tikkun Olam

What was the first command God gave to Adam and through him to all subsequent generations? We find it in Genesis 1:28, and it reads: "Be fruitful and multiply and fill the earth and subdue it, and have dominion over the fish of the sea, the birds of the heavens and all creeping things that creep upon the earth." As we have already explained, in order to fulfill the *mitzvah* of subduing the earth we must first study it. It is a biblical injunction that to the extent that it is humanly possible, we must master all there is to know about the nature of reality. Not only does this legitimize the pursuit of science; it classifies such a pursuit as the fulfillment of a *mitzvah* of biblical origin, and, having been given to Adam, the father of mankind, it pertains to all people. With mastery comes dignity, providing it is coupled with responsibility. There can be no dignity without responsibility.

The Jew has been charged by the Almighty with a dual responsibility. In the words of Rabbi Soloveitchik:

> We Jews have been burdened with a twofold task; we have to cope with the problem of a double confrontation. We think of ourselves as human beings, sharing the destiny of Adam in his general encounter with nature, and as members of a covenantal community. . . . We believe that we are the bearers of a double charismatic load, that of the dignity of man and that of the sanctity of the covenantal community.[30]

In the Talmud, man's responsibility to work for the welfare of society is called *tikkun olam*, literally, "the perfection of the world." It is invoked quite frequently with regard to a variety of matters of Jewish law. Whether we consciously accept this responsibility or not, the fact remains that Jewish ideas from the Torah and the Talmud have been and continue to be a formative factor in the legal systems as well as the ethics of Western civilization. What's more, history testifies to the fact that Jews have ranked prominently among the foremost thinkers and innovators in the field of science and technology.[31]

Of course, it must be understood that the way in which one pursues the responsibility of *tikkun olam* and the extent to which it is pursued varies from individual to individual, depending upon his talents, his intelligence, and his interests. Also to be taken into consideration is the culture in which one lives, the matter of anti-Semitism, and the opportunities that are open to Jews to become involved in the welfare of society. Assuming, however, that at a given time and place, involvement in the welfare of society is a viable option, one becomes obligated to actualize that option and contribute to the welfare of society to the best of one's ability.

Ecology: A Jewish Responsibility

Let us take, for example, the matter of the environment. In today's society, environmental protection is of major concern. We have reached the point where pollution of our rivers, lakes, and streams is widespread and the very air we breathe is threatening our existence. Unless something significant is done about pollution in the near future, we are all headed for disaster. To become actively involved in environmental protection would certainly come under the rubric of *tikkun olam*. But this is not all.

It can be established from the Torah as well as from rabbinic law that Judaism relates to environmental issues even more directly. In Genesis 2:15 we are told that man was placed in the Garden of Eden "to till it and to protect it." The *Midrash* adds:

When the Holy One, blessed be He, created man he took him to view all the trees in the garden and said to him: "Look at My works, how good and pleasant they are! All that I have created, was created for you. Make up your mind that you will not ruin or destroy My world. For if you will ruin it, no one will repair it after you."[32]

The earth was created by God for man. No sooner was man created, he was given the charge to subdue the earth and master it. But this blessing and charge was coupled with the warning that he must act responsibly to nurture the world and to preserve it. Let us look at a more specific example of man's responsibility for the preservation of nature.

The Torah forbids wanton destruction of fruit trees. In the book of Deuteronomy we read:

> When you shall besiege a city a long time, in making war against it to take it, you shall not destroy its trees by wielding an axe against them: for you may eat of them, but you shall not cut them down; for is the tree of the field man that it should be besieged by you? Only the trees of which you know that they are not trees for food, them you may destroy and cut down, that you may build bulwarks against the city that makes war with you, until it falls.[33]

The violation of nature is treated very seriously in the Torah. Even in war there are limitations to what may be destroyed in the process of conquest. That which was created to sustain man may not be destroyed for the purpose of annihilating him. But *Halakhah* goes beyond the confines of war. What appears in the Torah as a law with limited application has been interpreted by rabbinic law to apply to all forms of wanton destruction. The wanton destruction of anything that can be of use to man is prohibited by this law.[34]

Air and noise pollution is discussed in rabbinic sources, not from the perspective of environmental protection but as nuisances perpetrated upon one's fellow man. For example, carrion graves and tanyards must be kept fifty cubits from town.[35] A person who does the kind of work that makes loud noises, raises a great deal of dust, or emits an objectionable odor must do so at a reasonable distance from his neighbor so that he will not harm or annoy him in the process.[36] Just imagine how much good could be accomplished for the protection of the environment if a law like this were applied to industry.

Now it is important not to misconstrue the Jewish approach to environmental protection. Clearly, the focal point of *Halakhah* is man. Nature worship is idolatry, a cardinal sin in Judaism, and beauty for beauty's sake is a concept that is foreign to Jewish thinking. Man is obligated to protect the environment because everything in nature in some way enhances his life. It would be logical to assume that the rationale for extending the prohibition against the destruction of fruit trees in time of war to all kinds of wanton destruction is that most things have some value to man. In point of fact, the law states that a fruit tree that bears little fruit may be cut down and sold for fire wood if it would bring man greater profit.[37] Of course, an object that has no value may be dispensed with in whatever way one sees fit.

Man's responsibility for the welfare of his fellow man is not limited to the prohibition against improper behavior. Endangering our fellow man by refraining from proper action is likewise prohibited. For example, in Deuteronomy 22:8 we find: "When you build a new house, you shall make a parapet (railing) for your roof, so that you do not bring bloodguilt on your house if anyone should fall from it." Here again, it is self-evident that the law is not limited to its simple literal meaning. We are charged to remove any hazardous conditions that exist in our homes or on our property, such as an uncovered live electric wire, a slippery floor, an open pit in our backyard, or a vicious dog, so that no one is injured because of our negligence. Yes, inaction when action is necessary can be as unacceptable as improper action.

Finally, let us note the words of Rabbi Hanina, assistant to the High Priest in the Temple: "Pray for the welfare of the government, for without the fear of it men would swallow one another alive."[38] Left to their own designs, many people would be prone to engage in pursuits that are unethical and immoral. Others would have no qualms of conscience in pursuing the acquisition of wealth and power at the expense of their fellow man. And there are those who would not think twice about taking the lives of others for personal gain. Of course, one must keep in mind that power corrupts, and government officials are not at all immune to such corruption. Man needs the strong arm of government to keep him in line, but government needs the attentive eye of the people to keep it in line as well. Pray for the welfare of the government, says Rabbi Hanina, let the people be at peace with the government and let the government be at peace with its citizens.

We must always be mindful of the fact that the security of the Jew is dependent upon the security, the integrity of government officials, and the power of the government of the country in which he lives. We know all too well that in times of national unrest, whether this is initiated by war, economic depression, or some other national disaster, a scapegoat is always sought to blame for the bad times. History testifies to the fact that the scapegoat has inevitably been the Jew. Now while it is true that the most significant force in preventing this from happening is a government with integrity, Jewish loyalty to that government must likewise be recognized as an important factor. The Jew must be a loyal citizen to his country. He must recognize that Jewish law has always encouraged such loyalty. When Jerusalem was destroyed in 586 B.C.E. and the Jews were exiled to Babylonia, the prophet encouraged the people to seek the welfare of the government. In Jeremiah 29:7 we find the following words: "Seek the welfare of the city to which I have exiled you and pray to the Lord in its behalf; for in its prosperity you shall prosper." A Jew must respect and honor the law of the country in which he lives. As the Talmud states: "The law of the land is law."³⁹

There is another point that must be made in the context of this discussion. Rabbi Hanina teaches us to be concerned not only with ourselves and our families but with all of humanity. One should be concerned for the welfare of all people, and to some extent be personally saddened by the sadness of any decent human being. One should pray for the welfare of the government, for this will ensure peace in the world.⁴⁰ This, too, is *tikkun olam.*

There is a great deal more to Jewish ethics and morality than what we have discussed ever so briefly at this session. My purpose was merely to demonstrate the importance Judaism gives to interpersonal relations and the establishment of an ethical society. I'm sure that you now realize that the principles of ethics and morality that you have culled from society and have of your own free will adopted into your lifestyle derive from the Torah. Whether you are aware of it or not, you are an observant Jew by virtue of the fact that you are fulfilling many of the *mitzvot* in the Torah.

I would like to continue our discussion on Jewish ethics, and devote our next session to Jewish medical ethics. It will surprise you to know how much has been written through the ages, but especially in the last few decades, on this very relevant topic.

Session V
Some Considerations
in Medical Ethics

If there is one profession with which Jews throughout history have been identified more than any other, it is medicine. I believe that Jewish literature will corroborate the notion that the reason for this phenomenon is because Jews have always believed that a healthy body is a most fitting receptacle for the human soul, and the human soul is man's most precious possession. Jewish tradition teaches us that health and sickness emanate from God, and just as He inflicts illness so does He heal. As we find in Deuteronomy 32:39: "See, then, that I, I am He; there is no god beside Me. I deal death and give life; I wounded and I will heal: none can deliver from My hand." Given this, one cannot help but question the right of man to consult a physician and the right of the physician to attempt to heal. Should one not rely on God to cure man's ills? If God does not want an individual to be cured, what can the physician do? We will deal with this matter first.

One of the fundamental principles in Jewish philosophy is that man has a measure of free will. Human behavior is at least to some extent based on freely chosen actions. The parameters of human freedom are, of course, unknown to us, and they vary from person to person depending upon a multiplicity of factors, genetic and environmental. What about health and the human life span? Is this realm reserved exclusively for God, as the verse in Deuteronomy seems to indicate, or can man intervene? The position taken by the Karaites and Christian Science is that one must rely on God alone to heal one's ailments. Is this position in consonance with Jewish law or does Jewish law posit that man has both the ability and the right to improve his health, conquer disease, and thereby extend his life span?

If the answer to these questions were an unequivocal "yes," it would imply that the medical profession is simply "off limits" for Jews. If man is not permitted to seek healing from a physician, neither may he choose to be a healer. For by attempting to heal, he becomes an accessory to a transgression, and this is clearly prohibited by Jewish law. Of course, the answer to our questions is a definitive "no." Although our health and our life span are in God's hands, we have both the right and the ability to affect our physical and mental condition, to seek healing for ourselves, and to heal others. However, this does not preclude the possibility that illness and disease are inflicted upon man by God (as punishment) and may not respond to even the most noble efforts of expert physicians.

In point of fact, we know that in biblical times man sought healing from God. Abraham prayed to heal Avimelekh[1] and Isaac prayed to heal his wife Rebecca.[2] What, then, is the source for the right of a physician to heal and the right of man to seek healing?

The Physician's Right to Heal

In Exodus 21:18, 19, we find the following: "And if men quarrel, and a man smite his fellow man with a stone or with his fist, and he does not die but becomes bed ridden: if he then gets up and walks outdoors upon his staff, the assailant shall go unpunished except that he must pay for the loss of his time and his cure."

The words "his cure" refers to the physician's fee.[3] The fact that medical expenses must be paid by the assailant clearly indicates that a physician must be consulted. From this we infer that a physician has the right to attempt to heal. The Talmud states specifically: "From here we learn that permission was given for the physician to heal."[4] The commentators added that even if it is suspected that a particular illness or disease is the result of Divine punishment, the physician has permission to intervene and attempt to cure.[5] Now we must keep in mind that Jewish tradition regards the physician merely as God's messenger; God alone is the healer of the sick. Permission having been granted, however, the responsibility for proper care rests heavily upon the physician. Shoddy medicine bears severe punishment.

Having established the right of the physician to heal, let us discuss several timely medical issues and discover how these matters are addressed by Jewish law. It should be understood at the outset, however, that our discussions will be purely academic. Actual cases must be referred to responsible rabbinic authorities who will judge them on an individual basis.

Abortion: When Does Life Begin?

We have already established that there is nothing that carries higher priority in Jewish law than the preservation of a human life. But when does human viability begin? Is it the moment of conception or the moment of birth? Is a fetus viable? If not, does it have any status at all? If a fetus has full status as a viable human being, abortion would be murder. If it does not, one could make a good argument to permit abortion for almost any humane consideration.

The Talmud speaks of four stages of life: from conception until the fortieth day; from the fortieth day until birth; from birth on (when the infant is full term); from the thirtieth day after birth on (when the infant is not known to be full term).[6]

The basic source for abortion is the *Mishnah*,[7] where it is taught that if in the process of birth both the child's life and the mother's life are being threatened, and it has been determined that only one of them can survive, the mother's life takes precedence. The rationale for this ruling is that the mother is a viable human being but the fetus, while it is still in the womb, does not yet have full status as a living human being. If the greater part of the fetus has emerged from the womb, however, no action may be taken, for one may not set aside one life to save another.[8] Of course, the *Mishnah* speaks of a situation wherein the fetus is full term and viability is established on the day of birth.[9]

There is another principle in Jewish law that is prominent in the matter of abortion. It is the law of *rodef* ("pursuer"), which states: If one person is in pursuit of another with the intent to kill, whatever possible must be done to save the potential victim even at the cost of a limb of the pursuer, and if need be his life. According to Maimonides, in the first case of the *Mishnah*, the fetus assumes the role of a pursuer; the mother, that of the victim. This is the only consideration that prompted the sages to rule that the life of the mother takes precedence over the life of the fetus, says Maimonides.[10] Were it possible to clearly establish that the fetus is not in pursuit of its mother's life, abortion would be prohibited. In such a case, no action may be taken by man; the matter must be left to God. There is one exception, however. If it is the considered medical opinion that by refraining from taking any action, both mother and child will die, the mother must be saved.

Euthanasia: Mercy or Cruelty?

When setting priorities for saving a human life, should suffering not be taken into consideration? Jewish law demands that we do our utmost to alleviate pain and suffering. To ease a patient's pain, we may even violate the laws of *Shabbat.* Now it should be understood that the rationale for this ruling is not that we are lenient with regard to the laws of *Shabbat.* Quite the contrary: we are strict about *Shabbat* law. It is rather that we adopt a position of stringency in the matter of easing human suffering.

How does the Jewish attitude toward human suffering affect the matter of euthanasia? Would the pain and suffering of a terminally ill patient be sufficient to permit ending his life? Let us first define the term *euthanasia.*

Positive euthanasia is to actively bring about the death of a terminally ill patient by administering drugs or the use of other devices.
Negative euthanasia is to refrain from taking positive action by not administering life-prolonging drugs or putting the patient on mechanical devices, thus allowing him to die what is termed a "natural death."

It is important to note that the ability to prolong life almost indefinitely through mechanical devices is a rather recent phenomenon. In the days of the Talmud this was impossible. Nevertheless, there are precedents in the Bible and sufficient rabbinic rulings with regard to the care of a dying person for us to establish a halakhic position on the matter of euthanasia.

The law states that no action may be taken to hasten the death of one who is critically ill. Even the confession recited by a dying person must be worded in a way that will not make him lose all hope for recovery. It reads:

> I give thanks to you, Lord, my God and God of my fathers, in whose hands rest my healing and my death. May it be Your will that I be healed with perfect healing, but if I die, may my death serve as an atonement for the sins and the iniquities and for the transgressions, that I have sinned and committed iniquity and transgressed against You. Grant my portion in Paradise and enable me to enter the World to Come that is prepared for the righteous.[11]

In determining the position of Jewish law on euthanasia rabbinic authorities make reference to two cases that serve as precedents. The first case is found in the book of Samuel.

Saul, the first king of Israel, was in battle with the Philistines, and he was critically wounded. Turning to his arms-bearer he said, "Draw your sword and run me through, so that the uncircumcised may not run me through and make sport of me" (1 Samuel 31:1–5). His arms-bearer refused and Saul grasped the sword and fell upon it himself. In 2 Samuel 1:1–10, 13–15, some important details are added to the story. We are told that after the death of King Saul a man from his camp came before David and flung himself on the ground and bowed low. When David inquired from where the man had come, he told him that he had escaped from the camp of Israel. He had been at Mount Gilboa and had witnessed King Saul leaning on his spear and the enemy approaching. King Saul asked the man to finish him off because he was in agony, and he did so. Enraged by the act, David inquired, "How did you dare to lift your hand and kill the Lord's anointed?" and he had the man killed.

The second case is found in the Talmud.[12] It is the story of Rabbi Hananya ben Tradyon, one of the ten martyrs of Israel who was killed by the Romans in the sanctification of God's name. Wrapping his body in a Torah scroll, the Romans placed bundles of branches around him and set them on fire. Then they brought tufts of wool that they had soaked in water and placed them over his heart so that he would not die quickly. His disciples begged him to open his mouth so that the fire would enter and he would die more quickly, but Rabbi Hananya refused to contribute to his own death. The executioner then offered to raise the flame and take away the tufts of wool so that he would die more quickly. To this Rabbi Hananya acquiesced.

While Rabbi Hananya would not hasten his own death, he did agree to have that which was preventing him from dying removed. This act set an important precedent, for in a halakhic work written in the thirteenth century by Rabbi Judah *HaHassid* of Regensburg, Germany, we note the following: "One may not unduly prolong the dying process. For example, where someone was chopping wood outside the home of a dying person—the noise preventing his soul from departing—he may be told to leave."[13]

Now the precise parameters of what is termed "preventing the soul from departing" have not been spelled out by the sages nor have any guidelines been set forth by contemporary rabbinic authorities. It is clear, however, that actively or passively bringing about the death of a critically ill patient is strictly prohibited by Jewish law unless it can be shown that the action is merely removing that which is preventing the soul from departing.

An interesting comment in this regard is found in a contemporary work on medicine and *Halakhah*:

> The discontinuation of instrumentation and machinery such as a respirator or cardiac pacemaker, which are specifically designed and utilized for the treatment of critically ill patients, would only be permissible if the physician is certain that in so doing he is not interrupting life. Such a determination seems impossible for the physician to make with absolute certainty, and, therefore, once instituted, instrumental support of vital life processes should not be interrupted, unless and until halakhic death is established. If the patient is in extreme pain and no therapeutic protocol holds any hope for his recovery, it may be proper to withhold any additional non-routine medical services so as to permit the natural ebbing of the life forces.[14]

Cosmetic Surgery

While Judaism posits that God is Master of the universe, we have already indicated that it puts a great deal of the responsibility for the maintenance of the world on man. Man's foremost responsibility is to stay alive and preserve the life of other human beings. As we read in Genesis 9:5, suicide is clearly forbidden: "For your life-blood, too, I will require a reckoning: of every beast will I require it; of man, too, will I require a reckoning for human life, of every man for that of his fellow man." And Rashi states: "Though I have permitted the taking of the life of an animal, I will require your blood from he who spills his own blood."

What is meant by "spilling blood" in this context is the taking of life, but Jewish law likewise prohibits spilling the blood of a human being by wounding him. For that matter, merely striking an innocent person in a way that would shame him is equally forbidden.[15] If the process of healing involves wounding the patient, as is done in an operation or any other surgical procedure, would it be permissible according to Jewish law? The answer is an unequivocal "yes." The end would clearly justify the means. Special dispensation has been given to physicians because what they are doing is for therapeutic purposes.

Given this principle, would cosmetic surgery be justifiable? One could offer a convincing argument that a procedure of this sort is not really necessary and as such no special dispensation of the law against wounding should be granted. One contemporary rabbinic authority differentiates between cosmetic surgery that is performed simply to reverse the normal manifestations of the aging process and that which is performed to repair a congenital defect or blemish. While the former is to say the least highly questionable, he rules that the latter is clearly permissible.[16]

This lenient ruling is based on a discussion in the Talmud concerning the validity of a betrothal based on a false premise. The case is that of a man who betrothed a woman on the condition that she had no physical defects or blemishes. It was subsequently found that she had such a physical blemish at the time of the betrothal. As such the betrothal is invalid, says the Talmud, even if that blemish had later been *healed* by a physician.[17] Now the fact that the Talmud refers to removing a blemish as an act of "healing" excludes it from the prohibition against "wounding" and makes it a permissible act.[18] Another rabbinic authority permits surgical procedures to alleviate physical pain and permits cosmetic surgery even for psychological reasons—that is, when the person shuns normal socialization or cannot get adequate employment because of a disfiguring blemish.[19]

Autopsy and the Dignity of Man

The human body is a sacred entity; it must be treated with respect and dignity. If for no other reason than the fact that it once housed the human soul, the body of a deceased human being retains its sacredness, and it must be treated with respect and dignity as well. In Deuteronomy 21:22, 23 we read:

> If a man is guilty of a capital offense and is put to death, and you impale him on a stake, you must not let his corpse remain on the stake overnight, but must bury him the same day. For an impaled body is an affront to God: you shall not defile the land that the Lord your God is giving you to possess.

Although these verses refer to a criminal, it stands to reason that if the body of a criminal must be handled with respect, all the more so the body of every other human being. From these verses, the Talmud derives the following laws. It is a positive command to bury the dead. Whoever keeps the dead unburied overnight transgresses a negative command. If possible, the body should be buried whole.[20] Maimonides qualifies the ruling and posits that it is permitted to keep the body overnight in order to procure a coffin or a shroud.[21]

Now on face value these rules clearly pose a serious objection to the practice of autopsy. How can a body be autopsied if it must be buried whole? Although we recognize that autopsy is a procedure of vital importance to confirm or reject a diagnosis made before the death of a patient, and as such an invaluable aid in understanding and in treating disease, it is clearly and undeniably a procedure that desecrates the human body. How could Jewish law permit such a procedure? But even if permission were granted for autopsies, what would be the parameters of such procedures? Should they be performed routinely or only under certain conditions? May a physician comply with the wishes of the deceased on this matter? For example, if he had a rare disease and, knowing the benefit that could be derived for mankind, he had requested that an autopsy be performed after his demise?

Virtually all rabbinic authorities agree that where it can be established that an autopsy performed would benefit a particular person at hand, it would be permissible. One contemporary rabbinic authority in Israel extends this lenient ruling by adding the following:

> Autopsies are permitted in the case of hereditary diseases just as if the person whose life would be saved is at hand. If a person gave his consent for an autopsy to be performed after his demise, it is likewise permitted. On the other hand, he rules that dissection purely for medical studies or autopsies performed merely to establish the cause of death are prohibited.[22]

In those instances where autopsies are permissible, the care and respect for the human body prescribed by Jewish law must be scrupulously upheld. The autopsy must be done with dignity, affording the deceased the same respect that one would accord to a living person in an operation. Organs should be left in the body unless the information needed can only be obtained by removal of the organ, in which case the removed organ should subsequently be returned to the body for burial. Finally, if it is at all possible, the autopsy should be performed in the presence of an observant Jewish physician, a rabbi, or some other knowledgeable person to ensure that these requirements are followed meticulously.

The Definition of Death

In 1981, the president of the United States appointed a commission for the study of ethical problems in medicine. This commission recommended that a person be considered dead when he has suffered either irreversible cessation of respiratory and circulatory functions or irreversible cessation of all functions of the entire brain including the brain stem. In 1984, a task force appointed by the governor of New York State came up with the same definition of death and the same recommendation.

The classic definition of death in Jewish law is the absence of spontaneous respiration in a person who shows no movement and who is unresponsive to stimuli. Nonetheless, if resuscitation is deemed possible, it should be attempted no matter how remote the chances of success. One of the foremost contemporary halakhic authorities on medical issues has defined death as follows: "A person who has no evidence of either spontaneous respiration or heart action for ten minutes or more of continuous observation is considered mechanically dead provided resuscitation is deemed impossible."[23] Dr. Fred Rosner, a highly reputed physician and a renowned scholar on Jewish law as it relates to medicine, adds the following:

> Jewish writings provide considerable evidence for the thesis that the brain and the brain stem control all bodily functions, including respiration and cardiac activity. It, therefore, follows that if there is irreversible total cessation of all brain function including that of the brain stem, the person is dead, even though there may still be some transient spontaneous cardiac activity.[24]

Since it is the brain and brain stem that control respiration and heart activity, says Dr. Rosner, the total cessation of brain activity should be acceptable as death, according to Jewish law. Arriving at this decision is not a simple matter, however. It would be of interest, therefore, to briefly review the halakhic sources for the definition of death.

The *Mishnah* rules that if a building collapses on *Shabbat* and it is suspected that someone may be trapped under the debris, one must probe the debris for his sake. The Talmud adds that the search to ascertain whether he is dead or alive must continue until one reaches his nose. (Some say until his heart is reached.) Rashi explains that if no air emanates from his nostrils, it is certain that he is dead.[25] Although he does make mention of the fact that some suggest that the heart be examined, he does not require it. Neither is there any mention of examination of the heart in the writings of Maimonides or the Code of Jewish Law. Nevertheless, two contemporary rabbinic authorities insist on the examination of the heart.[26]

The matter of brain death is discussed in a responsum written by the late Rabbi Moshe Feinstein, considered by many the foremost contemporary rabbinic authority.[27] He defines death as the cessation of respiration and adds that if it can be determined by physicians that blood circulation to the brain has ceased, the person in question is to be considered dead. For all intents and purposes, such a person is no different than a decapitated person who, according to Maimonides, is unequivocally dead.[28]

There is a difference of opinion among present-day rabbinic authorities, however, as to the precise ruling of Rabbi Feinstein. Some interpret his position to be that cellular death follows organismal death and that the latter is sufficient to indicate the onset of death.[29] Concurring with this interpretation, Rabbi Dr. Moshe Tendler explains:

> Absent heartbeat or pulse was not considered a significant factor in ascertaining death in any early religious source. Furthermore, the scientific fact that cellular death does not occur at the same time as the death of a human being is well recognized in the earliest biblical sources . . . Complete destruction of the brain . . . can be considered physiological decapitation and thus a determinant per se of the death of the person.[30]

Nonetheless, it should be noted that some quite reputable rabbinic authorities do not consider this interpretation of Rabbi Feinstein's position to be accurate. Consequently, they rule that brain death is not in accordance with the definition of death in Jewish law.[31]

Organ Transplants

We have discussed the dignity and respect that must be afforded to the human body in life as well as in death, and we have pointed out the high priority given to saving a human life. Under ordinary circumstances, the dead must be buried with all their parts, but what if an organ of the deceased could be used to extend the life of a living person? We must address the question of whether saving a life takes priority over the laws of handling and burial of the dead. To be specific, would organ transplantation be permissible according to Jewish law?

There are direct and peripheral considerations that must be taken into account in determining the law. To whom does a transplanted organ belong, the donor or the recipient? What is done with the diseased organ that is removed? Must it be buried? Can it be used for research or merely discarded? We have already ruled that cosmetic surgery to remove blemishes would not be prohibited under the rubric of unnecessary wounding. Would this ruling apply to the operative procedure that is necessary in order for the recipient to receive the organ transplant? Does the donor meet the Jewish criteria for death? How would the prohibition of deriving benefit from the dead affect the whole matter of transplantation? These are the major considerations that must be taken into account in determining the law.

It is the consensus of opinion among contemporary rabbinic authorities that saving a life sets aside all prohibitions of deriving benefit from the dead, desecrating the dead, and delaying burial of the dead.[32] Most rabbinic authorities consider blindness a life-threatening situation and rule that eye transplants would be permissible. It would seem that kidney transplants would likewise be permissible since they are only performed when both kidneys are not functioning, and a person cannot live unless at least one kidney is functioning.[33] But this raises another question. Given that a person can live with only one kidney, is it permissible for him to submit to the dangers of surgery in order to donate one of his kidneys to a dying person? Would the responsibility one has to preserve one's own life override the obligation to save the life of another?

The commonly accepted ruling on transplants is that a person may submit to the limited risk of surgery in order to donate an organ that would save the life of another human being.[34] A diseased organ that is surgically removed from a living person does not require burial. It may be handled as one sees fit.[35] Unlike organ transplantation, it is permissible to donate blood to a blood bank even though it is not known who will be the recipient, since the danger to the donor is minimal if at all.[36]

Artificial Insemination

We have thus far dealt with the preservation of life and the respect that must be afforded to the dead. Let us now deal with the ethical questions that arise when the creation of life takes place through artificial methods of impregnation. Modern medicine has reached the point where it is possible to impregnate a woman by depositing semen in her genital tract artificially—that is, without sexual intercourse. The process can be successful whether semen is procured from her husband or from any other donor. In this regard, it is important to note that the possibility of a woman being impregnated artificially was already recognized in talmudic times.[37]

Almost all rabbinic authorities prohibit artificial insemination when the donor is not the husband. Among the many questions that arise regarding this procedure is whether a married woman impregnated in this way would be considered to have committed adultery, in which case she would be prohibited to her husband. According to most rabbinic authorities, she would not be considered an adulteress because the law of adultery applies only to sexual relations. As such, a child born through artificial insemination is considered perfectly legitimate.[38] Others feel that artificial insemination through a donor other than the husband is at least akin to adultery.[39] Where the husband is the donor, however, many contemporary authorities rule that the procedure is permissible in the first instance.[40]

Contraception

On the periphery, the issue of contraception might seem to be a highly personal matter between a man and a woman which is of no concern to society. In point of fact, the issue has ethical implications that are of universal relevance. To illustrate: As members of society we might be concerned with overpopulation and starvation statistics. Should the use of contraception be enforced after a couple have a specified number of children, in order to preserve the world? In light of the shrinking birth rate among Jews, on the other hand, should not all Jewish married couples consider it their responsibility to have larger families?

In terms of the morality of contraception, there are two basic arguments: the secular and the religious.

The secularist claims that there is no moral difference between preventing the natural process of conception through the use of contraceptives and preventing the natural process of obesity by diet. The religionist claims that there is an objective standard of right and wrong that is of Divine origin, by which it must be determined whether or not contraception is permissible.

To procreate, according to Jewish law, is not merely a privilege left to the discretion of a married couple; it is a *mitzvah* and a responsibility.[41] One has fulfilled that responsibility after having given birth to a male and a female child.[42] Sexuality is a manifestation of the closest personal relationship between husband and wife. As such, sexual relations are permitted even when the wife is sterile or has reached menopause.[43] However, where procreation is possible, sexual relations should be directed primarily toward that goal.

The classic discussion of contraception is found in the Talmud.[44] It is referred to in the subsequent halakhic literature as the *"Beraita* of the Three Women." The sages ruled that three married women may use an absorbent in their marital intercourse: a minor because she may become pregnant and die; a pregnant woman because she may cause her fetus to degenerate; a nursing mother because she might have to wean her child prematurely. But there are differences of opinion among the rabbinic authorities as to the meaning of this ruling. Some say that the Talmud merely gave these as an example and rule that in cases of a threat to the mother's life arising from pregnancy, there would be no objection whatsoever to the use of contraceptives. Others understand the Talmud to have ruled that the use of contraceptives is only permissible in these three cases.[45]

In the final analysis, contemporary rabbinic authorities have ruled that contraceptive devices are permissible only when pregnancy would endanger the life of the mother. In terms of which device is most preferable, we find the following: "Jewish law grades methods of contraceptive techniques from least to most objectionable in the following order: oral contraceptives, chemical spermicides, diaphragms and cervical caps to be used by the wife, condoms, and coitus interruptus [withdrawal]."[46]

Cryogenics

With the knowledge we now have in cryogenics, that is, the study of the effect of very low temperatures on matter, modern science has for some time pondered the possibility of freezing people who die from incurable diseases. Such persons would be placed in a vault instead of burying them so that the bodies do not decay even over a period of many years. Later, when a cure for the disease has been discovered, they would be revived and cured.

At present, revival is still in the primitive stages. Animals have been revived, but due to cell damage in the freezing process, they have only lived for briefs periods afterward. Before this procedure can emerge from theory to practice, a number of important ethical issues must be addressed. For example: Would a person frozen in this way be considered dead or alive? Would the familial relationships change in any way? What would be the family status of such a person after he is revived? Would freezing be a violation of the laws of burial? If it would be required that the freezing process be done when the person is technically still alive, would it be permissible?

There are early rabbinic authorities who ruled that a person who died and was subsequently revived retained his former status.[47] Others disagreed with this ruling, but this is because in those years there was virtually no hope for the deceased to be revived. In the case of a person who is frozen, given that the process for revival has been perfected, there is every reason to assume that he will be revived. Consequently, all rabbinic authorities would agree that such a person would not be considered dead, and his status would be retained. Were this not the rule, it would present a monumental problem today. A person who dies on the operating table and is revived, an occurrence not unheard of these days, would lose all status, causing him great complications when he resumed his normal life.

We have made it sufficiently clear that the obligation to attempt to save a human life applies even if the person involved is not expected to live for more than a few moments thereafter. Now, when a person dies, one would assume that the obligation is irrelevant. This is not so, however. Jewish law states that the obligation to save a life applies even after death, so long as there is a remote possibility for revival.[48] Such being the case, why wouldn't it be permissible for the deceased to be frozen until such time as a cure is found for his ailment, if there is good reason to believe that he could then be revived and cured?

One rabbinic authority rules that a dangerous drug or treatment may be administered to a patient who is approaching death, knowing full well that the drug will cure him if it takes effect but will hasten his death if it doesn't.[49] Accordingly, if and when revival becomes a viable option, it should theoretically be permissible to freeze a person who has reached the last stages of a terminal illness in the hope that he will later be revived and cured.

Animal Experimentation

Have animals been put in this world to be used by man entirely at his discretion? Even a cursory knowledge of the Bible and Talmud precludes an affirmative answer. There is no question that Jewish law prohibits cruelty to animals. Whether this prohibition has been promulgated solely or even primarily out of concern for the life of the animal is open to discussion.

There are many verses in the Bible that speak of God's concern for animals. In Psalms 145:15–16 we read: "The eyes of all look to you expectantly, and You give them their food when it is due. You give it openhandedly, feeding every creature to its heart's content." In Psalms 147:9 we find: "He gives to the beast his food, to the raven's brood that for which they cry." If for no other reason than i*mitatio Dei*, that is, the Divine imperative to walk in God's ways, we should be kind to animals.[50]

There is a specific principle referred to in the Talmud as *tsa'ar ba'ale hayyim* ("the pain of living creatures"), which forbids cruelty to animals.[51] The use of animals for medical purposes, however, is excluded from this prohibition.[52] The rationale is quite clear. In animal experimentation, man is the primary beneficiary. What right have we to assume that the pain of animals is of greater consideration than the pain of humans who might be helped as a result of animal experimentation? Nonetheless, care should be taken to limit the amount of pain and suffering the animal must endure. On the other hand, Maimonides and many later rabbinic authorities have ruled that hunting animals for sport only is prohibited.[53] It is important to note that while it is permissible to slaughter animals for food, it has been scientifically demonstrated that *shehitah*, the method of slaughter prescribed by Jewish law, is the method least painful to the animal.[54]

Notwithstanding all that has been said, it is important to note that according to many rabbinic authorities, the prohibition against cruelty to animals is meant primarily to cultivate the attribute of kindness in man and is not predicated on the notion of animal rights.[55]

The field of medical ethics should be of concern to each and every member of society, for sooner or later just about all of us are confronted with decisions of this nature that must be made concerning a parent, a spouse, or even ourselves. The advances in medical research and technology in the last fifty years stagger the mind. But with this monumental progress there have emerged many difficult ethical questions. These questions have all been addressed by our contemporary rabbinic authorities, many of whom are themselves men of science. Judaism is a living religion. There is a resolution in *Halakhah*, or at least an approach from which a resolution can be derived, to every problem that relates to life.

There is a great deal more to Jewish ethics than what we have discussed in the past two sessions. My purpose was not to exhaust the topic, but merely to demonstrate the emphasis that Judaism puts on the establishment of an ethical society. What I said to you last session is worthy of repetition. Many of the principles of ethics that you believe you have culled from society and have of your own free will adopted into your lifestyle derive from the Torah and the Oral Law. You are an observant Jew by virtue of the fact that you are fulfilling many of the *mitzvot* in the Torah. But be careful not to misconstrue my words. You still have a long way to go in terms of what would be considered full commitment to the Torah way of life.

Yes, Moshe, you are a practicing member of what the Torah terms the *chosen people.* This designation has caused our people much pain and suffering because it has been misinterpreted by Jews and non-Jews alike. We will spend the next session discussing the true meaning of this badge of honor and outline the responsibilities that come with it.

Session VI
The Meaning and
Significance of the
Chosenness of Israel

Now that we have established that you are not only a member of the Jewish people, but that by virtue of the fact that you have committed yourself to many ethical principles that appear in the Torah as *mitzvot*, you are a practicing member, we must discuss the further ramifications of such membership. As you well know, the Jewish people have been unjustly attacked through the centuries, even vilified, because they profess to be God's "chosen people." Misunderstood and misinterpreted to imply that they are inherently better than any other nation and as such more beloved to God, this designation has aroused much jealousy and hatred. As a Jew, it is important for you to understand the true meaning of "chosenness" and to learn when and why the Jewish people were given this designation. What is the meaning of "chosenness" in the context of the Torah and what does it mean to be a member of the "chosen people"? This will be our topic for today.

The Treasured Nation

The Torah tells us the following:

> And Moses went up to the Lord God. The Lord called to him from the mountain saying, "Thus shall you say to the house of Jacob and declare

to the children of Israel: You have seen what I did to the Egyptians, how I bore you on eagles' wings and brought you to Me. Now then if you will obey Me faithfully and keep My covenant, you shall be My treasured possession among all peoples. Indeed, all the earth is Mine, but you shall be to Me a kingdom of priests and a holy nation. (Exodus 19:3–6)

For you are a people consecrated to the Lord your God. The Lord your God chose you from among all other peoples on earth to be His treasured people. (Deuteronomy 14:2)

The Jewish people are clearly designated in the Torah as an *am segulah*, ("a treasured nation"), but this designation is not simply an honorary title. It makes specific demands on our behavior and our lifestyle. Rabbi Samson Raphael explains:

Segulah indicates a possession which is a special property of one sole owner . . . a unique treasure over which nobody else has any rights . . . so the use of this word for the fundamental condition which is demanded of us in our relationship with God indicates that we must become completely and exclusively His possession in every phase of our being, that our whole existence and all our desires be dependent on Him, that we give no place to ought but Him to have any influence to the direction of our lives and actions.

Being designated by God as His exclusive treasure is not merely a proclamation; it is a mission. It is to be continually aware of the unique and awesome responsibility for the enlightenment of mankind that we bear by virtue of that proclamation, says Rabbi Hirsch. God's chosen people must live the way of life ordained for them by God and by doing so set the example of ethics and morality for all mankind. As God's chosen people, we must focus our lives entirely on Him; the fulfillment of His will must be uppermost in our minds.

The Talmud says something interesting about the relationship between the Jewish people and the Torah. "Israel is of all nations the most willful or headstrong one, and the Torah was to give it the right scope and power of resistance or else the world could not have withstood its fierceness."[1] Does this mean that Jews are headstrong by nature, and the Torah serves to sublimate their stubbornness for the good of mankind? Does it mean that God has entrusted the mission to be a kingdom of priests and a holy nation to the Jewish people because their obstinacy would enable them to withstand the abuse of the nations and survive? Perhaps it means simply that stubbornness and truth are an ideal marriage that will ensure fulfillment, and this is why God has given the Torah to the Jewish people.

The Lifestyle of the Chosen

By no means is chosenness to be understood as racial superiority. What makes the Jewish people elite is not some genetic predisposition that is passed on from generation to generation. There is no master race! Every human being has his faults; every nation does as well. Witness God's words to Moses after the sin of the golden calf, "I see that this is a stiff-necked people. Now let Me be, that My anger may blaze forth against them and that I may destroy them and make of you a great nation" (Exodus 32:9).

It is the lifestyle to which the Jewish people would commit themselves, and the ethics and morality of the Torah that they would live by, that would make them an elite nation. A nation that chooses to live a moral life, one ordained for man by God, while society at large focuses on wealth and power, is indeed a very special nation. It should be made perfectly clear, however, that God's expressed love for Israel would manifest itself with equal measure on all people and all the nations of the world were they to choose to live ethical and moral lives.[2]

Why was it necessary for a whole nation to have been chosen for the task of teaching ethics and morality to the world? Were there not individuals in every generation who exerted an influence on their fellow man in this regard? Why was this insufficient? Why and when did the masses of the people go wrong?

To answer these questions we must refer to the Torah, the earliest record of human history, and focus on man's uniqueness, that which differentiates him from the beast. This will enable us to comprehend the demands that God has put upon man, why he failed, and finally, the role of the Jewish people in the attempt to bring man back to his original condition.

The Dilemma of Adam and Eve

In the story of creation, Genesis 1:27 tells us, "And God created man in His image, in the image of God He created him, male and female He created them." Adam and Eve, the first human beings, were endowed by God with a precious and unique gift—freedom of will. From among the multiplicity of God's created creatures man alone shares this attribute with his Creator. Freedom of will means the ability to choose what has been Divinely ordained as the proper ethical or moral response in any given situation.

Adam was placed in the Garden of Eden. In consideration of his free will, God charged him with the command not to eat from the tree of knowledge of good and evil that stood in the middle of the Garden. Whatever their motivation may have been, Adam and Eve chose to disobey God's command, and they ate from the forbidden tree of knowledge and were consequently banished from the Garden.

Let us begin our analysis with an important principle. Just as the commandments of the Torah are eternal, which means that they are and always will be relevant to man so, too, are the lessons that are derived from the Torah narratives. Needless to say, had the story of the Garden of Eden no relevance to subsequent generations, it is doubtful that so much space would have been given to it in the Torah. Every word of the Torah is the word of God; every letter is counted, and there are no redundancies. As such, it behooves us to study these narratives in depth, with as much careful analysis as we do the legal sections of the Torah.

Before they ate from the tree of knowledge, Adam and Eve did not know of good and evil. What they did know, according to Maimonides, was the difference between what is true and what is false.[3] In Genesis 2:1–17 it is revealed that Adam was charged: " . . . of every tree of the garden you are free to eat; but as for the tree of the knowledge of good and evil you must not eat of it; for as soon as you eat of it you shall be doomed to die." With this charge, man began to probe the legitimacy of his desires and thus gain insight into his psyche. Adam was free to choose whether or not to obey God's command. Had it been predetermined by God that he would either eat or not eat from the tree, the charge would be meaningless.

With this charge, man was initiated into "humanhood," with its virtues and its vices, attributes that would enable him to reach the height of dignity or sink to the depths of depravity. Rabbi Eliezer Berkovits explains:

> When God addressed Adam and gave him his first commandment, He called him from the innocence of complete thinghood in an eternal *now* into the personal reality of the not-yet and revealed to him human freedom as the source of responsibility. Only because man is forever not-yet, because his humanity consists of self-transcendence can he be the recipient of Divine commandments. A tree, an animal and a man when he shuts himself into the satisfied self acceptance of the eternal *now*, knows of no thou shalt or thou shalt not. Responsibility is the freedom of self-transcendence. Only because of that can man be entrusted with the revelation of God's word to him.[4]

Having charged Adam not to eat from the tree of knowledge God limited his freedom and confronted him with what must have been a perplexing dilemma. Should he obey the Divine charge or should he please his palate?

In point of fact, the dilemma was much more profound and of far greater consequence than one could expect from choosing to eat or not to eat from a particular tree. A precedent would be set that would affect not only Adam but all subsequent generations. On the one hand, Adam could heed the word of God and commit himself permanently and without qualification to Divine ethics, a system designed to bring the greatest satisfaction and fulfillment to the greatest number of people. On the other hand, he could opt for hedonism, a way of life that is independent of God, that defines *good* as any action or behavior that brings man pleasure and *evil* as that which brings him pain or displeasure. This would, indeed, be a pace-setting decision. Would the philosophy of every man for himself triumph or would Adam be willing to control his appetites for what would ultimately be his own benefit and the benefit of his fellow man? Think for a moment. Has this not been man's dilemma throughout history? Are we not faced with this choice every day of our lives?

The Choice and Its Ramifications

One would have hoped that man's freedom of will and his superior intelligence would have inspired a heightened sense of responsibility to

God, his Creator. Unfortunately, this was not the case. Adam was free to decide whether to control his appetites or give in to them. He chose the latter.

By eating from the tree of knowledge, Adam and Eve chose hedonism and self-determination over Divine ethics and morality. In consequence of that choice they were denied eternal life, and they were driven out of the Garden of Eden. A world populated with human beings who choose hedonism as a way of life is in imminent danger. A society that is not rooted in a Divinely ordained system of ethics, but believes in moral relativism, would eventually self-destruct. But such a catastrophe would be contrary to the Divine scheme of things. To save the world from destruction and to give every generation the opportunity to start anew, God limited man's life span. In Genesis 3:19 He addressed Adam with the discomfiting words: "By the sweat of your brow shall you get bread to eat, until you return to the ground, for from it you were taken: for dust you are and unto dust you shall return."[5] It was some time later that man's mortality was spelled out more precisely, and in Genesis 6:3 we read: "Then the Lord said, 'My spirit shall not shield man forever, since he is but flesh; let the days allowed him be one hundred and twenty years.'"

What were the immediate effects of Adam's choice and what were the long-term effects of man's choice of the hedonistic way of life and self-determined ethics?

Rabbi David Tzvi Hoffmann, the early twentieth-century halakhist and Bible commentator, draws our attention to the fact that the forbidden tree is not called "the tree of knowledge of *the* good and *the* evil." The definite article would have indicated objective good and objective evil. This could not be, for God alone is the source of objective ethics. Had man heeded the charge given to him by God and not eaten from the tree of knowledge, thus allowing Divine ethics to determine his behavior, had he not capitulated to hedonism, his destiny would have been "nourished" by the tree of life. But this was not the case. To ensure man's survival and the survival of the world when he ate from the tree of knowledge, God endowed man with a "proclivity toward the truly ethical."[6]

It is difficult to know precisely how man acquired what Rabbi Hoffmann considers "the proclivity toward the truly ethical," but I would like to venture an interpretation. I don't believe that Hoffmann meant to imply that there was something in the fruit of the tree of knowledge, a drug of some sort, that acted on Adam's brain and had an influence on his thinking and his behavior, although from what we know today about the effect of mind-altering drugs on the human personality, one dare not outrightly dismiss the possibility. Even so, how could what Adam had experienced affect subsequent generations? What Hoffmann meant is that after Adam ate from the tree of knowledge, his life began to change, and eventually he came to some important decisions on how he wanted to live and what his relationship to God should be. He realized that by eating from the forbidden tree he had acted irresponsibly, and he felt guilty for having disobeyed the Divine charge simply to satisfy his appetite.

Parenthetically, it is interesting to note that it was Adam's appetitive faculty to which he finally succumbed. For in Genesis 3:6 we read: "When the woman saw that the tree was good for eating and a delight to the eyes, and that the tree was desirable as a source of wisdom, she took of its fruit and ate, and she gave some to her husband also, and he ate." The power of man's basic biological drives is portrayed quite vividly in this statement. Indeed, the sequence of the phrases in this verse teaches us that to Eve's way of thinking, gratification of the palate and pleasing the senses were of even greater value than wisdom.

The feeling that he had acted irresponsibly by disobeying God's charge initiated a change in Adam's way of thinking. He tried to see beyond himself, beyond egotistical considerations, and he began to recognize his responsibility to God and to his fellow man. This is the seed from which the proclivity toward truly ethical behavior must have grown. This seed exists in every human being and in every generation. Who knows, perhaps there is even a genetic factor involved. In some people the seed blossoms into a beautiful flower. Not only do they lead truly ethical and moral lives, but they influence others to do so as well. These are the righteous of the world. In many people the seed lies dormant until something in their lives inspires them, and it begins to grow. These are the masses of society. Regrettably, there are still others in whom the seed lies dormant for so long that it withers away and dies. These are the wicked.

Cain and Abel: Differing Perspectives

It would not be unreasonable to assume that Adam and Eve tried to imbue their new way of thinking into the hearts and minds of their children, for our sages tell us that the seven Noahide laws had already been revealed to him.[7] From what we know of their children, it would seem that Abel was loyal to the teachings of his father, while Cain preferred to live a self-determined life. Although there is very little told about Cain in the Torah, even less about Abel, careful attention given to the text will reveal these traits: "In the course of time, Cain brought an offering to the Lord from the fruit of the soil; and Abel, for his part, brought the choicest of the firstlings of his flock. The Lord paid heed to Abel and his offering, but to Cain and his offering He paid no heed . . . " (Genesis 4:3–5).

Cain became a farmer while his brother Abel chose to be a sheep-herder, the Torah tells us. Crops cannot grow without rain, and rain comes from heaven. Cain brought an offering to God. What was his motivation? Would it be presumptuous to say that he had an ulterior motive? Having witnessed the importance of rain to the harvesting of successful crops, Cain realized that it would be in his best interests to bring a gift offering to God. "I'll give God a smidgen," thought Cain to himself, "and keep the rest for myself."[8] This is, indeed, the thinking of a truly self-determined man.

Abel recognized God to be the Creator and Master of the world in which he lived. God was, indeed, responsible for everything he had. In turn, God deserved Abel's total and unqualified commitment. The Torah tells us that Abel likewise gave a gift offering to God, but his offering came from the best of his flock, for only by giving the best to God did Abel feel justified in keeping the rest for himself. Parenthetically, this attitude became the accepted rationale by the sages for the recitation of blessings before partaking of food. We recognize that the food we eat belongs to God. What grants us permission to eat it is our acknowledgement that it comes from Him.

God was pleased with Abel and his offering because it was motivated by pure and honorable thoughts; He rejected Cain and his offering because it was a self-centered gesture, motivated primarily by greed. Friction ensued between the two brothers, whereupon Cain rose up against his brother Abel and killed him.

Why had Cain killed his brother? The biblical text doesn't reveal an argument or any harsh words between them. Had the story ended there, we would have been left bewildered. Fortunately, it did not. God confronted Cain with Abel's absence, "Where is your brother Abel?" and Cain answered, "I do not know; am I my brother's keeper?"

This simple response to God's query explains everything. It betrays Cain for what he really is, a greedy, self-centered, insensitive human being who answers only to his own appetites. Cain needs neither God nor man, and he acts accordingly. He was able to kill his brother without feeling any remorse. Quite the contrary. He resented the insinuation that he should in any way be responsible for his brother's well-being. In no way did Cain represent "man," that sublime creature who was formed by God in His image and in His likeness on the sixth day of creation. In no way would Cain fulfill the noble expectations God had for His representatives on earth.

The Corruption of the Generations

With few exceptions, the generations that followed walked in the footsteps of Cain. They lived egocentric, self-determined lives, shunning even the seven Noahide commandments. This was not God's intent when He created man. True, there were selected individuals, such as Enoch, Methusaleh and Noah, who were able to rise to the charge of the Almighty, but these men had little influence on the masses.[9]

The earth became filled with violence. Corruption and injustice reigned supreme, and God decided to destroy that which He had wrought and begin anew. But why? History would only repeat itself. If man is by nature a corrupt and unredeemable creature, what purpose would be served in creating a new world? The answer to this question is found in Genesis 6:8, the concluding words of the weekly portion. "But Noah found favor with the Lord." Noah was a righteous man. He had not succumbed to the corruption that was pervasive in his society, and this meant that there was hope that the Divine experiment with man might prove to be worthwhile after all. If one man could actualize the spiritual potential with which he was endowed by the Creator, others might do so as well, and perhaps some day all people would willingly choose righteousness over wickedness, Divine ethics and morality over hedonism and self-determined ethics. And so, God saved Noah and his family from the flood, and He renewed His experiment with man.

Unfortunately, the hope for the salvation of mankind did not materialize. Once more, hedonism became the dominant philosophy of society. The drive for independence from God and for self-determination once more reared its ugly head, spreading among the people like a plague. The masses did not need God. In point of fact, they believed that they were more powerful than God, in consequence of which they were determined to build a tower that would reach up to heaven and invade, so to speak, God's very domain.

On Genesis 11:1, "And the whole world was of one language and few words," Rashi comments: "They came with one plan, saying: He has no right to select the heavenly regions exclusively for Himself; let us ascend to the skies and make war upon Him."

But God had promised never again to destroy the world through a flood. Never again would He cleanse the earth of its corrupt human dross in the way He had previously chosen. Annihilate the corrupt thinking rather than the corrupt person became the Divine watchword. Education became God's tool for the betterment of mankind. The medium through which God would bring His plan to fruition was to be man himself. Regarding the tower builders, God confounded their language so that they could no longer communicate adequately with one another, and they were forced to separate and abandon their profane project.

Abraham's Mission

Education began with Abraham. It was Abraham who attempted to bring man back to ethical monotheism, a mission he fully and willingly accepted upon himself and to which he dedicated his whole life. The *Midrash* tells us that his tent was always open to travelers, passersby whom he would invite in for some respite and to whom he would preach about God. Abraham's efforts did not go unnoticed by God. In Genesis 12:2, 3, we read: "And I will make of you a great nation, and I will bless you and make your name great . . . and in you shall all the families of the earth be blessed."

Designated as the first of the patriarchs, Abraham was the seed from which the nation of Israel was to grow. His son Isaac and his grandson

Jacob and their families were the first Hebrews. Indeed, the calling of Abraham, Isaac, and Jacob was to become the calling of the nation of Israel. It is interesting to note that unlike the other nations of the world, Israel began its nationhood without a land of its own. Perhaps this was to establish in the mind of all Jews in every generation that a land of their own, as important as it might be, prestige-wise, is not and should never be the highest priority of the nation of Israel. But this was not to be a permanent condition. During Abraham's lifetime, God promised him many times that Canaan would eventually become the homeland of his descendants, the nation of Israel. As the Torah records:

> And the Lord said to Abraham after Lot had parted from him, "Raise your eyes and look out from where you are, to the north and south, to the east and west, for I give all the land that you see to you and your offspring forever. . . . Rise up, walk about the land through its length and its breadth, for I give it to you." [10]

The land of Canaan was indeed to be the inheritance of the Jewish people, but first they had to accept the Torah, the Law that was to be revealed to them by God through Moses. As important as the land may be to the attainment of national status and national dignity, the Torah is of greater importance, for without the Torah there is no nation of Israel. In point of fact, if the people of Israel relinquished their commitment to the Torah, the land itself would expel them. As we read:

> You shall not copy the practices of the land of Egypt where you dwelt, or of the land of Canaan to which I am taking you; nor shall you follow their customs. . . . But you must keep My laws and My norms, and you must not do any of those abhorrent things . . . for all those abhorrent things were done by the people who were in the land before you, and the land became defiled. So let not the land spew you out for defiling it. . . . [11]

The Mission of Israel

A new nation dedicated to a Divine calling, could one anticipate anything but a wonderful future for this nation? Alas, it seems that this unique people was destined to suffer from its very birth as a nation.

Witness the words of God to Abraham in Genesis 15:13, 14: "Know well that your offspring shall be strangers in a land that is not theirs, and they shall be enslaved and oppressed four hundred years . . . and in the end they shall go forth with great wealth."

One cannot help but wonder why enslavement was necessary. Why could the land not have been inherited by Abraham and his family immediately? One would have hoped that the infancy of Jewish nationhood would be marked by more pleasant national experiences. Be that as it may, there is something to say for growing up in the world of "hard knocks." For what applies to the individual applies to nations as well. It does tend to build character and to engender an appreciation for some of the more important things in life. Rabbi Samson Raphael Hirsch expands on this idea. When the nation of Israel was formed, writes Hirsch, "it needed to be deprived of all which constitutes ordinarily the glory of nations. . . . it had to lose all but morality, religion and hope, in order that it might receive all its life's treasures from Him [God] alone."[12] Yes, whatever nobility we possess as a nation derives from the Torah and is sanctioned by the Almighty. Our ethics and our morality, our cause, and even our national homeland are the gifts of God to His people Israel.

The Crucible of Egypt

Egypt was destined to be the crucible in which the nation of Israel would be refined. With seventy souls did our forefather Jacob come to Egypt. He intended it to be a brief sojourn, but it lasted for 210 years. In the beginning the family of Jacob flourished; the Pharaoh had great respect for Joseph and saw to it that his family was well provided for. But before long, a new king arose in Egypt who did not know Joseph and would not acknowledge what he had done for Egypt and its people. Things began to change. Envy and fear took hold of the Egyptians as they witnessed this nation in their midst growing by leaps and bounds. In Exodus 1:9, 10 the Torah records the paranoid thoughts of the Egyptian masses: "Look, the Israelite people are much too numerous for us. Let us, then, deal shrewdly with them, lest they increase and, in the event of war, join our enemies in fighting against us and gain ascendancy over the country." Thus began the horrendous history of Jewish suffering.

The process of "dealing shrewdly" with the Israelites was a gradual one. As God had revealed to Abraham, it was a three-step process: estrangement followed by enslavement and finally by oppression. First, the Israelites were alienated and treated like second-class citizens; then they were enslaved; and finally, they were made to endure physical abuse and spiritual degradation. When the appropriate time arrived, God intervened in the process of history and redeemed His people. The Israelites emerged triumphantly from the physical and spiritual bondage that had beset their lives for 210 years, and they went forth on the journey to Canaan.

In the third month after their departure from Egypt, the wandering Israelites became the nation of Israel. But unlike every other nation whose nationhood manifests itself first and foremost in a homeland, it was not territory that marked the entry of the Jewish people into nationhood; it was the Torah and the universal mission that came with it. In the words of Rabbi Samson Raphael Hirsch:

> It became a body whose soul was the Torah, and, therefore, could truthfully be called a kingdom of priests, for as the priest in the midst of a single people was this nation to be in the midst of universal mankind, preserving the law of God and practicing and fulfilling its holy precepts.[13]

The Jewish nation was to dedicate itself to the proposition that God alone is the source of ethics and morality. Rooted in the Divine, Torah ethics are absolute and eternal. The mission of Israel was to practice Torah ethics and by example teach mankind that the survival of the world is dependent on man's acceptance of Divine ethics, and that the happiness and contentment of each individual is dependent on his full commitment to the seven Noahide laws. Dedicated to this cause, the nation of Israel was to put man back on the road to his Divinely ordained destiny.

In a commentary on the Torah written by Abraham, the son of Maimonides, the matter is put quite succinctly. On the biblical verse "You shall be unto Me a kingdom of priests and a holy nation" (Exodus 19:6), he writes: "Through the observance of My Torah you shall be leaders of the world. You will be to them as the priest to his flock.

The world will follow after you, imitating your acts and walking in your path."[14]

Many of us fail to recognize that in the final analysis, ethics and morality are the major themes of the commandments. Even the wars that God waged against idolatry were to foster better relations between man and his fellow man, for history will testify that from the beginning of time idolatry went hand in hand with immorality. What better example do we have than the corruption that existed in the world in the time of Noah. What were the conditions that precipitated the flood that destroyed the world? The Torah records:

> The earth became corrupt before God; the earth was filled with injustice. When God saw how corrupt the earth was, for all flesh had corrupted its ways on earth, God said to Noah, "I have decided to put an end to all flesh for the earth is filled with violence because of them: I am about to destroy them with the earth."[15]

On these words Rashi makes the following clarification: "Corrupt," this means lewdness and idolatry; "violence," this means robbery.

It is of the utmost importance to recognize that knowledge does not always inspire commitment. Would that it did; we would have a much better world. Rabbi Isidore Epstein explains the important difference between knowledge of ethics and its practice.

> The cause of the human failure lay . . . in the heart rather than in the head. It was moral rather than intellectual. This problem of how to make man's impulses keep pace with his ethical knowledge is one that has perplexed moralists of all ages: it is one thing to teach man what is right and good, but it is another to make him disposed and willing to obey and live up to the ideal. . . . This moral problem which philosophy is incapable of meeting is taken over by religion.[16]

The Jewish people were chosen by God and designated to be *am kadosh*—not a "holy nation," which to some might imply a kind of superiority, but a "unique nation," which means a people separated by God to be different in their customs and rituals and in their general way of life in order to fulfill a specific calling. As Rabbi Samson Raphael Hirsch explains: "It was to be separate even in happiness, from the nations, in order that it might not learn of them to revere well-being and fortune as the goal of life, and, like them, sink into the

worship of wealth and lust."[17] As we have stated repeatedly, Israel
was to teach man by example that an objective system of values that
takes the welfare of every human being into consideration in determining what is appropriate behavior is not merely a goal toward which
man must strive, but a reality. That system is the Torah; its tenets
are the *mitzvot.* While it is true that man is incapable of creating such
an objective system, the Torah is not man's creation. The Torah is
God's creation, and in His abundant kindness He saw fit to reveal it
to man.

It is important to note that while both Judaism and Christianity are
dedicated to teaching Divine ethics to the world, the approach of the
former is entirely different from that of the latter. Christianity postu-
lates that for all intents and purposes, the only thing worthwhile in man
is his spiritual component. With Adam's decision to disobey God's
charge not to eat from the tree of knowledge of good and evil, he committed his greatest blunder, and with it he lost favor in God's eyes. He
became a fallen creature, hopelessly corrupt and continuously engaged
in a battle between his body and his soul. In further explanation of the
position of Christianity, Rabbi I. Epstein writes:

> The only good in man is that which proceeds from the soul—and that
> only insofar as it is kept free from the taint of the body. Hence the Chris-
> tian doctrine of the irreconcilable antagonism between the flesh and the
> spirit, the body and the soul, material pursuits and the holiness of life,
> and its consequent commendation of asceticism as providing the only
> means of escaping the horrors of sinful matter which are a bar to the
> fullness of moral and spiritual life.[18]

Judaism, however, has put great faith in human nature. It posits that
both the human body and the human soul are good, for they were both
created by God. Rather than a dichotomy, the body and the soul are
partners in man; they operate together in the pursuit of *kedushah* ("sepa-
rateness"), which is the Jewish ideal. Harmony between body and soul
is attained through the fulfillment of the *mitzvot*, the commandments
of the Torah. These biblical norms superimpose the soul over the body.
Unlike Christianity, which denigrates the body and man's natural
drives, Judaism respects man's body and his natural biological drives,
but it limits them. It puts man's intellect in control over his instincts.
By doing so, man transforms that which begins as a purely biological

drive into a *mitzvah*, an act that is in conformity with God's will. Again, Rabbi Epstein writes:

> The Jew is thus able to attain moral and spiritual perfection without fleeing from the world, without sealing his senses hermetically to the beauties and blessings of existence. His spiritual victory involves no suppression of the rightful use of the body, but rather its cultivation with due self-restraint resulting in a condition of mental adjustment in which all deeds . . . are performed for the sake of heaven.[19]

Clearly, the Jewish people were to march to the beat of a different drummer. Settled in the Promised Land, they were to live the Torah way of life. This meant a life that was infused with spirituality, in conformity with the *mitzvot* that are addressed to man vis à vis God and those addressed to man vis à vis his fellow man. In consequence of their fulfillment of the *mitzvot*, they would be at peace with both themselves and each other. What an awesome lesson to the rest of the world!

Regrettably, the mission of the Jewish people in the Promised Land was short-lived. The prosperity they enjoyed, a blessing granted to them by God to lighten their burden, blinded them to their responsibility, their raison d'etre. How interesting that Moses had predicted their folly before they even entered the land. He knew his people well. In the words of Deuteronomy 32:15: "So Jeshurun grew fat and kicked— you grow fat and gross and coarse—he forsook the God Who made him and spurned the Rock of his support." On these words Rabbi Samson Raphael Hirsch comments:

> Here for the first time we meet the name Jeshurun. It designates Israel after the ideal of its moral calling which in *yashar*, straight, never deviating in any way from the straight path, corresponds to this name. . . . But when the destined Jeshurun people got an abundance of all the good things on earth for the purpose of fulfilling this mission . . . then it became fat and kicked. . . .[20]

The chosen nation of Israel forgot God and abandoned His Torah. Seeking wealth and pleasure, Israel sank to the level of its idolatrous neighbors and became oblivious of its Divinely ordained mission. But this could not be! The vices that God tolerates in the rest of society are simply unacceptable for the nation that He has chosen to represent

Divine ethics and morality to the world. The status quo could not and would not continue. Drastic measures had to be taken: the Jewish people were twice exiled from their homeland.

Had the spiritual mission for which Israel had been created come to an end? No longer worthy of being considered the light unto the nations, would God choose another nation to replace it? Not at all! Such was not the Divine plan. The mission of Israel would remain intact, but the field of operation would be extended. For what began with exile eventually resulted in the dispersion of the nation of Israel to all parts of the civilized world. Israel lost its homeland but maintained its nationhood and its mission.

Despite anti-Semitism that manifested in prejudice, degradation, persecution, and even expulsion from many of the lands to which they were exiled, the Jewish people survived. Defying logic and the unwritten rule in history that only the mighty survive, the Jewish people, the smallest of nations, lives on. Suffering martyrdom when this was their lot, the religious leaders never relinquished their commitment to Torah and their love for and their devotion to God. Through the generations, nation after nation perished, becoming relics of history, but the Jewish people have endured to this day. Many ask, "What is the secret of Jewish survival?" The definitive answer can only be—the Torah. The unwavering, unimpeachable commitment of the nation of Israel to the Jewish way of life has earned it immortality. Israel has endured the wrath of the world and has survived, in a sense even prospered, and this without a land of its own.

There is an interesting analogy in the *Midrash*. The nation of Israel is like the olive that grows there so plentifully. Just as the olive yields its precious oil only after it is squeezed, so is the destiny of Israel one of great oppression and hardship in order that it might thereby give forth its precious illuminating wisdom to the world.[21]

Must the Jewish people endure persecution for all time? Is there no option open to them? In point of fact, there were many opportunities for individual Jews and for the entire nation of Israel to be accepted among the nations of the world as an equal. These opportunities came with one proviso—assimilation. The people of Israel had merely to give up their religion and abandon their mission, and they would be accepted among the nations of the world as an equal. Needless to say, this option was not a viable one. So the nation of Israel endures, undaunted by the "slings and arrows of outrageous fortune," until the time for its redemption arrives.

Perhaps the best evidence of the existence of a benevolent Supreme Being is the survival of the Jewish people in exile through almost twenty centuries of persecution, only to return home in 1948 to reestablish the State of Israel. Miracle of miracles! In the eyes of the secular world, the survival of Israel and the establishment of the State are inexplicable; they present a perplexing and vexing enigma. But to the Jew who has made Torah his life, it is the fulfillment of a Divine promise . . . a dream come true.

The Torah tells us that because of Adam's disobedience, God closed off the path that leads to the ancient Tree of Life, but this was only a temporary measure, meant to keep Adam from partaking of its fruit. Just as God formed man, He formed the "chosen people." By revealing the Torah to them, God planted within them a new "tree of life." He bade them to partake of its fruit, thus setting an example for all the world of how God wants man to live. Mission accomplished, God would reopen the path to the ancient Tree of Life for all humanity and grant the world the blessing of eternal life and eternal peace.

Let me make it perfectly clear that the designation of Israel in the Bible as the chosen people is by no means meant to denigrate non-Jews. This point cannot be overemphasized. We firmly believe that God loves every human being. Our sages taught: "The righteous of the nations of the world have a place in the World to Come."[22] The Torah reveals that *man* is created in the image of God; it does not limit that title of nobility to Jews. Every human being, of every race and every nationality, can attain a measure of greatness by actualizing the intellectual and spiritual potential with which he or she has been endowed by God and, by doing so, will earn God's blessings. The contention of some that Jewish law is blatantly unfair to non-Jews is simplistic and essentially untrue. We shall devote the next session to an analysis of the approach of Judaism to the non-Jew and hopefully put to rest this erroneous and dangerous contention.

Session VII
The Attitude of
Jewish Law
Toward Gentiles

From time to time I am asked by Gentiles to enlighten them as to their role in the world and their obligations to God as defined by Judaism. Among the most common questions are the following:

1. If Judaism has a universal message, should it not have something to say about the obligations and the destiny of Gentiles?
2. Must one be Jewish to win Divine approval?
If so, why does Judaism discourage conversion? If not, how does one become a righteous Gentile?
3. How should Jews relate to Gentiles?

The Torah, as well as the Oral Law and the Responsa literature, do indeed, speak to the issue of Jewish–Gentile relations, and define in no uncertain terms what is considered appropriate behavior for a Jew toward a Gentile. The responsibility Gentiles have to God and to society is defined as well. We will begin with the Torah laws.

Name Terminology

The term most commonly found in the Torah for a non-Jew is *nokhri* ("foreigner"); thus in Deuteronomy 15:3 we read, "You may dun the *foreigner*; but you must remit whatever is due you from your kinsmen." We also find the term *ben nekhor* ("outsider"), as in the phrase in Genesis 17:12: "the one bought from an *outsider* who is not of your seed."

The term *goy* ("nation") is generic, the nation of Israel inclusive. Thus in Exodus 32:13 we find the words, "consider, too, that this *nation* is Your people." The sages of the Talmud referred to non-Jews individually and as a group, but it was always clear to them to which nation they were referring. To simplify matters, however, they began to use the term *goy* or *goyim* to refer to any males who were not from the nation of Israel. A non-Jewish woman was referred to as a *goya*.[1] An important qualification of the usage of these terms in the Talmud is made by one of the early commentators. Whenever the discussion pertains to the desecration of the Sabbath or to the subject of intermarriage, the term *goy* applies to all non-Jews, but when the subject is idolatry or murder, it refers only to the ancient uncivilized peoples of the world who did not observe any of the Noahide laws.[2] But let me make it perfectly clear that in the Torah, as well as in halakhic literature, the term was never used in a derogatory sense. The term *akum*, an acronym for *oved kokhavim u'mazalot* ("star worshiper"), is found in rabbinic literature as well, as are the terms *mitzri*, *canaani*, and *kushi*, but they were only used because of the problem of censorship.

It is important to note that a non-Jew does not lose these terms of designation unless and until he has been fully converted to Judaism. According to Jewish law, a child born to a Jewish male and a non-Jewish female is considered a non-Jew. Most halakhic authorities posit that a child born to a non-Jewish male and a Jewish female is considered a Jew, and this is the accepted ruling. Conversion for males is a twofold process: it means circumcision and immersion in a *mikvah* ("ritual bath") for the specific purpose of conversion. For females, only the latter applies. Upon the fulfillment of these requirements, a convert is considered Jewish, with all the rights and privileges thereof. Needless to say, whether the prospective convert is male or female, intensive study of Jewish law and training in Jewish practices is required. An examination to ensure that the material has been assimilated is administered before the official conversion can take place.

The Noahide Laws

We have mentioned the Noahide laws many times in our discussions, in light of which some further explanation is in order. The Noahide laws are seven principles of ethics and morality that were revealed by God to Noah and were designated to be followed by all subsequent generations. According to one opinion in the Talmud, these laws had already been revealed to Adam. This is hinted to in the verse "And the Lord commanded the man saying: Of every tree in the garden you are free to eat, but as for the tree of the knowledge of good and evil you must not eat of it; for as soon as you eat of it you are doomed to die" (Genesis 2:16–17).[3]

Most of the sages agree that the seven Noahide laws consist of one positive command, to establish courts to administer justice in accordance with the general laws of morality, and six negative commands prohibiting blasphemy, idolatry, murder, robbery, illicit sexual relations, and eating a limb from a living animal.[4] With the exception of the single positive command to administer justice, the Noahide laws apply to men and women alike. It is important to note that these commands are obligatory to Jews as well, some of them with even greater stringency. The Talmud clarifies that with the revelation of the Torah at Sinai, Israel became obligated to a total of 613 commandments. With few exceptions, the Noahide laws that were repeated at Sinai apply to both Jews and non-Jews alike, but those that were not repeated at Sinai were henceforth applicable to Jews alone.[5]

An interesting comment was made by Maimonides. A non-Jew who commits himself to the Noahide laws, not because he finds them to be reasonable and as such worthwhile but simply because he recognizes them as Divine, is designated one of the righteous people of the nations of the world. He is rewarded with a portion in the World to Come.[6]

Equality before God

There are many people who are of the opinion that Jews are blatantly prejudiced against non-Jews and that this prejudice is expressed in Jewish law as well. This is a very dangerous position, and it is impor-

tant that we set the matter straight. To begin with, one must differentiate between "Jews" and "Jewish law." Jews are human, and like all humans their attitudes and opinions are shaped to a great extent by experience. Their behavior is most often guided by their intellect, but it
is at times a spontaneous response to their emotions. Such is the nature of man. As we have already pointed out, Torah ethics are objective; they are absolute and irrevocable truth. They favor no one and
respect the rights of everyone. Their only preconceived agenda is the
welfare of mankind, Jew and non-Jew alike. Hillel, the great sage of
whom we spoke last session, made an important statement in this regard: "Be of the disciples of Aaron, loving peace and pursuing peace,
loving your fellow creatures and drawing them near to the Torah."[7]
The renowned Rabbi Joseph Hertz, former chief rabbi of the British
Empire, comments:

> The word *creatures* connotes the whole human family: there is one hu-
> manity on earth, even as there is One God in heaven. . . . Hillel did not
> advocate love of Jews only, or only of the righteous. He demanded love
> for all, Jew and non-Jew, those under the Torah and those far from the
> Torah.[8]

The Shameful Record of History

All of what we have said notwithstanding, Jews who speak unkindly
about Gentiles have good reason. It is perfectly clear to every student
of history that anti-Semitism abounds in the world. As we pointed out
in our last session, from earliest times many Gentiles have been hos-
tile, cruel, and inhumane in their treatment of Jews. With very few
exceptions, Jews have been treated as second-class citizens wherever
they have lived, despite their contributions to the welfare of the society in which they lived.

It is no secret that directly or indirectly, whether overtly or covertly,
Gentiles have been responsible for the murder of millions of Jews
through the centuries. These acts of evil reached their apex in our own
time with what is perhaps the most horrendous crime ever perpetrated
by man against man, the greatest stain on man's character, and the
greatest insult to his intelligence—the Holocaust of European Jewry

only half a century ago. Indeed, there is good reason for Jews not to speak kindly of Gentiles. The survivors of the Holocaust are still with us; their wounds are still open, and their pain has not yet subsided. But let it be made perfectly clear that the resentment and hostility many Jews justifiably feel toward Gentiles in light of world history is in no way reflected in Jewish law, nor should it be.

Let us make another important point here. In a multi-ethnic society such as ours, every person must be given the right to believe and to worship as he chooses. Judaism would have it no other way. One does not have to be Jewish to win favor and reward in God's eyes. The law requires only that he be a good person. We have already pointed out that Jewish law posits that every human being has a potential share in the World to Come, regardless of his or her religion. It is also well-known that Judaism does not encourage conversion. In point of fact, conversion is forbidden unless it has been ascertained that the perspective convert has no ulterior motive and is sincere in his desire to commit himself to the observance of Jewish laws and customs. Parenthetically, neither Christianity nor Mohammedanism takes this position.

Let us recognize that to be tolerant is not to entertain the notion that all religions have the same validity, that they are merely different paths that ultimately lead to the same destination. No one who is firmly committed to his religion could entertain such a notion. There are fundamental differences between Judaism and other religions in theology and morality, and we believe with perfect faith that on these matters Judaism is the only authentic word of God. To think otherwise would be absurd. For if all religions posit the same basic principles and have a common goal, differing from each other only in approach, why choose one religion over the other? Why would one choose to be Jewish and thereby submit oneself to the horrendous effects of prejudice and second-class citizenship unless one believes that there is a fundamental difference between Judaism and the other religions? Should one feel obligated to practice Judaism only because one was born a Jew? Only one who believes with perfect faith in Divine revelation and the absolute truth of the Torah way of life would be willing to commit oneself in body and soul to its rigorous demands.

To ascertain the position of Jewish law vis à vis the Gentile, one must examine Jewish legal texts through the ages. To do so will prove definitively that the prevailing attitude has always been fair and considerate. Let me illustrate this with several examples.

The Law: Ways of Pleasantness

We have already discussed *tikkun olam,* the responsibility of Jews for the welfare of society. Although there is a difference of opinion among the sages as to the precise meaning and parameters of this responsibility, there is no question that it is incumbent upon Jews to play a formidable role in the humanitarian causes of society. To what extent these causes relate specifically to Jews in comparison to the rest of society is irrelevant.[9] In point of fact, the assigned mission of the Jewish people to effect an ethical and moral change in society is a prime example of the concern Jews must have for all people. Also to be recognized is that, according to tradition, it is Israel who will bring about the Messianic Era, a period in history that will be marked by universal peace. This blessing is one that will be shared by all people, Jews and Gentiles alike. But let us consider some principles in Jewish law that relate more directly to Gentiles.

There is an important principle found in the Talmud termed *darke shalom* ("ways of peace"). Our sages did not live in "ivory towers." Their relentless devotion to Jewish law did not cause them to retreat from society, as is common among scholars. Quite the contrary; they lived and functioned within it. Keenly aware of the effect of jealousy, envy, vanity, the pursuit of honor, and other such human foibles, they instituted precautionary measures to avoid conflict among people.

Similar in nature is the principle termed *darke noam* ("ways of pleasantness"). The expression derives from the words of King Solomon. In referring to the beauty of the Torah, he wrote, "Its ways are ways of pleasantness and all its paths are peace" (Proverbs 3:17). When there is some question as to the meaning or intent of a commandment, said the sages, an interpretation that would render the commandment unduly harsh or unpleasant is considered unacceptable because the ways of the Torah are ways of pleasantness; they are meant to promote peace and harmony among people, not uneasiness and difficulty. In light of these principles our sages ruled that it is proper to support the poor of the Gentile community, to visit their sick, to bury and to eulogize their dead, and to comfort their mourners.[10]

Another principle frequently applied to relations between Jews and Gentiles is *evah* ("enmity"). To prevent enmity or hostility between one Jew and another, the sages enacted certain principles. For example, under ordinary circumstances, a found object, unless claimed by someone, belongs to the person who found it. However, in situations where adult children live with their parents and are dependent upon them for support, a special ruling was made. In order to avoid *evah*, enmity between parents and children that may cause the parent to relinquish his support, the sages ruled that any unclaimed objects found by such children belong to the parents.[11] Understandably, where the children do not live with their parents and are not supported by them, anything they find belongs to them.

The principle of *evah* has been applied to Gentiles in the following manner. The law states that a Jew may not accept a gift from a Gentile if it is given on one of his holy days for fear that he has an ulterior motive. However, if the Jew feels that the giver has no ulterior motive, and that he would be offended if the gift is not accepted, causing enmity between them, it is permissible for him to accept it.[12] In the land of Israel, it is forbidden to do business with Gentiles three days before their holy days. In the Diaspora (where Jews and Gentiles live and work together), the law applies only to the holy day itself, so as not to cause enmity.[13] Although some of the sages ruled that selling a *mezuzah* to a Gentile is prohibited, this ruling was remanded because of the fear of enmity.[14]

A Gentile living in Israel who has accepted upon himself the seven Noahide commandments is accorded special status. Although he is not a Jew, he is given special consideration. Termed a *ger toshav* ("resident alien"), the Torah, in Deuteronomy 23:17, states, "He shall live with you in any place he may choose among the settlements in your midst, wherever he pleases; you must not ill-treat him." A resident alien must not be made to wander in the land from place to place like an unwelcome stranger. He must be permitted to live wherever he chooses. The Jewish residents of a community may not force him to move away by complaining that he is competing with them. (How different this is from the horrendous way Jews have been treated throughout history in the lands of their exile.) It is incumbent upon the Jewish community to assist the resident alien to establish himself and care for his family.

The Talmud makes an important clarification with regard to the treatment of Gentiles. A Gentile who commits himself to the Noahide commandments is deemed a good person and must be treated as such. It goes without saying that this principle applies as well to all nations and societies whose governments are based on the ethical and moral principles of the Torah and that are disciplined in the ways of religion and civilization.[15] Maimonides adds that with the exception of certain immigrant rights, our obligations to any and every Gentile who accepts upon himself the seven Noahide commandments are the same as they are to a resident alien, whether or not he is living in the land of Israel.[16] Similarly, Rabbi Zevi Hirsch Chayot, the renowned nineteenth-century halakhist, states:

> The seven [Noahide] commands are the natural laws which both Christians and Mohammedans apply in their courts, and both see that they are fulfilled. . . . everyone who keeps the seven commands because they were given in God's Torah by the hand of Moses is [treated like] a resident alien.[17]

Finally, the late Rabbi Joseph Henkin, perhaps the leading and most respected authority on Jewish law in contemporary times, made the following comment:

> "Beloved is man for he was created in the image of God." This applies even to idolaters. Certainly the people of the world in our time are not idol worshipers, and with the passage of the generations, idolatry has progressively been uprooted from their hearts . . . and even if there are some who worship idols, in my opinion, the overwhelming majority are in the category of resident alien.

> As for the talmudic ruling that a resident alien must accept the seven commands before a tribunal of three as a decree from God through Moses, this is only with respect to our obligation to provide him with a livelihood and the privilege to reside in the land of Israel. But insofar as being removed from the class of idolaters is concerned, anyone who denies idolatry and acknowledges that the seven commandments are obligatory is a resident alien.[18]

All Too Popular Misconceptions

There are some people who are of the opinion that the commandment in Leviticus 19:11 that forbids theft applies only to Jews. This misconception is not only erroneous, it is a distortion of Jewish thinking that can have serious repercussions. Let it therefore be made perfectly clear that Judaism forbids stealing. The law does not distinguish between Jew and Gentile.[19]

Another common misconception concerns the *Shabbat.* We have already explained that with the exception of the three cardinal principles (murder, illicit sexual relations, idolatry), the saving of a life takes precedence over every law of the Torah. Some contend that this ruling applies only to Jews, and that the *Shabbat,* for example, may not be violated to save a Gentile. Misinformation and misinterpretation has been responsible not only for confusion concerning this matter but for much enmity as well.

We have many friends in the Gentile world, but we also have many enemies. As painful and depressing as it is, we have learned to accept this condition as a fact of life. What most of us find to be even more painful and distressing is the fact that in every generation there are self-hating secular Jews who, out of pure ignorance, point accusing fingers at the Talmud and other books, claiming that the law is prejudiced against Gentiles. Despite the sources that indicate clearly that the Gentiles of today are not the heathens of which the Talmud spoke, in consequence of which the laws that apply to heathens simply do not apply to today's Christians and Moslems (or, for that matter, to any civilized members of society), these self-hating Jews do not desist from their false accusations.

The Shahak Affair

In December 1965, a shameful incident took place in the State of Israel. It is known as "the Shahak Affair." A letter by Dr. Israel Shahak, sent to the Israeli newspaper *Haaretz,* made an inexcusable and vicious charge. He considered it a disgraceful form of prejudice that, according to Jewish law, it is permissible to violate the *Shabbat* in order to save a Jewish life while it is forbidden to do so in order to save the life of a Gentile. To strengthen his charge, Dr. Shahak claimed to have witnessed an incident himself where an Orthodox Jew refused to allow his telephone to be used on *Shabbat* in order to call for help to save a Gentile who had collapsed. When he inquired as to whether this was in accordance with Jewish law, writes Dr. Shahak, he was told by the rabbis that it was so, indeed.

Needless to say, this letter caused a furor in Israel. Embellishments of the story abounded. Jewish law was labeled primitive, and the rabbis were designated as inhumane bigots. Conveniently overlooked in the press was the fact that when Dr. Shahak was challenged to substantiate his story, he was unable to do so and in the end he admitted that the story was a total fabrication. He had invented the incident simply to give credence to his claim. What also eluded the press was the fact that Rabbi I. J. Unterman, chief rabbi of Israel at the time and one of the leading authorities on Jewish law, had ruled on this matter. In a responsum concerning proper behavior on *Shabbat*, Rabbi Unterman ruled unequivocally that the *Shabbat must* be violated to save the life of a non-Jew no less than for a Jew.[20]

The reasoning of Rabbi Unterman is quite interesting. Theoretically speaking, *Shabbat*, being one of the fundamental principles of the Jewish religion, should be treated like one of the three cardinal sins (idolatry, murder, and illicit sexual relations) for which the law demands martyrdom, that one suffer death rather than violate the law.[21] In point of fact, *Shabbat* is testimony to the fact that God created the world in six days and rested on the seventh day. Violation of the *Shabbat* is an implicit denial of this fact, in consequence of which it carries the same penalty as the sin of idolatry—execution.[22]

Considering the intrinsic value that Judaism puts on human life, would Jewish law also demand martyrdom for violation of the *Shabbat*? In an attempt to resolve this question, the sages sought some implied sanction in the Torah to warrant violation of the *Shabbat* in order to save a human life.[23] It was found in Exodus 31:16, which reads, "The Israelite people shall keep the *Shabbat*, observing the *Shabbat* throughout the generations as a covenant for all time." Desecrate the *Shabbat* once for a dangerously ill person (to save a life), said the sages, and thus enable him to observe many *Shabbatot* in the future.

Let us understand clearly what is implied in this rationale. The leniency with regard to the laws of *Shabbat* is not predicated on the premise that a human life is of greater importance than the laws of *Shabbat*. Had that been the case, it would apply to all people, Jew and Gentile alike. It is not in man's province to make such a judgment. It is rather the prospect that this person for whom the *Shabbat* is being violated will, as a result, have the opportunity to observe many *Shabbatot* in the future that the sages ruled leniently. As such, the ruling could not possibly apply to Gentiles, for they are not charged with the duty to observe the *Shabbat*.

Parenthetically, this stringency applies only to biblical law. It would certainly be permissible to violate rabbinic law in order to save the life of a Gentile. Be that as it may, says Rabbi Unterman, today the law of *evah* ("enmity") would warrant even the violation of biblical law in order to save the life of a Gentile.[24] In point of fact, Jewish law rules that in a situation where conditions prevail that would warrant the violation of *Shabbat* in order to extinguish a house on fire, it makes no difference whether the house is owned by a Jew or a Gentile.[25]

Teaching Torah to Gentiles

It would not at all surprise me if one were to ask, "How are Gentiles supposed to know about the Noahide laws and their obligation to follow them? Is one permitted to teach these Torah laws to non-Jews?" In point of fact, the Talmud records discussions between the sages and prominent non-Jews on issues of Jewish philosophy, and we do know of important debates that took place later in history between Jews and Gentiles on such issues. One of the more prominent ones is the debate between Nahmanides and Pablo Christiani that took place in the thirteenth century. Teaching Torah to Gentiles is a multifaceted and complicated matter, however. Let me simplify matters somewhat by categorizing the material in response to the following questions.

 1. Is a Gentile forbidden to study the Torah? If so, does this prohibition also apply to the Noahide laws?

 2. If a Gentile is permitted to study the Torah, does this apply to the Oral Law as well? May he be taught by a Jew?

We will begin with a biblical verse, Deuteronomy 33:4, with which even the youngest Jewish schoolchild is familiar. "The Torah, which Moses handed down to us, is the heritage of the community of Jacob." An interesting interpretation of this verse is given by Rabbi Samson Raphael Hirsch. Emphasizing the important role that the Torah plays in Jewish life and the exclusive rights that Jews have to the Torah, Rabbi Hirsch comments:

> The Teaching which Moses commanded us, so runs the national creed which is to be the heritage of Israel from generation to generation. It is *this* Torah which is *morashah*, the real inherited estate, not the land and what that offers; the Teaching is the national Jewish heritage; land and power are only the conditional consequences of this treasure.[26]

The sages of the Talmud are even more emphatic about the exclusive rights the Jewish people have to the Torah. Witness the following:

> Rabbi Johanan said: "An idolater who studies the Torah deserves death, for it is written, 'Moses commanded *us* the Torah for an inheritance.' It is *ours*, not theirs." Then why is it not included in the Noahide laws? [It is!] On the reading *morashah* [an inheritance] he steals it. On the reading *m'orasah* [betrothed] he is guilty as one who violates a betrothed maiden, who is stoned. [Both of these are forbidden to a Gentile by the Noahide laws]. An objection was raised. Rabbi Meir used to say, "From where do we know that even an idolater who studies the Torah is as a high priest? from the verse, 'You shall therefore keep My statutes and My judgments which if a man do, he shall live in them'" (Leviticus 18:5). Priests, Levites and Israelites are not mentioned, but men. Hence you may learn that even a heathen who studies the Torah is as a high priest. [Response] That refers to their own seven [Noahide] laws.[27]

It is quite clear from this text that with the exception of the seven Noahide laws, which are the province of Gentiles as well, the Torah and the pursuit of Torah studies belong exclusively to the Jewish people. The analogies to stealing and to the violation of a betrothed maiden, however, need elucidation. An interesting interpretation of the former is made by Rabbi Jacob Emden, the renowned eighteenth-century German scholar, in his commentary on the Talmud.

The Talmud uses the term *morashah*, which literally means "an inheritance." The Torah and its in-depth interpretations are the inheritance of the Jewish people. An idolater who studies Torah is stealing from the Jewish people. Now, stealing implies one person's gain and the other's loss. What loss is incurred to a Jew when an idolater studies the Torah? Nothing has been taken from him. The answer, says Rabbi Emden, is that an idolater who studies the Torah, with its in-depth interpretations, at times even venturing his own interpretations, reveals the secrets of the Torah. He engages in an activity that has been reserved by God to be exclusively for Jews, and thus treads on Jewish territory.[28] In a real sense, this is stealing, says Rabbi Emden, no different than if that which was stolen were a material object.

Now let us move to the second analogy. The bond between the Jewish people and the Torah is likened to the bond between a bridegroom and his bride: she is betrothed to him, but they are not yet married. One might say that at this point in their relationship they belong to each other theoretically but not practically. Similarly, the Torah that was given to the Jewish people is betrothed to each and every Jew. If he studies the Torah and observes its commandments, he establishes a meaningful practical relationship with it, one that the sages likened to marriage. The Torah was not revealed to the idolater, in consequence of which he has no relationship with it whatsoever, neither a theoretical nor a practical one. If he studies it, therefore, it is analogous to his having relations with a maiden who is betrothed to a Jew.

It is interesting to note that notwithstanding the talmudic analogies and ruling, one commentator opines that the reason for the prohibition is the fear that the idolater might be studying the Torah to enable him to pass as a Jew and subsequently use his acquired knowledge to subvert Jews. However, if it can be ascertained that his only motivation for studying the Torah is to enable him to fulfill its precepts, he is permitted to do so with but a single caveat: he may not study the laws in depth. This limitation does not apply to the seven Noahide laws, however. He may study those laws to the full extent of his intellectual capacity.[29]

Clearly from what we have seen thus far, there are many things that must be taken into consideration in the matter of whether a Gentile may study the Torah. As in many situations, the law is not black or white. We have spoken of teaching "Torah" to Gentiles, but what is meant by this term? Is the prohibition limited to the Written Law, the Oral Law, or does it include both the Written and the Oral Law? Rabbi Zevi Hirsch Chayot opines that the prohibition applies only to the Oral Law. A Gentile may study the Written Law on his own, or it may be taught to him by another Gentile or a Jew.[30]

Rabbi Samuel Eliezer Idels, the renowned seventeenth-century commentator on the Talmud, takes a more stringent position, which he explains as follows:

> The Talmud says: The teachings of the Torah are not to be transmitted to an idolater. It does not say are not to be taught to an idolater, for surely he may be taught the seven commands that apply to him. If he studies the other commands, however, he forfeits his life. From the term *transmitted* we deduce that what is meant is in-depth study of the reasons and secrets of the law, and this applies to the seven commands as well. This is derived from the verse "He declares His word to Jacob, His statutes and ordinances to Israel" (Psalms 147:19), [the latter phrase] meaning the statutes and ordinances of God's law. "He did not do so with any other nation . . ." (147:20), meaning that even regarding the laws that apply to them, He has not revealed to them their reasons and secrets.[31]

From the use of the term *transmit*, rather than *teach*, the Talmud implies the Oral Law, says Rabbi Idels. The laws of the Torah that apply to an idolater, namely, the seven Noahide commands, are certainly to be taught to him, but they may not be taught in depth, revealing the reasons and secrets of the laws, which means the Oral Law that applies to them. The rest of the Torah is clearly forbidden to idolaters. One who does so forfeits his life. Of course, one must keep in mind that both the Talmud and Rabbi Idels address their prohibition to idolaters. Whether the Christians and Moslems of today are considered idolaters is open to discussion. Rabbi Joseph Henkin, whom we quoted previously, as well as many other rabbinic decisors of modern times, opines that they are not.

Converts to Judaism

Lastly, let us address the topic of converts. A male convert to Judaism is called a *ger*, technically, a *ger tsedek*; a female is called a *giyoret*. How are converts treated in Jewish law? Are they regarded as bona fide Jews, with all the rights and privileges that obtain thereof, or are they considered to be lower in status, more like second-class citizens of the Jewish nation?

Let me begin by stating that the key ingredient in a proper conversion is sincerity. As we mentioned earlier, a Gentile who sincerely desires to embrace the Jewish religion, who has been diligent in studying the laws that would enable him to practice Judaism properly, and who has proven himself to be knowledgeable in these laws becomes a bona fide Jew in the fullest sense of the term as soon as he or she immerses in a *mikvah* ("ritual bath"). Understandably, a male convert must first undergo circumcision.

In Exodus 12:49 the Torah teaches, "There shall be one law for the citizen and the stranger who dwells among you."[32] Our sages have explained that the covenant made between God and the nation of Israel in the valley of Moav included not only the Jews of that generation but those of future generations, as well as all future converts to Judaism. It is assumed, of course, that these converts are sincerely committed to the observance of the *mitzvot* and that they had made that commitment before they were accepted into the fold.

For all intents and purposes, a *ger* has become a new person; he begins a new life from the moment he is converted to Judaism. The Talmud likens him to a newborn infant whose "slate" is clean.[33] From the perspective of Jewish law, he no longer has any of his familial relationships. Now, there are many ramifications to this principle. For example, a convert could theoretically marry his own sister if she converts to Judaism. For a variety of reasons, however, rabbinic law prohibited such a marriage.[34] Court testimony would be a better example. Jewish law prohibits brothers from testifying for or against each other in court. Converts, however, would be permitted to offer such testimony because legally they are no longer related. Applying the same principle to the law of inheritance, a convert should not inherit the property of his parents for they are no longer related to him. Here again, the sages stepped in and promulgated a lenient position. They ruled in his favor, for fear that the loss of such an inheritance might make him have second thoughts about his conversion. He might choose to return to his former religion in order to get his inheritance.[35] It should be made perfectly clear that none of these laws apply to a child who was conceived in the womb of a non-Jewish woman but was born a Jew by virtue of the fact that his mother converted to Judaism when she was pregnant. In such a situation, the fetus becomes a Jew in the fullest sense of the term at the precise moment of his mother's conversion, and when he is born he has all the rights and privileges of every other Jew born of a Jewish mother.[36]

A convert is not required to observe the Jewish laws of mourning for his non-Jewish parents or siblings.[37] Married persons who convert to Judaism and want to continue their marriage are permitted to do so, providing they now go through a Jewish marriage ceremony. However, they must first separate for a period of three months in order to differentiate between a child who was conceived as a Gentile and one who was conceived as a Jew.[38] It is interesting to note that a convert who had children before he converted to Judaism is considered to have fulfilled the command to be fruitful and multiply.[39]

A Gentile who converted to Judaism as an adult and subsequently chose to return to his former religion is in violation of Jewish law. His decision notwithstanding, he remains a Jew, albeit a Jewish heretic.[40] On the other hand, someone who converted as a child and who chooses to return to his former religion when he reaches adulthood is permitted to do so, according to Jewish law.[41]

Let us close our discussion with two important statements, the latter being a comment on the former:

> I have witnessed many people enrich themselves by benefiting from a non-Jew's miscalculation, but in the end success was not theirs for they lost all they had, leaving nothing of worth after them. Others, who sanctified God's name by returning that which they had gained by mistake, attained success and prospered and had enough to leave for their children.[42]

> All the more so are we obliged today to our brethren of the nations [of the world] who recognize and honor the One God of the universe, who affirm their belief in Him . . . and keep the seven Noahide commands to which our Torah obligates them. Even more, they perform acts of kindness by providing for our poor . . . how then can we show ingratitude to them, God forbid, and not say as Joseph said, "How then can I do this most wicked thing and sin before God." (Genesis 39:9)[43]

This, my dear Moshe, is how Jewish law addresses the Gentiles of the world and treats the converts to Judaism. The Jewish religion respects all people who are committed to ethics and morality and who practice what they believe. Unlike Christianity, which has a history of forced conversions at the penalty of death, Judaism, for all intents and purposes, has never preached conversion as the only road to salvation. Quite the contrary. Judaism preaches that one need not be Jewish to be considered a righteous person, and designates the righteous of the nations of the world as worthy inheritors of a portion in the World to Come. Would that Gentiles had treated the Jewish people as it is incumbent upon the Jewish people to treat them. How different our lot would have been through the ages!

Now that you have been exposed to Torah, both the Written and the Oral Law, and you have acquired some knowledge of how Jews relate to God and to their fellow man, I would like to think that you are impressed. More important, I hope that the sessions we have had until now have affected your attitude toward Judaism in a positive way. Be that as it may, we will move on. In the next session, I would like to introduce you to the Torah approach to the more intimate relationships between people—friendship and marriage.

Session VIII
Friendship,
Sexual Ethics,
and Marriage

Judaism is a religion that speaks to every facet of man's existence. It is not reserved for the synagogue, nor is it confined to the home or the place of business. Proper interaction with one's fellow man in order to cultivate wholesome relationships is of major importance in Judaism. We will spend today's session on the significance and parameters of friendship, the meaning and application of sexual ethics, and the definition and value of a good marriage.

Man is a gregarious animal. He needs a friend with whom to communicate in order to survive, and he needs society in order to attain his maximum potential. Did not God Himself attest to this? No sooner was Adam created do we read in Genesis 2:18: "The Lord God said: 'It is not good for man to be alone; I will make a fitting helper for him.'" Looking about, it did not take Adam very long to realize that despite the multiplicity of living creatures with which the world was inhabited, he was alone. All life had been created in pairs, but he was a singular being. Indeed, it was not good for Adam to be alone; he needed a creature of his own kind with whom he could communicate and with whom he could share life's joys, its trials, and its tribulations.

Adam needed a friend, so God created Eve. It was a gift that Adam truly appreciated, for the Torah in Genesis 2:23 tells us that when this newly created creature was brought before him he exclaimed, "This one at last is bone of my bones and flesh of my flesh. This one shall be called woman for from man was she taken." Eve was, indeed, Adam's first and most beloved friend.

The Blessing of True Friendship

True friendship is as indispensable to man's well-being as the blood that pulsates through his veins. It is a blessing not to be underrated and never to be taken for granted. But one must be careful not to confuse or equate true friendship with friendliness. The latter is simply a gesture, a common courtesy that is the result of little if any personal feeling or commitment; the former, at its worst, is still a state of commitment. Needless to say, at its best, friendship is a relationship that is marked by unqualified devotion. True friendship is not easily won; it takes patience to cultivate and perseverance to maintain. It is based on many things, among which common interests and shared experiences rank highest. Common interests can be pursued by friends for a lifetime of pleasure, and common experiences can be pleasurably recollected time after time without fear of impending boredom. The Bible lauds the friendship between David and Jonathan and speaks of it as having a spiritual dimension. Thus, we read in 1 Samuel 18:1, "Jonathan's soul became bound up with the soul of David: Jonathan loved him as himself."

Friendship is among the many topics addressed in the Book of Proverbs, and we will focus on selections from this source as an opening for our discussion. In Proverbs 19:24, we read, "Many court the favor of a great man, and all are the friends of a dispenser of gifts." Our sages speak of two kinds of love: the love of another human being for himself, that is, the sum total of all aspects of his being, and the love of another human being for the personal benefit that one derives from him. Needless to say, the former is considered far more honorable than the latter. This distinction is true of friendship as well. Men in high places who have attained what society defines as "greatness" can pull the right strings and do favors. They will be courted by many, none of whom are true friends. One must also recognize the difference between friendship bought and friendship won. The former is a parasitic relationship in which only the desperate engage. It endures only so long as the gifts are forthcoming, for it is not the person who is sought out, but the gifts. A relationship of this sort should be discouraged; at the very least, it should be recognized for what it is, the sages tell us. For both the giver and the receiver will suffer in the end.

The Ramifications of Friendship

Friends face a serious dilemma, and the closer the friendship the more difficult it is to resolve this dilemma to the satisfaction of both parties. Should friends be critical of each other? Would criticism destroy the friendship or would it strengthen it? Is there a way to offer criticism to a friend that would not threaten the relationship? In Proverbs 27:6 we read, "Wounds by a loved one are long lasting; the kisses of an enemy are profuse."

Criticism is a double edged sword. When it comes from an enemy, it can be embarrassing to the recipient at first—there is no sharper blade than the tongue of an enemy—but given its source, the wise will readily dismiss it as baseless. Criticism that comes from a friend is another matter. All things being equal, it should be taken as well-meaning constructive criticism. By virtue of the fact that it is taken seriously, however, it is painful and often causes long-lasting emotional wounds. But much like the wound of the surgeon's knife, it is worthwhile pain, for it brings healing in its wake. Taken in the way it is given, it should strengthen a good friendship rather than weaken it. The praises and compliments of a known enemy are always suspect. All too often there is a dangerous ulterior motive to his words.

A good friendship is based not only on mutual interests but on mutual benefits. In Proverbs 27:17 we read, "As iron sharpens iron, so man sharpens the wit of his friend." A relationship that is one-sided, such as that of a brilliant scholar and his protege, where one is continually giving while the other only receives, has obvious advantages and even some merit. But it cannot compare to true friendship, a relationship in which each party has something to offer to the other. Through the years, the latter has a tendency to grow ever closer while the former will at best maintain the status quo. Two friends studying together, whereby one, by virtue of his superior knowledge, assumes the role of the teacher and the other that of the student, may for a variety of reasons work out well.

All too often, however, impatience and petty jealousies tend to put a strain on such a friendship and more often than not alienate one friend from the other. Two friends who are on a par with each other intellectually tend to challenge and stimulate each other's thinking when they study together, and with the passage of time the bond of friendship that exists between them becomes ever stronger. The Talmud records the words of Rabbi Nahman, spoken in the name of Rabbi Hanina, "I have learned much from my teachers, and from my friends more than from my teachers, and from my students more than all the others."[1]

Friendship means communication, not only on an intellectual plane but on an emotional one as well. In Proverbs 27:19 we read, "As face answers to face in water so does one man's heart to another." The heart is depicted as the seat of intelligence but also as the source of emotion in Jewish symbolic literature. Good friends know each other's thoughts, but they know each other's feelings as well. It is quite common to find kindred hearts reflecting each other in the way they react to stimuli. Good friends often reflect each other's values as well. It is not merely coincidence or a matter of mutual respect that motivates good friends (even more so, husbands and wives) to take the same side in a discussion. It is because they have learned from each other and think alike on many issues. Rabbi Samson Raphael Hirsch adds, "Just as the communication of minds results in mutual improvement, so, too, the association of similarly attuned hearts."[2]

A friend's counsel is like a good spice: too little accomplishes nothing; too much can spoil everything. In Proverbs 27:9 we read, "Oil and incense gladden the heart, and the sweetness of a friend is better than one's own counsel." Anointing oneself with oil and smelling the sweet aroma of incense are each soothing experiences; together, they are that much more pleasant. When faced with a difficult problem, two heads are better than one. A good friend's advice can be of great importance, but only when it is presented in the proper way. Unnecessarily harsh words are self-defeating; they will either be rejected outright or simply fall on deaf ears. A true friend's counsel and constructive criticism should be *sweetened* with words of encouragement so that it will be more readily accepted.

There is a qualitative difference between a companion and a friend, and it behooves us to recognize that difference and act accordingly. In Proverbs 18:24 we read, "There are companions to keep one company, and there is a friend more devoted than a brother." We all have companions or acquaintances with whom we socialize from time to time, and this is a good thing. However, it is of the utmost importance that we recognize that relations with companions are for the most part perfunctory; there is little if any commitment established, in consequence of which such relationships cannot be relied upon for much help in times of need. True friendship, on the other hand, is difficult to achieve; it demands careful attention and patience and giving of oneself, but as any true friends will tell you, the efforts are amply rewarded. Rabbi Samson Raphael Hirsch explains:

> The kind of harmony of mind and spirit that is the basis of friendship exists only between few. We can have many companions but only few friends. Someone who has succeeded in finding a long life treasure of a really true friend may be called fortunate indeed. However, a person who has many companions, being a friend of all the world, may be suited for sociability, but as a rule, he lacks the depth of feeling which makes for real friendship.[3]

Despite what we have said thus far, let us digress for a moment to note the following. There are times when one feels alone even in the presence of a friend, for there are limits to what can be shared even by good friends. A perceptive friend knows the parameters of true friendship, and he acts accordingly. He knows when he is needed and makes sure to be there, but he also knows when it would be best for him to absent himself. Our sages knew these parameters well, and they taught us: "Do not appease your friend in the hour of his anger, and comfort him not in the hour when his dead lies before him, and question him not in the hour of his vow, and strive not to see him in the hour of his disgrace."[4]

Friendship or Kinship?

Which is the greater bond, friendship or kinship? In Proverbs 17:17 we read: "A friend is devoted at all times, a brother is born to share adversity." Is King Solomon not telling us that as precious as true friendship may be, in times of adversity it takes second place to kinship? Indeed, when adversity strikes, there are few friends whose words are as comforting as those of a devoted brother or sister. A friend can be sympathetic, but only a family member shares the pain. In times of utter distress, one draws greater consolation from a partner than from a sympathizer.

The words "a brother is born to share adversity" have an interesting interpretation that I would like to share with you. As we all know, families are not always close. The vicissitudes of life will sometimes alienate brother from sister and parent from child to the extent that they don't even speak to each other. In such families the familial bond that kept them together when they were young and engendered a feeling of love and responsibility for each other is broken, with little prospect of being repaired. Suddenly, adversity strikes one of them, and for some mysterious reason the familial bond is reborn. The wound of the past that had once caused great pain is forgotten, for in its place there is a new wound, one that is shared by the whole family. Brothers and sisters who had almost been forgotten by each other are reunited and children are reborn to their parents. Indeed, in times of adversity when comforters are in desperate need, family is often the first to respond and the most supportive.

When we began our discussion today, we pointed out that Judaism relates to every facet of a person's life; sexuality is no exception. To put the Jewish view on sexuality into proper perspective, however, we must compare and contrast it to two other approaches that have had a major impact on civilization in this regard: hedonism and Christianity. Hedonism is defined as follows:

> Ethical hedonism is a doctrine as to what entities possess intrinsic value. According to it, pleasure or pleasant consciousness, and this alone, has positive ultimate value, i.e., is intrinsically good, has no parts or constituents which are not intrinsically good. The contrary hedonic feeling tone, displeasure or unpleasant consciousness, and this alone, has negative ultimate value, and is intrinsically bad. The intrinsic value of all other entities is precisely equivalent to the intrinsic value of their hedonic components. The total value of an action is the net intrinsic value of all its hedonic consequences.[5]

In essence, hedonism purports not merely that pleasure is *good* and displeasure is *bad*, but that all things are measured in terms of their pleasure component and judged accordingly. In point of fact, what is today termed "The New Morality" is nothing more than "old time hedonism."

In reaction to the lustful behavior of people in the early years of the Christian Era, the Christian fathers formulated a doctrine of ascetic antisexualism, which essentially pitted the body against the soul. The Apostle Paul reluctantly sanctioned marriage as a compromise for those who "cannot contain," but he advocated celibacy as the preferred state. This fundamental Christian approach to sexuality not only denigrates one of the strongest drives within the human psyche; it attempts to obliterate it. In no way could such a doctrine be maintained by the masses. Consequently, the New Morality, or at least some form of sexual revolution, was bound to come.

In reaction to today's sexual revolution, Eliezer Berkovits writes:

> It is the open manifestation of the rebellion against Christian sex ethics which has been occurring under the surface for several generations. It is a revolt against the Christian denigration of the human body and against the Christian approach to sexuality which for many centuries determined the official moral climate in the West.[6]

Let us summarize: The pagan pleasure principle that marked the period of late antiquity in history was acted upon by Christianity by its putting forth a doctrine of severe antisexualism, which is contrary to man's fundamental nature. This created an unbearable situation. Outwardly, some of the Christian masses conformed, but most others merely professed conformity and went on with their chosen lifestyle, somewhat frustrated and perhaps somewhat hypocritical and guilty. One can readily understand why this intolerable situation eventually resulted in the sexual revolution in Christian society.

Jewish Sexual Ethics

Jewish sexual ethics are an approach to sexuality marked by its fundamental differences from both hedonism and Christianity. To understand the Jewish approach, we must begin with the principle of creation. The very concept of creation endows the universe with meaning and purpose. Without the belief in a Creator and the principle of creation, we are confronted with the absurdity of existence. Life becomes meaningless, and we are left in the clutches of bleak existentialism—a depressing thought, indeed. Judaism purports that all that exists is the product of the Divine Mind, and all that is destined to be will be the result of the Divine Will. But of equal importance is the qualification in the Talmud "Whatever the all merciful God has done is for good."[7]

Man, the quintessence of creation, was designed by the Almighty to be a composite of the physical and the spiritual—in a sense a fusion of the Divine and the mundane, as Nahmanides in his Torah commentary explains:

> And God said, "Let us make man after our image, after our likeness . . . " (Genesis 1:26)

> Comment: That is, I and the aforementioned earth, let us make man, the earth to bring forth the body from its elements as it did for the cattle and the beasts . . . and He to give the spirit from His mouth . . . And He said, "in our image," as man will then be similar to both.

Nahmanides' interpretation is based on Genesis 2:7, where we read, "The Lord God formed man of dust from the earth, and He breathed into his nostrils the breath of life; and man became a living being." The "breath of life" here refers to the human soul, which came directly from God. In point of fact, Nahmanides' comment is already found in the Rashi commentary on the previous verse.[8]

The composite of heavenly and earthly matter, that is, body and soul, or the physical and the spiritual, is unique to man; it is what makes him human and should not be denigrated in any way. In contradistinction to Christianity, which pits the body against the soul in an eternal conflict for dominance, Judaism sees the body and soul working together harmoniously. We must keep in mind that just as the soul of man is inherently good by virtue of the fact that it was created by God, so is the body. Its needs are natural; its drives or appetites, sacred. To satisfy these needs is not merely permissible; it is a *mitzvah*. However, like all other *mitzvot*, it must be fulfilled in accordance with the rules and regulations set forth in the Torah and the Oral Law.

The Good and the Evil Inclination

The human soul is involved in every decision man makes as it is in every action he eventually takes. Our sages speak of the two inclinations in man: *yetser haTov,* "the good inclination" and *yetser haRa,* "the evil inclination." They teach us that as soon as a fetus begins to stir within its mother's womb, it is endowed with the evil inclination.[9] Strangely enough, we are told that the good inclination does not appear in the child until it reaches the age of maturity: for males, the age of thirteen, and for females the age of twelve.[10]

Now it is important to understand what our sages meant by the good and the evil inclinations. Clearly, what they termed the evil inclination cannot be taken to mean man's proclivity to commit evil by causing harm to himself or others. Why would the Supreme Being of the universe, of Whom it is said, "He is righteous in all His ways, long suffering and abundant in mercy," endow man with such a failing?

The *Midrash* reveals something interesting. Were it not for the evil inclination in man, says the *Midrash,* he would never marry, or build a home, or have children, or engage in business.[11] There is no civilized society in the world that would consider these natural human desires to be evil traits. What, then, is the evil inclination?

It is my contention that what our sages meant by the evil inclination is the drive within the human personality that is responsible for man's ambition and his progress. It is the force that inspires him to strive for the "brass ring" in life. It is a good thing, but like all good things, it must be handled with good sense and with care. Those who effectively harness this energy will maximize their Divinely endowed potential. Some will attain greatness. Be that as it may, if this energy is allowed total freedom, it will stop at nothing. It will influence man to commit all sorts of evil things under the guise of self-fulfillment, for it wields tremendous power. It is very much like a wonder drug. When taken in appropriate amounts, it can effect a miraculous cure! An overdose is deadly.

Every civilized society attempts to harness the evil inclination in man by establishing a system of law. In return for his being given the privilege of living freely in that society, man must be a law-abiding citizen. Of course, it is taken for granted that any system created by man is by its very nature imperfect, which means that it is in constant need of revision and modification. Judaism has its system of law as well. What differentiates it from every other system, however, (and we have repeatedly emphasized this difference) is that it is rooted in the Torah and the Oral Law, both of which were created by God and revealed at Sinai. It is not at all unlikely that this system is what our sages refer to as man's good inclination. As we have mentioned earlier, the evil inclination, or energy force, in man begins to function in the initial stages of life, while the embryo is still in the womb, but the good inclination does not begin to function until one reaches the age of responsibility and is mandated to obey the laws of the Torah. In males, it is at the age of thirteen; in females, the age of twelve.

There is a beautiful lesson in the Talmud that defines the role of the Torah in man's life.

> Our Rabbis taught: *ve-samtam*, read *sam tam* [perfect remedy]. This may be compared to a man who struck his son a strong blow, and then put a bandage on his wound, saying to him, "My son, as long as this bandage is on your wound, you can eat and drink at will, and bathe in hot water and cold water without fear. But if you remove it, it [your skin] will break out into sores." Even so did the Holy One, blessed be He, speak unto Israel: "My children, I created the evil inclination, but I also created the Torah. You will not be delivered into its hand, for it is said, 'If you do right will there not be special privilege . . . ' (Genesis 4:7). But if you do not occupy yourself with the Torah, you shall be delivered into its hand, for it is written, 'Sin crouches at the door.'" (Genesis 4:7)[12]

The laws of the Torah serve to sublimate man's driving force in life. So long as he keeps within the bounds of the law, he can satisfy his natural desires. He can pursue his ambitions to the utmost of his ability and maximize his potential. But if he lets loose the reins of control, there is no limit to the harm that he will cause to both himself and others.

Now one might understandably ask, "How is it possible for us not to be overcome by the abundant power and cunning of the evil inclination? Are we not products of our genes and our environment? Perhaps some of us simply have no control over our behavior. Should we be punished for our sins?"

On the surface, this question seems reasonable enough. Why punish the weak? In point of fact, however, it's a "cop out." Ultimately, every human being is responsible for his behavior. We were created in God's image. Our sages interpret this to mean that we all have the ability to reason, and, at least to some extent, we all have freedom of will. Granted, the interaction of our genetic code with the environment plays a major role in every decision we make, but we are capable of superimposing what some refer to as "our sovereign will" over these major influences and consciously choose to do otherwise. The Torah proclaims: "I call heaven and earth to witness against you this day: I have put before you life and death, blessing and curse. Choose life—if you and your offspring would live—by loving the Lord your God, heeding His commands and holding fast to Him" (Deuteronomy 30:19).

Were man totally determined by forces over which he has no control, unalterably programmed, as it were, by his genes and his environment, he would never have been commanded to *choose* a way of life. Indeed, under such conditions, choice would be impossible.

With this background, we can now proceed to the issue of Jewish sexual ethics and marriage. Let us begin with an important general statement by Nahmanides that will set the tone for our analysis.

> Sexual intercourse when it is done appropriately, in the appropriate time and with the appropriate attitude, is holy and pure. . . . From the Creator's part there is no aspect of human physiology that is ugly or corrupt for all was created with Divine wisdom and as such is good and perfect. When man sins, however, he brings ugliness to that which had none originally. When the sexual act is done in fulfillment of Divine law, there is no act of greater purity.[13]

The key words here are *in the appropriate time and with the appropriate attitude*. Sexual relations are a mutual affair; they are appropriate only when there is mutual consent. While it is true that sexuality is a drive that man shares with the animal kingdom, it is appropriate only when it is experienced as a totally human activity. To begin with, this means that if for no other reason than the fact that another human being is involved in this experience, it must be controlled by that which is uniquely human, namely, the will and the intellect of both parties. Let it be made perfectly clear, however, that humanizing sexuality does not mean spiritualizing it or in any way diminishing its pleasure. Human sexuality should by all means be appreciated and practiced as a pleasurable experience, but one must keep in mind that human beings need not act like animals in order to experience pleasure.

The first message of sexual ethics is hinted at in Genesis 4:1, where it is written: "And the man *knew* Eve his wife, and she conceived and bore Cain, saying, 'I have gained a male child with the help of the Lord.'" The verb *to know* in this context is obviously a euphemism for sexual relations, but to presume that this phrase is merely euphemistic is too simple and misses the point. What is really implied here is that the context within which human sexuality is appropriate is marriage. Even more, the greatest hope for a successful marriage is where husband and wife *know* each other—that is, they are harmoniously matched to each other in all facets of their psyches. As such, the biblical phrase is not merely descriptive; it is prescriptive.[14] And the precedent is set at the very beginning of the Torah narrative for a humanized sexual ethics. This is to say that the prerequisite for meaningful human sexuality is compatibility in three realms, the spiritual, the intellectual, and the physical, in that order.[15]

Man wills, the animal reacts. The satisfaction of the sexual drive in the animal, whenever and toward whomever it manifests itself, is normal—that is in accordance with the Divine Will. But the Torah ordains that man must behave differently in this regard. Human beings have freedom of will; their behavior must conform to the dictates of their intellects. Man can make his own decision as to whether a particular act is appropriate or not, and if he determines that it is appropriate, he can subsequently decide when and how to satisfy his desire to perform that act. This is what Nahmanides meant by the words *in the appropriate time* and *with the appropriate attitude.*

Consequently, human sexuality can be either sacred or profane, depending on how, with whom, and when it manifests itself. Unlike in the animal kingdom, sexuality in man is never neutral. It must be clearly understood that we are speaking of what *should be*, and this is not necessarily what *is* in our society. There is no question that sexual relations can be and often are a purely physical act. Man has both the ability and the freedom to perform sexually like an animal, but he must keep in mind that if he chooses to do so, the pleasure he will derive from the experience will be nothing more than animal pleasure.

This brings us to the matter of sexual promiscuity or premarital sex. Without going into the technical details of the Jewish laws of modesty and family purity, let it be made perfectly clear that Jewish law prohibits sexual activity before marriage. But we must understand the rationale of this stringent position.

Let us once more recall the story of creation. At the completion of each day, the Almighty evaluated what He had created and the Torah tells us, "And God saw that it was good." What this teaches us is that what exists conforms precisely with the qualities or the design that God had in mind for it. This positive value judgment is omitted after the creation of man, and one cannot help but wonder why. Is not man, the quintessence of creation, worthy of a positive evaluation? Perhaps the answer is that all other creatures can be evaluated on the day that they are created for they are destined to be exactly what God designed them to be. They lack the freedom of will to affect their destiny in any way. Not so with man.

Postponed Gratification

Man is free, and he is goal-oriented. He lives in the future of "becoming." What he is today, he need not be and may not be tomorrow. The wicked can be reborn and for all intents and purposes start a new life if and whenever they choose to do so. This is *teshuvah* ("repentance"), the powerful gift that God has given to man in consideration of which it can neither be said of him that he is good nor that he is bad until the day he dies. Then and only then can his life be evaluated by God and judged accordingly. Unlike any other creature on earth, man has the ability to control his behavior. "Who is truly strong," the sages tell us, "he who controls his passions."[16] Man need not be a slave to his desires. The point is succinctly put by Eliezer Berkovits:

> Whereas delay is frustration, postponement is growth; whereas delay is violence against the "now," postponement is care of tomorrow; whereas delay is denial, postponement is promise. Within the Jewish sexual ethics one should replace the term *inhibition* by that of *discipline*. Inhibition upon a creature of "now" is oppression while discipline chosen by the future-open man is liberation.[17]

The ability to postpone gratification is an essential ingredient in man; it differentiates him from the animal. We are taught to exercise this ability from childhood, from which time, theoretically, it should be assimilated into our personality.

"Mother, may I have a cookie?"

"Not now, dear, you must wait till after dinner."

"Mother, may I open my birthday present now?"

"No, dear, tomorrow is your birthday. You may not open it until tomorrow."

"But can you tell me what it is?"

"No, dear, it's a surprise. Be patient, you'll find out tomorrow."

Postponement is not denial; it is a lesson in control. Quite often, it promises even greater gratification at a designated time in the future. To illustrate: Most working people have the good sense not to spend all of their money on the day that they get their weekly paychecks. They save or invest some of it, which enables them to make a substantial purchase in the future. They recognize that postponement of gratification will enable them to experience much greater gratification in the future. This ability is unique to man. Now it stands to reason that the stronger the desire, the more difficult it is to postpone gratification. With most people there will be instances when, against their better judgment, they succumb to temptation.

The sexual instinct is one of the strongest drives in the human psyche. It cannot be ignored, but neither can it be allowed to run rampant. Contrary to the position of Christianity, which advocates celibacy as the preferred state for man and reluctantly sanctions marriage as a compromise for those who "cannot contain," Judaism has a very positive attitude on human sexuality. For Judaism, sexual fulfillment at the appropriate time is a *mitzvah*, a sacred precept. We mentioned earlier that Nahmanides designates sexual relations as an act that is holy and pure. As such, it is not at all surprising and very much in keeping with Jewish character for the "Song of Songs" to have been written by King Solomon in the sexual idiom. Even more! Note the words of the great Rabbi Akiva: "The whole world is not as worthy as the day on which the Song of Songs was given to Israel; for all the Writings are holy, but the Song of Songs is the holy of holies."[18]

Jewish sexual ethics are not merely about sexuality; they are about relationships. They define the rules and regulations that apply to a man and a woman in love. And what is true love? It is the closest possible relationship between a man and a woman, which eventually results in a mutual decision to enter into the sacred covenant of marriage. Think for a moment. Sexuality being the most intimate and the most pleasurable relationship between a man and a woman, should it not be reserved for marriage?

Let me put it this way. A man and a woman who are intellectually and spiritually compatible and are attracted to each other physically reach a point in their relationship where they are no longer content in being mere friends; they want to marry and raise a family. The Almighty, in His infinite wisdom and kindness, has seen fit to instill within their physiology the ability to attain the greatest possible physical pleasure in creating that family.

Dating and Engagement

When two people become engaged to be married, they must learn to postpone sexual gratification until marriage, when sexual relations become not only permissible but, as Nahmanides has written, an act of holiness. To do so is to engage in self-discipline of the highest order, to be sure. It is to put mind over body and demonstrate the power of the sovereign will. It is to dignify human existence and classify it as qualitatively different from that of the beast.

There was a time, not more than a generation ago, when society at large, Jew and non-Jew alike, looked at marriage as a beautiful and sacred bond between husband and wife. It was a time when most people looked askance at sexuality outside the bond of marriage. But times have changed. Today's young people live with great uncertainty regarding their place in society. They are confused and skeptical about the future. Life is too insecure to plan ahead. In today's secular society, the younger generation is hedonistic and narcissistic, focusing almost exclusively on pleasure and self-gratification. Young people think primarily in terms of the "now," for only the present is real. The institution of marriage has been discarded by many in favor of what is called "living together," a euphemism for what in reality is "sex without responsibility."

The words of the prophet who centuries ago depicted the attitude of the masses of his day as "Eat and drink for tomorrow we die" (Isaiah 23:13) could well have been written today, for it is the creed of a large segment of the secular society, indeed, the watchword of the exponents of the "New Morality." The threat of another world war and nuclear disaster looms up before us, and we act as if we are powerless to prevent it. Serious crime is rampant in our country and we are doing virtually nothing about it. Corruption and immorality manifest themselves even among the highest echelons of government and are dismissed by our citizens with a hopeless shrug of the shoulders. Perversion has come out of the closet and is practiced with pride; substance abuse is growing by leaps and bounds all over the globe, and humanity stands by and observes in silence. All of this is tolerated, by many condoned, in the name of "freedom," the catchword of the late twentieth century. For Jews to acquiesce to the "norms" of today's secular society and abandon morality, sexual ethics, and the sacred institution of marriage in these immoral times would be to reap the fruits of hopelessness and thus render the human experiment a failure. To abandon their sacred mission would indeed mark the beginning of the end of civilization.

Adherence to Jewish sexual ethics demands of a man and a woman that they exercise great control over their sexual desires when dating. Those who are engaged to be married must exercise even greater control. This is what was meant to be! Whether we are willing to admit it or not, control is what defines us as human beings and differentiates us from the animal, and it is of the utmost importance to recognize that this differentiation is by Divine design.

This notwithstanding, we must recognize that there is a difference in what is demanded of an engaged couple as opposed to a man and a woman who are merely dating for pleasure and have no serious intentions. Sexuality in dating is simply the hunger for one more pleasurable experience. Call it lust or the passion of the moment, it is instinctual and essentially no different than the hunger of an animal for its mate. The "date rape" phenomenon and the statistics on teenage pregnancy clearly confirm this. To refrain from sexuality is simply a matter of mind over body and obedience to the law. There are some experiences in life that must simply be recognized as inappropriate before marriage.

When a couple is engaged to be married, the prohibition against sexuality must be seen from an entirely different perspective. Marriage is the beginning of a new life. Two persons who are planning to be married live not only for today but for tomorrow. They are not told to refrain from sexual gratification but to postpone it, better yet, to reserve it for when they are married. In point of fact, one of the ways in which a marriage is consummated, according to Jewish law, is through sexual relations. As such, what would be a purely physical experience before marriage takes on holiness by becoming part of a marriage. We must also keep in mind that procreation fulfills a twofold *mitzvah*, to have a family and to propagate the earth. For Genesis 1:28 reads, "God blessed them and God said to them, 'Be fruitful and multiply, fill the earth and master it.'"

The Jewish Marriage

Marriage is a natural phenomenon, sanctioned and endowed with holiness by the Almighty Himself. In the second chapter of Genesis we read:

> The Lord God said, "It is not good that man should be alone; I will make a fitting helper for him." And the Lord God formed out of the earth all the wild beasts and all the birds of the sky, and brought them to the man to see what he would call them; and whatever the man called each living creature, that would be its name. And the man gave names to all the cattle and to the birds of the sky and to all the wild beasts; but for Adam no fitting helper was found. So the Lord cast a deep sleep upon the man and he slept; and He took one of his ribs and He closed up the flesh at the spot. And the Lord God fashioned into a woman the rib that He had taken from the man and He brought her to the man. Then the man said, "This one at last is bone of my bones and flesh of my flesh. This one shall be called woman for from man was she taken."[19]

It is sufficiently clear from the opening verse of this narrative that it was not man's destiny to be a singular creature. Had these words been meant merely to reflect on the depressed state of loneliness in which Adam found himself, the phrase would have read, "It is not good for man that he be alone."[20] It is also important to take notice of the words "I will make him a *fitting helper*," and to man's response when he saw the woman for the first time: "This one at last is bone of my bones . . . "

God brought the animals to man so that he would study their forms and their habits. In doing so, Adam must have observed that they had physical characteristics that were very much like his own. There is no doubt that he also observed that they came in pairs, male and female, and that they coupled for mating purposes. Yet he found no suitable partner among them. Is this not why the Torah proclaims, "But for Adam no fitting helper was found?" Surely he must have wondered why he was different?

To be alone was not natural for man, but he needed much more than a mating partner. He needed a "fitting helper." He needed companionship, a wife with whom he could create a family and with whom he could share life's goals, its joys, its trials, and its tribulations. Surely, this is the deeper meaning he wished to convey in the words, "This one at last is bone of my bones and flesh of my flesh." What follows is the inspiring message from the Almighty Himself, sanctifying the union of husband and wife in marriage. As we read in Genesis 2:24, "Hence a man leaves his father and mother and clings to his wife, so that they become one flesh."

A Significant Precedent

The importance of honoring parents, respecting their wishes, and caring for them when they are in need cannot be overstated. It is a fundamental principle in Judaism. Fifth of the Ten Commandments, in Exodus 20:12 it reads, "Honor your father and your mother, that you may long endure on the land which the Lord your God is giving you." We have already pointed out that the future of Judaism rests on the faithful transmission of its tenets from father to son through the generations. The respect and honor that a child must show to his parents for their having given him life is second to none, and the gratitude that he must feel for their having given him the wherewithal to function and to contribute to society must never wane. Nonetheless, the Torah recognizes that the commitment and the allegiance of husband and wife to each other must take precedence even over that of a child to his parents.

Let us explain this a bit further. It is only natural for the relationship between parent and child to undergo a series of transformations, qualitative changes, as the child becomes more and more self-reliant and emerges from total dependency to total independence. And when the adult meets his chosen mate in life, another change takes place. The child clings to his parents for support, but the Torah tells us that the adult clings to his spouse. The child acts primarily out of the need for self-preservation; the adult, out of love. This natural change does not mean that the adult no longer needs or loves his parents, nor does it mean that he is no longer obligated to honor them and respect their wishes. What it does mean is that his most intimate concerns, his needs, and his goals in life are now shared primarily with his chosen partner in marriage.

A Marriage Made in Heaven

In the ideal marriage husband and wife are like "one flesh." They act in harmony with one another, and each feels incomplete without the other. They cling to each other in times of joy, and in times of stress and tragedy they are each other's firmest support. In Deuteronomy 10:20 we read: "You shall fear the Lord your God; Him shall you serve, *and to Him shall you cling,* and by His name shall you swear." Isn't it interesting that the Torah uses the verb "to cling" to indicate how strongly we should relate to God?

The ultimate intimacy between husband and wife brings the ultimate fulfillment of their life together, the creation of a child. But with fulfillment comes the responsibility of raising that child properly. It is in this regard that harmony is of paramount importance. On matters of education, discipline, religion, and proper behavior, both parents must speak as one. Where there are differences of opinion between parents, those differences must be aired and reconciled early in the marriage before children come on the scene. For there is nothing more confusing and frustrating to a child than getting differing views from his parents on right and wrong.

We have already noted that marriage is a mutual decision by a man and woman to build a life together that begins as friendship and develops into love. In point of fact, the sixth blessing that is recited at a Jewish wedding refers to the bride and groom as "beloved friends." In a good marriage the friendship between husband and wife is viable, and it is continually adding new dimensions. Time brings with it more and more shared experiences: the joys and trials of living together, parenthood, new friendships, and new interests. These shared experiences bring husband and wife ever closer to each other.

True love inspires commitment, fidelity, and unwavering devotion, which are the hallmark of a successful marriage. Minimizing competition between husband and wife and maximizing the things that can be shared inspires true love. The notion that opposites attract in a relationship is illogical, and experience has proven it to be erroneous. While it is true that opposite personalities might be intrigued by each other initially, such relationships are usually short-lived.

Love, honor, and respect for one another are fundamental in a Jewish marriage. The Talmud speaks of a man who loves his wife as himself and honors her even more than he does himself, who guides his sons and daughters in the right path, and arranges for them to be married near the period of their puberty. Of him, it is said, "And you shall know that your tent is in peace" (Job 5:24).[21] The following comment is made: Regarding love, the Talmud says "as himself," for it is written, "You shall love your neighbor as yourself," which is interpreted to include one's wife. Man's body lives only in this world, but his soul, if it is worthy, may ascend into the next world. A man must honor his wife even more than himself for she keeps him from sin and thus brings his soul into the next world.[22]

A very strong statement was made by Rabbi Tanhum, in the name of Rabbi Hanilai: "A man who has no wife lives without joy, without blessing, and without goodness."[23] Perhaps what he wished to teach us is that joy shared with one's beloved wife is qualitatively different and far superior to joy experienced alone, even joy shared with a friend. One who is unmarried is deprived of that joy. The greatest blessing one can receive in life is pride in one's children. This, too, is qualitatively different from any other blessing one may enjoy in life. Finally, until a man finds his mate, goodness is lacking in his life. We have already explained that the term "goodness" can mean "completeness," as it does in the statement that closes each act of creation, "And God saw that it was good." These words are conspicuously missing after the creation of man, to indicate that until the woman was created man was incomplete. The point is confirmed by none other than King Solomon in Proverbs 18:22, where he wrote, "He who has found a wife has found good."

Notwithstanding the fact that no one other than the husband and wife really know whether a marriage has been blessed with true happiness, most people are impressed by couples who appear to be happily married. Such bliss is referred to as "a marriage made in heaven." In point of fact, Judaism teaches us that good marriages are, indeed, made in heaven. With the completion of the six days of creation, the Holy One, blessed be He, spends His time matchmaking.[24] It is a difficult process, says the Talmud. "To effect a union between a man and a woman is as difficult as dividing the Reed Sea."[25] Nevertheless, explains the Talmud, "Forty days before the creation of a child a heavenly voice issues forth and proclaims, 'the daughter of A is for B.'"[26]

An Interesting Analogy

In the light of all that we have said, it is understandable that the loss of one's mate is a devastating experience. How sensitive our sages were to the significance of such a loss. The Talmud says: "The death of a man is felt by none but his wife, and that of a woman by none but her husband."[27] This remark is not in any way meant to belittle the pain felt by parents for children or children for parents. It is just meant to emphasize that that which is felt by a relative of the deceased, painful as it may be, can in no way be compared to that which is felt by a spouse. The Talmud went still further and compared the loss of a spouse to the destruction of the Temple in Jerusalem. "He whose first wife has died," says the Talmud, "is grieved as much as if the destruction of the Temple had taken place in his days,"[28] and again, "The world is darkened for him whose wife has died in his days. . . . R. Yose ben Hanina said: His steps grow short . . . R. Abbuhu said: His wits collapse."[29]

Let us attempt to understand the analogy. Those who marry at a young age, and are fortunate enough to have been able to live together for many years, have a unique relationship. They can reminisce and recall the delights of their youth. Having virtually grown up together, they share each other's most intimate experiences: the gains and the setbacks, the good decisions and the bad ones, the joys and the sorrows. The intensity of love that is engendered by having shared so many of life's experiences for so many years can never be duplicated. When one mate passes on, the other is permanently affected.

The greatest national tragedy suffered by the Jewish people was the loss of the land of Israel, and their greatest spiritual tragedy was the destruction of the Holy Temple in Jerusalem. As a nation, they felt that their world had virtually come to an end. All that was left of the Temple was the memory that lingered in the minds of those who had seen it and had participated in the Temple service. Loneliness and despair prevailed among the masses. The analogy to the death of a spouse is therefore most appropriate. There is no greater tragedy to a person than the loss of a beloved mate, for he feels that he is bereft of his raison d'etre. He, too, feels that his world has virtually come to an end, and he, too, is left only with memories to recollect when he is in utter loneliness and despair.

Such is the significance of a Jewish marriage. It is a sacred trust, a binding covenant between two people that results from what is clearly the most important decision they will ever make in life. The decision to marry must be made wholeheartedly, with the full intent of making the marriage last for life.

Notwithstanding all that we have said, let it be clearly understood that when a marriage has gone bad, divorce is an acceptable option. There is no special merit in staying married if it means living a life filled with misery. Judaism recognizes that there are circumstances that vitiate the sacred and binding covenant of marriage, and that despite the aggravation it causes to both parties and the pain and trauma experienced by the children, there is a need to sever the relationship. Unlike in Catholicism, where it is clearly forbidden, Judaism recognizes divorce as legitimate, assuming that it is handled in full accordance with Jewish law. However, divorce should only be granted in situations in which all efforts for reconciliation have been exhausted. This is one more example of the insight Judaism has into the human personality, the grasp Judaism has on reality, and the flexibility of Jewish law.

In most cases, a successful marriage is usually blessed with children. What does Judaism have to say about the attitude of parents toward children and children toward their parents? This will be the topic for our next session.

Session IX
Parents toward
Children and
Children
toward Parents

Our topic for today is "Parents and Children," and we will focus on the Jewish approach to relating. One need not be a sociologist to know that relating marked by mutual understanding, consideration, and clear communication is the lifeblood of society. How many wars have been precipitated and how many innocent people have been killed and maimed because of greed and envy and the refusal of the leaders of one nation to recognize the rights or to understand the needs of another? How many international tragedies could have been avoided had there been proper communication between the leaders of nations?

The Nuclear Family

Society begins with the nuclear family, and the precedent for proper or improper "relating" is set by the father and mother. The interaction of the family that takes place in the home is a learning experience for the child; it makes an indelible impression upon him. This in turn influences the way he interacts with his peers early in life and greatly affects his approach to friendship and collegial relationships when he becomes an adult. The child is indeed father to the man.

None of us are so naive as to think that policy decisions, even those made on an international level, are based entirely on what takes place at the conference table on a particular day. The nature and nurture of the participants—their inherited traits and their cumulative experience, the seeds of which are implanted in the womb and shaped early in life—this is the background with which they come to the conference table. It is as important to the outcome of a policy meeting as that which is openly discussed. It is not at all unlikely that decisions made by leaders of nations, affecting multitudes of people the world over, are influenced, at least to some extent, by what took place at home that morning at the breakfast table. To be precise, the successes and failures experienced by both parents and children leave an indelible mark on their personalities, affecting their way of thinking throughout life and the way they relate to society at large.

Ideally speaking, with the exception of husbands and wives, there is no closer relationship than that between parents and children. Our parents merit our respect and honor, if for no other reason than because they are responsible for our being and are committed to sustaining us until we are able to care for ourselves. Where they have accomplished these responsibilities amiably, they have earned our love as well. Our children merit our love because they are the product of our love for each other and are in some ways an extension of our own lives. But they also merit our honor and and our respect as human beings, for they were created by God in His image.

Would that the love children have for parents were as intense and as pure as the love parents have for their children. In point of fact, one would expect the love of children for parents to be of far greater intensity than the love of parents for children. Is it not our parents who teach us the Torah way of life? Is it not they who dutifully and unhesitantly forgo many of the pleasures they could enjoy in life in order to care for us when we are young and nurse us when we are unwell? And is it not they who give us the moral and financial support to pursue the career of our choice, enabling us to accomplish something with our lives in this world? Be that as it may, experience teaches us that logic is not the sole determinant of human behavior even in the best of families. In point of fact, in most families the devotion of parents to their children by far exceeds that of children to parents. Such is life!

Parental Roles: Honor and Reverence

Let us examine two important biblical sources that bear on our discussion:

1. Honor your father and your mother, that you may long endure on the land which the Lord your God is giving you (Exodus 20:12).
2. You shall each revere his mother and his father and observe My sabbaths, I am the Lord your God (Leviticus 19:3).

It is interesting to note that when it pertains to honor, fathers are mentioned first, while mothers take precedence when it pertains to reverence. Why is this so? Our sages explain that it is to teach us that we must honor and revere both parents in equal measure.[1] Let me explain.

Parents have had definitive roles in the Jewish family from early times on. In many families, these roles have remained essentially the same to the present day. The attitude of children to their parents and the way they relate to them is to a great extent based on these roles. Even today, in most Jewish families, it is the father who is the main wage earner. He is usually away from home for the better part of the day. He may see his older children in the evenings, but he seldom has the opportunity to interact much with them other than on *Shabbat.* Given these conditions, how well can he know them, and how close can he be expected to be with them? As a result, the father is often seen by his children as the austere authority figure who lays down the law, inspiring fear and demanding obedience. Who among us cannot recall mother's threatening words, "When your father comes home, I'll tell him what you did, and he'll punish you."

Mothers, on the other hand, get to know their children well if for no other reason than that for the first five or six years in a child's life he spends most of his day with his mother. Under normal circumstances, mothers become close to their children. As a result, they are more aware of their needs, more sympathetic, more loving, and more forgiving. It is quite natural for a child to love and honor his mother more than his father. He knows her better and relates to her more easily than to his father. To teach the child that it is not enough for him to revere his father, but that he must honor him as well, fathers are mentioned first in the biblical text that speaks of honoring parents. To teach him that he must revere his mother as well as honor her, mothers are mentioned first in the biblical verse pertaining to reverence.[2]

It should be noted that honor and reverence are *mitzvot* that apply to God as well. In the book of Proverbs 3:9 we read, "Honor the Lord with your wealth," and in Deuteronomy 6:13 we are told, "Revere only the Lord your God." In many ways God is like a parent to us. In the Talmud it is stated: "There are three partners in man, the Holy One, blessed be He, the father, and the mother. When a man honors his father and his mother, the Holy One, blessed be He, says, 'I ascribe [merit] to them as though I had dwelt among them and they honored Me.'"[3] In His abundant kindness, God has graciously bestowed upon mankind the ability to co-create: man is a partner with God in the creation of a human life. Eve, the first mother of mankind, recognized this partnership with the Almighty, and after giving birth to her first child she expressed her feelings and reflected, "I have gained a male child with the help of the Lord."[4]

The Matter of Love

Let us ponder an interesting question. We are commanded to honor and revere our parents just as we honor and revere God. Yet there is no *mitzvah* in the Torah that obligates us to love our parents, nor is it prescribed by rabbinic law, whereas love of God is ordained in the Torah in no uncertain terms. In Deuteronomy 6:5 we are distinctly commanded: "You shall love the Lord your God with all your heart, with all your soul, and with all your might." What is the rationale for this? Why are we not commanded to love our parents?

Love is a complicated and multifaceted human emotion. In point of fact, it is a generic term whose definition is dependent upon the love object and a multiplicity of other variables. The love of a parent for a child, for example, is not based on the same feelings as the love of a child for a parent. The love of God is motivated by considerations that are definitively different from those that motivate the love of one's fellow man. The love of one's spouse is qualitatively different from the love of one's teacher or mentor, and the love of one's country is not at all like the love of one's chosen profession.

Maimonides speaks of the love of God as follows: "When a person contemplates His great and wondrous works and creatures and from them obtains a glimpse of His wisdom which is incomparable and infinite, he will immediately love Him, praise Him and glorify Him."[5]

Clearly, there is a qualitative difference between love of God and love of any other person or object. Love of God is awesome. Contemplation of the mysteries of the universe and the miracle of life are sufficient to inspire love of God. Perhaps it is for this reason that love of God can be mandated by the Torah.

Love of parents is an entirely different matter. Here we are dealing with a whole set of variables that at any given time can either contribute to or detract from our love. The terms *father* and *mother* attest to parenthood, a biological phenomenon that does not in and of itself elicit feelings of love. Proper relating breeds love. The relationship we have with our parents when we are young has a profound effect on the way we relate to them later in life.

Parenting is an extremely difficult task, and most of us are unprepared to handle that task skillfully. To love one's children comes naturally to most parents, and it brings them great satisfaction. But in order for parents' love to be meaningful, it must be expressed and demonstrated to their children frequently. None of us is perfect, and that includes parents. We make mistakes, and at times we are guilty of poor judgment. We have our idiosyncrasies, and the vicissitudes of life subject us to mood swings that make things unpleasant not only for us but for our children as well. Our personality traits, our manner, our interests, and the lifestyle we try to instill in our children may cause friction between us and irreparable damage to the parent–child relationship. Such incidents of friction can sour even the strongest feelings of love. Unlike the love of parents for children, which can weather most storms, a child's love is fickle; it must be earned and nurtured. It cannot be mandated by the Torah. But regardless of whether one loves his parents or not, one must honor and revere them. This much is mandated by the Torah.

The Promised Reward

The *mitzvah* of honoring one's parents is one of the Ten Commandments. There are two versions of this commandment: one appears in

Exodus 20:12, the other in Deuteronomy 5:16. The latter clearly links honoring parents to long life and reads, "Honor your father and your mother as the Lord your God has commanded you; that your days may be long, and that it may go well with you upon the land which the Lord your God gives you." The fact that this *mitzvah* is linked to long life highlights its importance, for the gift of a long life is the greatest reward man can receive. Isn't it strange, therefore, that another *mitzvah* found in Deuteronomy, one which would seem to be of minor importance in comparison, is also linked to long life? The *mitzvah* to which I refer is found in Deuteronomy 22:6. It reads: "If, along the road, you chance upon a bird's nest, in any tree or on the ground, with fledglings or eggs, do not take the mother with her young. Let the mother go and take only her young, in order that it may go well with you, and you may prolong your days."

At first blush, we are confused. How can this *mitzvah* be compared to honoring parents? A little reflection, and what they have in common becomes apparent: both *mitzvot* reveal the high regard the Torah has for motherhood. Rabbi Samson Raphael Hirsch explains:

> You are commanded to take up the mother bird—so that you see that you could take it—but to let it fly away into freedom. The fact that it is exercising its function of motherhood protects its independence and freedom. Do this in the consciousness that on the spirit of the *mitzvah* which you thereby fulfill, on the deep respect for motherhood which you express thereby, the happiness of the present and all the future depends.[6]

Perhaps there is another way of understanding the promise of long life to those who honor their parents. It is stated in the Talmud: "In the measure with which a man measures, it is meted out to him."[7] Among other things, this statement teaches us that God treats us the way we treat our fellow man. Children who fail to give their parents proper respect or who dishonor them by behaving unethically or immorally cause them great distress, embarrassment, and mental anguish. Parents tend to blame themselves for the character flaws and improprieties of their children. They feel that they have failed in the most important responsibility of married life, that is, raising children. Depressed over their failure, their lives are often cut short. Perhaps the Almighty metes out punishment to such children measure for measure and shortens their lives as well. Conversely, children who honor and respect their parents bring them great joy and pride. Such parents feel a sense of accomplishment, for they know that they have succeeded in their life's mission. The contentment and peace of mind they have gained often prolongs their lives. In reward for their exemplary behavior, the Almighty prolongs the lives of the children as well.

The Parameters of Honor and Reverence

As important as the *mitzvah* of honoring and revering one's parents may be, it does not always take precedence. Leviticus 19:3 is a good example. It reads: "You shall each revere his mother and his father and observe My sabbaths, I am the Lord your God." The text links reverence for parents to the observance of the laws of *Shabbat*. What this teaches us is that as important as the *mitzvah* of revering one's parents may be, it does not take precedence over the laws of *Shabbat*. Revere your parents and honor them, unless to do so would be to transgress the laws of *Shabbat*. Under those circumstances, obedience would be forbidden. This means that if our parents demand that we transgress the laws of *Shabbat*, we are forbidden to obey them. But there is something more that we can learn from this juxtaposition. It teaches us of the high esteem in which parents are held in the Jewish tradition. For were it not for this verse, we might have assumed, with good reason, that to honor one's parents takes precedence even over the laws of *Shabbat*.

It is interesting to note that despite the strictness of the law on these matters, our sages have suggested that parents be forgiving and look away from some of the improprieties of their children so as to protect them from severe punishment.[8]

Let us pose an interesting question. It is a *mitzvah* for a Jew to live in the land of Israel. The great sage Nahmanides rules that the source is biblical, deriving from Numbers 33:53, which reads: "And you shall drive them out of the land and settle it, for I have given this land to you to possess it."[9] One who has settled in the land may not leave, but must remain there permanently. Nonetheless, there are exceptions to this rule, enumerated by Maimonides as follows:

> It is forbidden to emigrate from the land of Israel and go abroad unless one goes to study the Law, to marry or to rescue property from hea-

thens, and then return to the land. So, too, one may leave on business. But one is forbidden to make one's home abroad unless there is famine in the land.[10]

Considering that there are extenuating circumstances in which one would be permitted to leave the land temporarily, would it be permissible to do so in order to honor one's parents? The Talmud records a situation in which one of the sages who had established permanent residence in Israel contemplated leaving the land temporarily in order to personally escort his mother there. Would this not be a matter of honoring his mother and, as such, take precedence over the law that forbids him to leave the land? Unsure how to act, he raised the question to his teacher. Not only was he answered in the affirmative, but he received his teacher's blessing.[11]

Let us now relate this material to a contemporary problem. Many young Americans are leaving this country and settling in Israel. In some cases, they are doing so against their parents' wishes. Does the *mitzvah* of going on *aliyah* (settling in the land of Israel) take precedence over obedience to parents in this regard? From what Maimonides has taught us, it is clear that living in the land of Israel presupposes relative comfort and excludes a life that would impose undue hardship. One is not obligated to settle in the land without ample food and shelter or if one cannot possibly earn a living there.[12]

While the objection of parents does not in and of itself release one from the *mitzvah* of *aliyah*, it may be a strong impediment to the proper fulfillment of this *mitzvah*. Separation from one's parents in order to settle in a distant land might leave them vulnerable in their old age. From a psychological perspective, one might say that an inability to assist one's parents in times of need could cause stress and initiate guilt feelings that at the very least would make life difficult. Just as inadequate food and shelter or the inability to earn a living would vitiate the conditions under which the Torah commands one to settle in the land of Israel, so would stress. Perhaps this is what motivated one of our contemporary sages to rule that a parent's objection to his child's desire to settle in the land of Israel must be honored.[13] Here again, we have an example of the seriousness with which the law of honoring parents is taken in Jewish tradition. Let me add that the age of the parents and the age and marital status of the children would also carry some weight in determining the position of the law on this matter.

Trustworthiness and Tradition

In our discussion of the meaning and significance of friendship, we often referred to verses in the Bible found in the book of Proverbs. This incisive work, which stresses commitment to God and to Torah ethics and morality, also addresses the relationship between parents and children. It sensitizes us to the way parents react to their child's intellectual and spiritual progress, and gives us some important advice on the proper discipline of children.

In point of fact, the book of Proverbs begins with the *mitzvah* of honoring parents. This is not at all surprising, for the future of Judaism depends to a great extent on the establishment of harmony and proper relations between parents and children. Our parents are our first teachers. They introduce us to Torah ethics, and we must honor and respect them for it whether or not they have earned our love. But every parent must recognize his responsibility to both his child and the Jewish people. If he wants to be taken seriously, not only must he acquire adequate knowledge; he must practice what he preaches. For children are very straightforward in their thinking. Unless they have faith in the integrity of their teachers, the principles that they are being taught will fall on deaf ears. Even more. Children must be willing to accept that what is being taught to them as Jewish tradition that dates back to the time of Moses, our teacher, has been faithfully transmitted from one generation to the next. This demands a great deal of trust and faith. Parents have been given the initial responsibility of teaching Torah to their children because there is no one a child trusts more than his parents. Witness the words of Rabbi Samson Raphael Hirsch:

> The knowledge and acknowledgment of historical facts depends solely on tradition, and tradition depends solely on the faithful transmission by parents to children and the willing acceptance by children from the hands of their parents. So the continuance of God's whole great institution of Judaism rests entirely on the theoretical and practical obedience of children to parents, and honor to parents is the basic condition for the eternal existence of the Jewish nation.[14]

It has been correctly noted that if people listened more intently to each other, much strife in the world could be avoided. Psychologists and educators insist that we must listen to our children, not only with open ears but with open minds. What some forget to emphasize, however, is that parents must also be heard, and it is important for children to learn to listen to their parents as well. To the toddler, listening simply means obeying. To the adolescent, listening means trying to understand the point of view of one's parents from their perspective and recognizing the merit in compromise. To the adult, listening means understanding what one's parents are saying from the perspective of their age, their lifestyle, and the generation in which they live, and responding accordingly. To listen to one's parents is also to honor them.

Teaching and Discipline: A Dual Responsibility

Let us now turn to Proverbs 1:8, 9: "Hear, my son, the discipline of your father and do not forsake the teaching of your mother; for they shall be a charm of grace for your head and gems about your throat." The choice of words here is terribly significant. It is the *discipline* of one's father and the *teaching* of one's mother that are being emphasized. Here again, we have an example of the text taking human nature into account. According to Jewish law, it is the father's responsibility to teach his son Torah. This is based on Deuteronomy 11:18, 19, which reads: "Therefore impress these My words upon your very heart: bind them as a sign upon your hand and let them serve as a symbol on your forehead, and teach them to your children [lit., 'sons'] reciting them when you stay at home and when you are away, when you lie down and when you get up." If he is qualified, a father may do so himself; otherwise, he is obligated to send his son to a school where he will study Torah. It is expected of the child that he pay attention to the teaching of his father.

As we have already pointed out, the mother's primary responsibility is to care for her son from birth until he is mature enough to care for himself. During this period, she must discipline him, train him in appropriate behavior, and teach him ethics and morality. Consequently, it is quite natural for the child to pay attention to the discipline of his mother.

In light of these responsibilities, one would have expected the verse to read, "the *teaching* of your father and the *discipline* of your mother." Not so, our sages tell us. A child can benefit greatly by paying attention to the ethics and moral discipline practiced by his father, and he can learn a great deal about Torah from the teachings of his mother. In point of fact, children must learn to embrace the teaching and moral discipline that comes from both their parents. The analogy here is an interesting one. The teaching and the discipline that the child learns from his parents become a *charm of grace* for his head and a *gem* about his throat. They become ornaments of beauty that manifest themselves in the way the child thinks (head) and the way he speaks (throat) and interacts with his fellow man.

Nature and Nurture

Is there a definitive way to raise children, a set of rules that will work on every child? Probably not! Raising children is an art, and just as every artist must find the medium that works best for him, so must every parent. Of course, the best approach is not necessarily the one that has worked for most children; it is rather the one that works for your child. In determining the way to go with regard to discipline, a parent must take two personalities into careful consideration, his own and that of the child, and tailor his approach accordingly. There are two cardinal principles in raising children: first, whatever the rules of conduct are to be, they must be agreed upon and strictly enforced by both parents; second, it is as important to reward as it is to punish.

Whether nature or nurture are most significant in the development of the child, in the final analysis both genetics and environment must be considered in setting the rules of conduct for the family. But to avoid disappointment and disillusionment, it is important to keep in mind that no matter how good we are at parenting, there are and always will be things that are beyond our control. Perhaps this is why some people who appear to be ideally suited for parenthood fail miserably, while others who seem to lack the most basic qualifications are very successful. The bottom line is that we must make a concerted effort to treat each and every one of our children fairly, but on an individual basis.

Pride or Shame and Sorrow

Some children bring an abundant measure of pride to their parents; others bring sorrow. Do both parents experience pride and sorrow in equal measure? In some families, perhaps they do. Nevertheless, in Proverbs 10:1 we read: "A wise son brings happiness to his father; a foolish son is his mother's sorrow." Now we have already explained that, according to Jewish law, it is the obligation of the father to teach his son Torah. When a child attains academic excellence and becomes known for his wisdom there is no doubt that both parents feel a sense of pride. Yet the father of a wise child experiences an additional measure of happiness for, as the child's first teacher, it is an indication that he has not only met his responsibility, but that he has fulfilled it admirably.

But what of the foolish, inept child who becomes known as the class clown and just doesn't measure up to the other children? While it is certainly true that such a child brings sorrow to both his parents, one cannot compare the disappointment felt by the father to that which is felt by the mother. In many families, a mother's life revolves around her children, especially if she has no career of her own. Personal interests and aspirations must of necessity take second place in her life, especially when the child is very young. In some families the mother is compelled to give up her career in order to care for her children. Most mothers feel that it was all worthwhile when the child grows up to be a fine adult. But when the child is a simpleton and is treated like a fool, the mother may experience a sense of personal failure. She may blame herself even for things over which she had no control. Her sorrow is beyond compare. Rabbi Samson Raphael Hirsch writes:

> It follows that if the child turns out to be well brought up, and the parents are fortunate enough to find joy in a wise and successful son, the father has won a big prize in return for a comparatively low stake. If, on the other hand, the child becomes a foolish inept person, then who can fathom the grief of his mother? She is forced to admit that she has wasted years of anxious days and sleepless nights, that she has spent the best part of her physical strength and mental energy, and all this for what result?[15]

In a similar vein in Proverbs 17:25 we read, "A foolish son is vexation for his father and bitterness to her who bore him." There is a definitive difference between vexation and bitterness. A foolish son is particularly frustrating to his father, who is responsible for educating him. Yes, he becomes impatient and annoyed with his son, but even more annoyed with himself. Nevertheless, this cannot be compared to the bitterness suffered by the mother. It is she who carried the child in her womb, and she alone gave it birth. No love can be greater than a mother's love, and no pain can be more intense. When society looks upon the child as a fool, she is not merely frustrated; she becomes bitter about her lot in life.

For these very reasons, some Bible commentators contest that the mother derives even greater happiness in her son's intellectual excellence that does the father. For it is she who will be given the accolades for having nurtured him from birth. Why then is the father singled out in Proverbs 10:1? Not to exclude the mother, but rather to point out that fathers also derive happiness in their son's intellectual excellence, albeit to a lesser degree.[16]

Righteousness or Wisdom

Which son brings his parents greater joy and happiness? Is it the one who is honored by the community for his righteousness or the one who is respected for his great wisdom? In Proverbs 24:23 we read: "The father of a righteous son will be joyous; he who begets a wise son will be happy with him." It would seem that the Bible didn't differentiate between the two. But let us ponder the matter a bit.

Jealousy and envy manifest themselves in many people when they see good things in others that are conspicuously missing in themselves. This is true in all realms: the material, the intellectual, and the spiritual. Under normal circumstances, parents are not jealous of their children. The greater the child's accomplishments, the greater the parents' pride. Our sages put it quite simply, "Of everyone a man is jealous except his son and his disciple."[17] Righteousness and wisdom are the most noble qualities of man. When they manifest themselves in one's child, they bring immeasurable joy and happiness. This is confirmed by the biblical text. But let us probe still further.

From one perspective, parents derive greater joy from the wise child than from the righteous one, for with the exception of the misfortunes of illness or old age, wisdom once attained remains with the recipient throughout life. As such, it is a continuous source of joy to his parents. This is not necessarily true of righteousness. By virtue of the fact that righteousness is a chosen lifestyle, it is subject to the vicissitudes of life, which could affect not only its fervor but its viability. If the winds of experience that inspired the "good life" change their course unexpectedly, bringing disappointment or tragedy, today's righteous man may become tomorrow's scoundrel.

Seen from a different perspective, however, righteousness is superior to wisdom by virtue of the fact that it focuses on others rather than oneself. It is one thing to think noble thoughts, to speak or write them; it is quite another to put them into practice. What is the old adage? "Action speaks louder than words." Besides, experience has taught us that knowledge and intelligence do not always lead to ethics and morality. Parents can only hope and pray that the wisdom that their children have attained will motivate them to do good deeds. Seen from this perspective, one might say that a righteous son will bring greater joy and happiness to his parents than a wise one.

The Parameters of Discipline

Observation plays an important role today in studying the behavior of children. Psychologists tell us that children at play already exhibit personality traits, and one can discern these traits in a child by observing him carefully. Of course, the Bible revealed this about children many centuries ago. In Proverbs 20:11 we read: "A child is known by his doings whether his actions are pure and honest." A good parent is a good observer; he monitors the behavior of his child very carefully. Is he greedy or prone to anger? Does he tend to be jealous of other children? Is he disrespectful of the property of others? A concerned parent will address these problems himself. Where he feels unqualified to do so, he will seek advice from a qualified psychologist or educator.

There are some educators who believe that a child should be given as little discipline as possible. They feel that he should be left free and uninhibited, that he should be allowed to discover life on his own and determine his own priorities. Others disagree and maintain the need for training and discipline. For despite outward appearances, every child seeks direction, whether he is consciously aware of it or not. Unless it is presented to him properly, however, he will tend to reject it. Presentation becomes increasingly important in the pre-adolescent and adolescent years.

William Wordsworth once wrote, "The child is father of the man."[18] I believe that what he meant to teach us is that the personality traits and inclinations of the adult are formed early in life and are to a great extent the result of the nurture he receives and the experience he gains in childhood. It would not merely be unwise to leave these choices to the inexperienced child; it would be cruel. There are just too many ways to go in life, too many irreversible choices to be made, and too many dangerous pitfalls. The naive must be led by the experienced; the adult must train the child. This is confirmed in Proverbs 22:6, where we read: "Train the child in the way he should go, and even when he is old he will not depart from it." Every child has special needs. His education and his moral training should be geared to these needs.[19] Ideally, every child should be evaluated by his parents and his teachers periodically. His educational and recreational programs should be revised if his needs change. As a result, good learning and recreational habits acquired early in life will become second nature to him, and in all probability they will endure even in old age.

Raising children is not for the weak-willed. There are situations when firm disciplinary measures must be taken, which are usually far more painful to the parent than to the child. Before taking any disciplinary action, however, one must examine one's motivation very carefully. Punishing a child for no other reason than to vent one's emotions is not merely off-target; it is outright cruelty. On the other hand, to fall prey to a child's contrived weeping is to lose both one's power and one's respect in the child's eyes, and in effect, encourage disobedience. Compassion is a noble virtue, without which society could not be maintained, but unless it is used wisely it can do more harm than good. Indiscriminate compassion is not merely foolishness; it is blatant injustice and a sign of weak character. Thus, we read in Proverbs 13:24: "He who spares the rod hates his son, but he who loves him disciplines him early."

Forgiving and forgetting all improprieties is a sign of ineffective and inadequate parenting. It betrays an attitude of disconcern. Strong discipline, on the other hand, builds character. Administered to children at an early age, discipline is an indication of true love and proper parenting. Thus, we read in Proverbs 13:24: "He who abstains from chastisement hates his child, but he who loves him disciplines him diligently."

The Meaning and the Role of Punishment

Punishment must be custom-tailored to the recipient, however, or it will do more harm than good. In Proverbs 17:10 we read: "More penetrating is a rebuke to one who understands than a hundred blows given to a fool." Rebuke is not merely punishment; it is an appeal to one's intelligence. Assuming that it is a calculated intelligent response to unacceptable behavior and not merely a spontaneous outburst of anger, rebuke can be a far more effective means of motivating change than corporal punishment. Understandably, the recipient must comprehend the meaning and significance of the rebuke. Corporal punishment simply relies on the recipient's ability to recollect the physical pain he suffered as an inducement to obedience. Rebuke is embarrassing; it lingers in one's memory and is a far more devastating experience for both adults and children than corporal punishment. The fear of a repeat performance is an inducement to obedience.

Considering its shortcomings, should corporal punishment be abandoned or is there a place for it? As we have already pointed out, rebuke can only be effective when it is tailored to the personality of the recipient, and its message is understood. A boor and a stubborn fool in whom animal-like characteristics and a base nature dominate will not be very much affected by rebuke, if at all. In Proverbs 26:3 we read: "A whip for the horse, a bridle for the donkey, and a rod for the back of fools." The child who is too young and naive to be affected by rebuke or too stubborn to heed its message, should he merely be given his way? Absolutely not! Every child must be disciplined. Where rebuke would be ineffective, corporal punishment may be the only recourse.

In Proverbs 19:18 we read: "Discipline your child while there is still hope, and do not pay attention to his crying." As we have pointed out, the stubborn and unreasonable child must be forced to conform. We must be willing to recognize that there are times, however rare, when the psychology book will serve the interests of the child best when it is used on his other end. Nevertheless, says Rabbi Samson Raphael Hirsch, "Hitting should occur only as a rare and unfortunate exception. . . . parents whose ordinary means of discipline is beating will undoubtedly have cause for alarm at the results of their education."[20]

The Threefold Cord

A family in which true love and respect prevails among all family members and each person takes pride in the accomplishments of the others is surely to be admired. One cannot overemphasize the importance of the family bond to the emotional well-being of both parents and children. But how do grandparents fit into the picture? In Proverbs 17:6 we read: "Grandchildren are the crown of their elders and the glory of children is their parents." A crown is placed on top of the head. In this context it symbolizes the epitome of joy experienced by elders who live to see grandchildren with whom they are able to interact comfortably. But there is much more implied in this verse.

In Ecclesiastes 4:12 we read: "A threefold cord is not readily broken." The Talmud adds the following insightful comment: "He who is himself a scholar, and his son is a scholar, and his grandson as well, the Torah will never depart from his seed."[21] This can be understood as follows. Where one has succeeded in transmitting Torah knowledge and the love of Torah study to one's child so that as an adult he not only retains it but is able to successfully transmit it to his own children, it is a sign that Torah values have become so ingrained within that family that, in all but extenuating circumstances, they will be retained through the generations. Seeing that the Torah values they hold to be so important are being implanted within the hearts of their grandchildren gives grandparents an added measure of joy and satisfaction, for such values secure the future of Judaism in their family. Yes, grandchildren are indeed the crown of their grandparents.

Considering the generation gap and the frequent episodes of confrontation between parents and children that so typify our society, the words "the glory of children are their parents" are somewhat strange. Much to our chagrin, only in rare families would this be the case today. Some will say that the Bible is speaking of the ideal, the Messianic Era when interpersonal relationships will be more wholesome. Perhaps the generation gap that has separated parent and child since early times will at long last be spanned or at least substantially narrowed, and a great bonding of the hearts will ensue. Listen to the words of Malachi 3:24: "Lo, I will send the prophet Elijah to you before the coming of the awesome, fearful day of the Lord. And he shall reconcile fathers with sons and sons with their fathers." Elijah will enlighten parents and children so that they see eye to eye. Where the sons have strayed from the path of Torah, he will prevail upon them to reevaluate their lives and with free will return to the Torah way of life taught to them by their fathers. And where it is the sons who walk in the ways of Torah and the fathers who have strayed, Elijah will prevail upon the latter to adopt the teachings of the former.[22] At such time, the parents will indeed be the glory of their children.

There is another way of understanding these words. A good parent wants only the best for his child. He will often make great personal sacrifices to provide a wholesome environment and the proper education for his child, in the hope that he will walk in the ways of his forefathers and become a committed and observant Jew. Teaching children Jewish values in today's hedonistic society is not at all an easy task. It is very difficult for a child to understand the value of control and to recognize that when his parents impinge upon his freedom, it is for his own good. Limiting a child's freedom in the adolescent years, when he considers himself old enough and mature enough to act independently, precipitates episodes of confrontation even in the best of families. With the passage of time and the onset of maturity, many sons and daughters recognize the propriety of their parents' teachings and discipline, and they respect them for it. At no time does this become more evident than when they themselves become parents, and, confronted with a plethora of methods and value systems, they choose to follow in their parents' footsteps. They raise their children in the path of Torah, the way they themselves were raised. Indeed, there comes a time when "the glory of children is their parents."

Let me conclude our session with a beautiful parable from the Talmud that illustrates what it means to be truly blessed. We are told that Rabbi Nahman and Rabbi Isaac were studying Torah together. When they were about to part, Rabbi Nahman turned to Rabbi Isaac:

"Pray, master, bless me." He replied: "Let me tell you a parable. To what may this be compared? To a man who was journeying in the desert; he was hungry, weary and thirsty, and he came upon a tree the fruit of which were sweet, its shade pleasant, and a stream of water flowing beneath it; he ate of its fruit, drank of the water, and rested under its shade. When he was about to continue on his journey, he said: 'Tree, O tree, with what shall I bless you? Shall I say to you, May your fruit be sweet? They are already sweet; that your shade be pleasant? It is already pleasant; that a stream of water may flow beneath you? Lo, a stream of water already flows beneath you; therefore [I say], may it be God's will that all the shoots taken from you be like you.' So also with you. With what shall I bless you? With the knowledge of the Torah? You already possess the knowledge of the Torah. With riches? You already have riches. With children? You already have children. Hence [I say], 'May it be God's will that your children be like you.'"[23]

Indeed, there is no greater blessing for the righteous than to witness their children and grandchildren following in their footsteps, relating to God by embracing righteousness and pursuing the path of Torah. Yet there is another medium through which Jews relate to God: it is prayer. We will spend the next session in an analysis of prayer as a spiritual and emotional experience and a means of legitimate communication with God.

Session X
The Jewish Approach to Prayer

In the nine sessions that we have spent together, Moshe, we have devoted a great deal of time to the matter of "relating." We have discussed relating to our fellow Jews, relating to Gentiles, relating to our parents, and relating to our children. We have not discussed relating to God, and I would like to spend today's session on this topic.

Should you wonder why have we waited so long to discuss so important an issue in religious life as prayer, the answer is quite simple. Before we can relate to God, we must learn to believe that He exists and that He is concerned with mankind. I had first to present the logical arguments for the existence of God and to show the credibility of the Torah as a Divinely revealed document. To gain your respect for Torah-true Judaism, or at least to convince you to look objectively at the religion into which you were born, I had to give you some concrete examples of Torah ethics and demonstrate the relevance of Torah in today's society. Having achieved that objective and having shown that it is through the revelation of the Torah that God relates to man, we may now proceed to the matter of man relating to God.

The Posture of Prayer

Man relates to God through prayer. But what is prayer? In contradistinction to revelation, which is a confrontation between God and man
in which God takes the initiative, in prayer man takes the initiative and
confronts God. Given this definition, isn't the posture of prayer rather
presumptuous? What gives man the right to initiate a confrontation
with God? Ultimately, we rely on precedent. Abraham, Isaac, and Jacob
prayed. They have set the precedent for all time. The Talmud teaches:

> The prayers were instituted by the Patriarchs . . . Abraham instituted
> the morning prayer, as it says, "And Abraham arose early in the morn-
> ing to the place where he had stood" (Genesis 19:27), and "standing"
> means only prayer, as it says, "Then Pinhas stood up and prayed" (Psalms
> 106:30). Isaac instituted the afternoon prayer, as it says, "And Isaac went
> out to meditate in the field in the evening" (Genesis 24:63), and "medi-
> tation" means only prayer, as it says, "A prayer of the afflicted when he
> faints and pours out his meditation before the Lord" (Psalms 102:1). Jacob
> instituted the evening prayer, as it says, "And he came upon [Heb.
> *vayifga*] the place . . . " (Genesis 28:11), and *p'giah* means only prayer,
> [or pleading] as it says, "As for you, do not pray for this people, do not
> raise a cry of prayer on their behalf, do not plead with Me" (Jeremiah
> 7:16).[1]

Moses prayed, as did the prophets who came after him. In Psalms
55:18 King David wrote: "Evening, morning, and noon, I complain and
moan, and He hears my voice," and Rashi comments: "This refers to
the evening, morning, and afternoon services." In point of fact, even
the angels pray. Isaiah 6:3 records the words "Holy, holy, holy is the
Lord of Hosts: the whole earth is full of His glory" as the prayer of the
angels, and Ezekiel 3:12 adds: "Blessed be the glory of the Lord from
His place."

Here again, one might ask, "Isn't it rather presumptuous for us to
establish our right to confront God in prayer on a precedent set by the
great prophets of old? Do we dare put ourselves on their level?" The
answer is *yes* and *no*. In no way would we have the audacity to compare
our wisdom to the wisdom of the prophets nor would we consider our
knowledge of God in any way comparable to their knowledge. In no
way do we liken our righteousness to their righteousness. But there is

a common thread that unites us; it is our humanity. We are all created human beings. Our days are like a fleeting shadow, here today and gone tomorrow. It is our dependency that legitimates our behavior, our creaturely needfulness. Intellectual and spiritual accomplishments are irrelevant in this regard.

The thought is expressed quite succinctly in Psalms 102:1: "A prayer of the afflicted when he is overwhelmed and pours out his plea before the Lord." Every human being who is overwhelmed by life comes to God as one who is afflicted. And as we read in Psalms 142:2, 3: "I cry aloud to the Lord: I appeal to the Lord loudly for mercy. I pour out my complaint before Him; I lay my trouble before Him." Every human being has a right to appeal to God for mercy. Let it be made perfectly clear, however, that whether we can establish a logical argument or not, whether we can find a precedent or not, we confront God in prayer because we must. Indeed, we have no alternative way to deal with the vicissitudes of life other than prayer.

It is interesting to note that there is a difference of opinion between the two great halakhic authorities, Maimonides and Nahmanides, as to whether the obligation to pray is of biblical or rabbinic origin.

The Obligation of Prayer

According to Maimonides, the obligation to pray is biblical, based on the words in Exodus 23:25: "You shall serve the Lord your God . . ." Service to God is prayer, says Maimonides; our sages deduced this from the words in Deuteronomy 11:13, "to serve Him with all your heart and with all your soul." Service of the heart is prayer, they said. However, the number of prayers to be recited, as well as the set times for prayer and the texts that make up the service, are all of rabbinic origin.[2]

Nahmanides was of the opinion that under ordinary circumstances, the obligation upon an individual to pray is of rabbinic origin. As a manifestation of Divine kindness, God listens and responds to the prayers of all who call out to Him. The words "You shall serve the Lord your God" are of a general nature and mean to teach us that whatever we do should be in the service of God. However, there is a biblical obligation upon the community to cry out to God in prayer and blasts of the trumpet in times of distress or tragedy and to have faith that He listens and comes to their aid. The source of this obligation is the verse in Numbers 10:9: "When you are at war in your own land against an aggressor who attacks you, you shall sound short blasts on the trumpets that you may be remembered before the Lord your God and be delivered from your enemies."

The Prayer Par Excellence

What is the character of formal Jewish prayer? The Jewish prayer service was formalized about the fifth century B.C.E. (Before the Common Era) by a group of sages and prophets known as "The Men of the Great Assembly." The term "prayer," as it is used in the Talmud, usually refers to the prayer par excellence, the *Amidah* ("standing"), so named for the position one assumes when reciting this prayer. It is also known as the *Shemoneh Esre* ("eighteen") because it originally consisted of eighteen benedictions. The *Amidah* is the central prayer of every service. It consists of three parts: praise, petition, and thanksgiving.

We mentioned earlier that we have the right to confront God in prayer because the precedent has been set by our forefathers. It is only logical, therefore, that when the *Amidah* was put together, it would be patterned after one of those prayers. Now, what prayer could serve as a better model than the prayer of Moses, our teacher? In the Talmud we find the following:

> Rabbi Simlai expounded: A man should always first recount the praise of the Holy One, blessed be He, and then pray. From where do we know this? From Moses, for it is written, "O Lord God, You Who let Your servant see the first works of Your greatness and Your mighty hand, You Whose powerful deeds no god in heaven or on earth can equal! Let me, I pray, cross over and see the good land on the other side of the Jordan, that good hill country and the Lebanon." (Deuteronomy 3:24)[3]

Moses opened his prayer with words of S*hevah* ("praise") to God and subsequently put forth his petition. His style became the model for the *Amidah*. Although the *Amidah* for *Shabbat* and Festivals does not include prayers of petition, it does begin with words of praise to God.

The opening paragraph of the *Amidah* has an additional theme, the precedent for which was set by Jacob, the third Patriarch. About to confront his brother Esau, Jacob feared for his life and the lives of his wives and children. In Genesis 32:10, 12 we read that he turned to God with the words: "O God of my father, Abraham, and God of my father, Isaac . . . deliver me, I pray from the hand of my brother, from the hand of Esau; also, I fear, he may come and strike me down, mothers and children alike." Before making his request, Jacob made mention of his grandfather and his father. Our sages explained the rationale for this move as follows.

The acts of righteousness performed by the Patriarchs were of such merit before God that they could never be fully requited in their life-time, in consequence of which it is imparted to their children and chil-dren's children throughout the generations. It is interesting to note that when the nation of Israel sinned, Moses appealed to God for forgive-ness on its behalf. It was not until he referred to Abraham, Isaac, and Jacob, however, that we read in Exodus 32:14: "And the Lord renounced the punishment He had planned to bring upon His people." Reference to the merit of the Patriarchs in prayer is referred to as *Zekhut Avot* (lit., "merit of the forefathers").

Praise: The Opening Section

Shevah, the opening section of the *Amidah*, is a unit consisting of three benedictions. *Zekhut Avot* was considered of major importance by the sages, and they made it the opening theme of every *Amidah*. *Gevurot* ("mighty acts") is the theme of the second benediction. Rain in the natu-ral realm, and the resurrection of the dead in the supernatural realm, are examples of these mighty acts.

The third benediction, *Kedushat Hashem* ("sanctification of God"), declares the sanctity of both God's Name and those who praise Him. Before putting forth our prayers of petition, we acknowledge the unique-ness of both God and the people of Israel. The uniqueness of God is self-evident. The uniqueness of the Jewish people consists in their com-mitment to God and to the 613 commandments of the Torah. Reflect-ing these ideas, the third benediction of the *Amidah* reads: "You are holy, and Your Name is holy, and the holy ones proclaim the praise of Your mighty deeds each day." In his commentary on the Prayer Book, Rabbi Samson Raphael Hirsch comments: "Only those who themselves are holy or who at least aspire to holiness may praise God. . . . To praise

God while leading a life that is at variance with His holy and sanctifying will would be gross blasphemy."

The significance of praise as a forerunner of petition is often misunderstood, and it is of the utmost importance to clear the air on this matter. The skeptic and the individual who is ignorant of Jewish tradition might consider praise to be man's way of ingratiating himself with God before petitioning Him. After all, flattery works well with many people. In point of fact, nothing could be further from the truth. Had this been the intent, it would be most disappointing, for such a notion would indicate a shallow image of the Supreme Being of the universe, quite unbefitting the sages of Israel. Besides, on what logical premise would it even be conceivable that God resembles man, in that He succumbs to flattery? The introduction of praise in the *Amidah* must be understood as follows.

Formal obligatory prayer, in contradistinction to informal voluntary prayer, deals with the existential condition of man rather than an immediate crisis situation. Its regularity (three services daily) and the fact that it is obligatory, whether biblically or rabbinically, make this self-evident. As put by Rabbi Eliezer Berkovits: "Free of the urgency of the immediate experience, in obligatory prayer one does not approach God with what life has done to one, but with the knowledge of what God means to man."[4] The recitation of praise to God in the *Amidah* is not meant to affect God; it is meant to affect man. God does not need our praise; we need it. We acknowledge Him as "the great, mighty, and awesome God," to contrast His omnipotence with our impotence, His independence with our dependency. We refer to Divine providence with the words "who bestows loving kindness . . . remembers the fathers' acts of devotion and who, in love, will bring a redeemer to their children's children for His Name's sake," to correspond His concern with our need. Only then can we consider prayers of petition.

Petition: The Intermediate Benedictions

It is important to note that our sages considered petition to be the most essential part of the *Amidah*, of greater importance than praise or thanksgiving, and there is good reason for this. As with praise, petitioning God for the general needs of mankind demonstrates not only man's inadequacy and thus his dependency upon God, but by contrast,

God's omnipotence, omnipresence, and omniscience as well. For to fulfill the multiplicity of human needs, one must turn to an omnipotent God. To turn to Him three times a day, He must be omnipresent as well, and in order for Him to perceive our silent prayer, He must likewise be omniscient. This is the essence of prayer.

The Hebrew term for petition is *tehinah* (literally, "unearned favor").[5] We must always be mindful of the fact that our posture in petition is not as one who asks for that which is rightfully due him, but rather as one who implores God to grant him unearned favor. There are no words that express this thought more poignantly than those we recite daily in the morning service:

> Master of all worlds! It is not on account of our righteousness that we offer our supplications before You, but on account of Your great compassion. What are we? What is our life? What is our goodness? What our righteousness? What our helpfulness? What our strength? What our might? What can we say in Your presence, Eternal One, our God and God of our fathers? Indeed, all the heroes are nothing before You, men of renown as though they never existed, the wise as if they were without knowledge, the intelligent as though they lacked understanding . . .

The thirteen petitions in the *Amidah* address the following needs: knowledge and understanding, repentance, forgiveness, deliverance from affliction, healing, and want; the reunion of Israel and the righteous reign of God; the destruction of the wicked (slanderers, informers, and traitors); mercy for the righteous; the rebuilding of Jerusalem; the coming of the Messiah; and the hearing and acceptance of our prayers. Since these petitions simply enumerate the needs of society at large (unless, of course, a personal prayer has been inserted before the benediction), they should be recited in a calm and collected manner.

It is interesting to note that each of the thirteen petitions of the *Amidah* is followed by an acknowledgment. We ask God for understanding, and before it is granted, we acknowledge Him as He Who grants understanding. We ask God to gather our dispersed people to the land of Israel and before our request is granted, we acknowledge Him as He Who gathers the dispersed of Israel. We ask for redemption and call Him the Redeemer of Israel, yet Israel has not yet been redeemed. What is the rationale for this formula?

The petitions in the *Amidah* are not merely requests on behalf of the people of Israel; they are affirmations of God's existence, His providence, and our faith that just as He has shown His concern in the past, He will continue to show His concern in the future. We ask God for understanding, and we have faith that He will grant our request because the precedent, namely, that He has given man understanding in the past, has been established. As such, we speak of Him as though He has already fulfilled our request.[6] The same is true of all of the petitions of the *Amidah*; they have all been established by precedent.

Thanksgiving: The Closing Section

The last section of the *Amidah* is called *Hoda'ah* ("thanksgiving"). It is composed of three benedictions, but only the middle one, which opens with the words "we give thanks to You," is an actual expression of gratitude. The first is a petition for the restoration of the Temple service, and the last is a prayer for peace. Now one might ask, "Where in the Bible is the precedent for thanksgiving found?" Yet is there a need for such a precedent? If petition is permissible, is it not self-evident that when a request is granted, thanksgiving should follow? Nonetheless, it is interesting to note that somewhat of a precedent is found in the Torah narrative quite early in human history, the story of Cain and Abel.

In Genesis 4:3, 4 we read: "In the course of time, Cain brought a gift offering to the Lord from the fruit of the soil, and Abel, for his part, brought the choicest of the firstlings of his flock." A gift offering is, among other things, an expression of thanksgiving. Of course, as with every offering, the motivation and the sincerity of the gift giver are of paramount importance. Our Bible commentators explain that this is the rationale for Abel's gift being favored by God while the gift of Cain was rejected.[7]

The Shema and Its Related Benedictions

The recitations that precede the *Amidah* serve as an introduction and are of a preparatory nature. We have already explained that the uniqueness of the Jewish people consists in their commitment to God and the

613 commandments of the Torah. We introduce the *Amidah* by focusing on the uniqueness of the Jewish people. The *Shema* is recited immediately before the *Amidah*. It consists of three paragraphs taken from the Torah, and is introduced and closed by benedictions. The recitation of the *Shema* is a *mitzvah* and an exercise in the study of Torah, a most fitting preparation for the *Amidah*. In the opening paragraph we express our commitment to God and His rule, termed *kabbalat ol malkhut shamayim* ("acceptance of the yoke of the kingdom of heaven"). This is followed in the second paragraph by a "commitment to observe the commandments," termed *kabbalat ol mitzvot*. The last paragraph has two themes: the *mitzvah* of *tsitsit* ("fringes") to remind us of the commandments, and the *mitzvah* of remembering the redemption from Egypt.

In *Shaharit* ("morning service"), the *Shema* is preceded by two benedictions and concluded by one. The theme of the first benediction is "light," the luminaries that bring light and life to the world; the second theme is "Torah," as a source of spiritual light to its inhabitants. The concluding benediction attests to the truth of the themes of the *Shema* and affirms the redemption from Egypt in conformity with the halakhic ruling that one must adjoin the theme of redemption to prayer. In the evening service, the *Shema* is also preceded by two benedictions. Although the wording there is different, the themes are identical with those of the morning service.

The Verses of Song

Chapters from the Psalms, called *pesuke d'zimrah* ("verses of song"), precede the *Shema*. The introduction of these Psalms is based on the words of Rabbi Yose, who said: "May my portion be of those who complete the *Hallel* every day." The term *complete* means Psalms 145–150, which are the last five chapters of the book, said the sages.[8] The *pesuke d'zimrah* is also related to the *Amidah*. In the Talmud we read: "One should not stand up to say *the prayer* while immersed in sorrow or idleness . . . but only while still rejoicing in the performance of a *mitzvah*."[9] This refers to *pesuke d'zimrah*, the recitation of which is a fulfillment of the *mitzvah* of studying Torah.[10] The *pesuke d'zimrah* section also has an opening and closing benediction, the theme of which is praise to God. On *Shabbat*, on the Festivals, and on the High Holidays, the *pesuke d'zimrah* is extended and special prayers that indicate the significance of the day are added to the *Amidah* of all services.

The Afternoon and Evening Services

The afternoon service is called *Minhah*. It is the shortest service of the day. In all likelihood this is in consideration of the fact that it is difficult for most people to spare much time for prayer in the middle of the working day. *Minhah* begins with Psalms 145, which serves as introductory praise to the *Amidah* that follows. *Minhah* concludes with *Alenu*, a prayer of praise to God, the Creator of all things, and anticipates the day when He will be acknowledged by all people and His Name will be One.

The evening service is called *Maariv* or *Arvit*. The *Amidah* is its central theme. It is preceded by the *Shema*, which is introduced and followed by two benedictions. The first introductory benediction focuses on the function of the heavenly luminaries and praises God through Whose word the luminaries function; the second benediction focuses on God's love for Israel, the gift of the Torah, and the commitment of the Jewish people to study the Torah by day and by night. In the first of the benedictions that follow the *Shema*, we affirm all that is included in the three paragraphs of the *Shema*, and praise God to Whom none can be likened. We enumerate some of the great miracles that He has wrought for us and finally, we praise Him as the redeemer of Israel. In the second benediction, we petition God to preserve us through the night and protect us from adversity and from all those who wish to do us harm. In about the ninth century a series of eighteen verses, corresponding to the eighteen benedictions of the *Amidah*, was added to the service.

Now that we have established the right to pray, and we have briefly discussed the content of the *Amidah*, the prayer par excellence of every service, let us turn again to the philosophy of prayer and raise an important twofold question.

The Efficacy of Prayer

How do we know that our prayers are heard? And even if we are to assume that they are heard, what guarantee have we that our prayers will be answered? Here again, we rely on precedent. The Bible teaches us that prayers are indeed answered. Even a cursory reading will make this sufficiently clear. Let us illustrate with but two examples.

The Israelites were enslaved in Egypt. In Exodus 2: 23, 24 we read: " . . . The Israelites were groaning under the bondage and cried out; and their cry for help from the bondage rose up to God. God heard their moaning . . . God looked upon the Israelites, and God took notice of them." When the Israelites brought their first fruits to the Temple in Jerusalem, we read in Deuteronomy 26:7, 8 that they recalled the redemption from Egypt with the following words: "We cried to the Lord, the God of our fathers, and the Lord heard our plea and saw our plight, our misery and our oppression. The Lord freed us from Egypt by a mighty hand. . . . " Clearly, their prayers were answered.

When traveling in the wilderness to the land of Canaan, the Israelites sinned and forced Aaron, the priest, to build them a golden calf that was to replace Moses and lead them to the Promised Land. God was angered by this and threatened to annihilate them, but Moses intervened on their behalf. He prayed for them, invoking the names of the Patriarchs, and we read in Exodus 32:14: "And the Lord renounced the punishment He had planned to bring upon His people."

No prayers go unheard, and no prayers remain unanswered. However, there is no guarantee that the answer that is given to a prayer will please the recipient, even though it may be for his or her benefit. In situations where the Divine response is negative, the recipient may be angered. He may find the response incomprehensible or consider it unacceptable. Let us create two scenarios.

Should All Prayers Be Answered?

A patient is critically ill with cancer and is in extreme pain. He prays for death. Should his request be granted? It would certainly seem to be the merciful thing for God to do. But what if there is a drug that could cure him that is in the process of being approved for use. If he bears his pain for a little while longer he can be cured and live a normal life thereafter. Of course, he is not privy to this information. Under those circumstances, should a beneficent God have granted his request?

On his way to his first interview, a job applicant who is inadequately prepared for the position prays to God to help him make a favorable impression on the interviewer so that he is hired for the job. Should God grant his request? Why not? Consider the following: If he gets the job, it will not take very long for his inadequacy to be discovered, leading to an unpleasant dismissal. This could wreak havoc with his self-image and scar him for life. Were he not to get the job, he would surely be disappointed, but when the initial reaction wears off, he will be forced to face the reality of his incompetence. Under normal circumstances, this would motivate him to do whatever it takes to qualify for the position so that on his next interview he is successful. Here again, should a beneficent God have granted his request?

Now in these two situations we have been made aware of the ramifications of the Divine response, and we are able to comprehend Divine justice. In real-life situations, however, we are not privy to all the facts and the potential ramifications of the Divine response. Consequently, there are countless situations, scenarios far more complicated than these, that are totally incomprehensible to us because we are intellectually unequipped to analyze them. We are unqualified to judge the propriety of the Divine response. In our ignorance, many of us reject God's providential hand.

An Interesting Dilemma

To entertain the notion that the Divine response to our prayers is positive presents an interesting philosophical problem. Rabbi Joseph Albo, the fifteenth-century Spanish philosopher, poses the following question:

> Either God has determined that a given person shall receive a given benefit or He has not so determined. If He has so determined, there is no need for prayer; and if He has not so determined, how can prayer avail to change God's will that He should now determine to benefit the person, when He had not so determined before?[11]

We have the right to praise God and to thank Him for His kindness and mercy, but in light of Rabbi Albo's question how, can we petition Him? To petition God is to plead with Him to alter His will. In light of our understanding of Divinity, is this a rational request? The notion that God's will is alterable contradicts the very definition of God. On the other hand, if we must accept the principle that everything has been predetermined and that all our efforts for self-perfection are in vain, there is little hope for the future of humanity.

The resolution of the problem lies in our understanding of the meaning of petition, says Rabbi Albo. Petition presupposes sincere repentance, regret over the past, and resolve to improve one's ways in the future. Seen from any other perspective, petition is not even a "shot in the dark;" it is simply a wasted effort. Repentance brings about a transformation in man, and prayer reflects that transformation. For the person who turns to God in sincere prayer affirms thereby not only God's existence but His omniscience, His omnipresence and His omnipotence as well.

Prayer Is a Transformation

Ideally, the experience of prayer makes man reflect upon his condition. It motivates him to recommit himself to his responsibility to God, to himself as a Jew, and to society. David the sinner becomes David the penitent, a transformed human being with a new perspective on life. The Divine decree that punished David the sinner by withholding his needs is null and void, for he no longer exists. He has been replaced by David the righteous penitent. It is not the Divine will that has been altered; it is the personality of the man that has been recycled. One further point, says Rabbi Albo. The Divine decree of punishment to the sinner is made with a proviso that renders it inoperable should he repent his sins.[12]

Let us close our discussion on the significance of prayers of petition with a remark made by Rabbi Eliezer Berkovits. Appealing to logic, he writes: "If the Divine plan allows a measure of importance to man's actions, why should it not be conceivable that the same plan may have a provision by which human suffering may be considered as a matter of some importance."[13] As such, petition to God is most definitely in place.

Spontaneous versus Obligatory Prayer

We must now confront what is perhaps the most frequently posed objection to obligatory prayer. Why are we obligated to recite a set service composed of prayers that were written centuries ago and not at all addressed to modern problems and concerns facing man in today's times? Would it not be preferable to address God in our own words at such times as we are moved to do so? For example, an overwhelming phenomenon of nature might evoke within us the feeling of awe and inspire a prayer of praise to God, the creator of nature. A time of personal distress might inspire us to turn to God for help. And when help comes, thanksgiving would be a natural and most meaningful response. Surely, there is no question of the sincerity of prayers of this sort. Why can't we rely on voluntary spontaneous prayer?

Let us begin by pointing out that our sages not only recognized the value of spontaneous prayer, they made provision for it in the *Amidah.* The Talmud teaches us the following:

> Even though it was said that one should pray for his private needs only at [the benediction] "Who hears prayer," nevertheless, if he is disposed to supplement any of the benedictions [by personal supplications] relevant to the subject of each particular benediction, he may do so.[14]

The sages were well aware of the tendency of man to be overwhelmed by nature and they composed special benedictions to be recited at such moments of grandeur. On seeing trees blossoming for the first time during the year, we bless the name of God "Who has withheld nothing from His world and has created beautiful creatures and beautiful trees in it, so that men may delight in them." On taking possession of a new home or tasting any fruit for the first time in the season, we bless God "Who has kept us alive and sustained us and enabled us to reach this season." These are just two of a host of benedictions composed for special occasions.

To confront God *only* in times of overwhelming grandeur, impending tragedy, or profound gratitude, however, is to imply that only at such times is He relevant to our lives, and turning to God only in matters that are personally significant implies that the rest of life is not worthy of our prayer. Given its fervor and sincerity, there is certainly a time and a place for spontaneous prayer in the Jewish tradition, but it is simply not enough. Our sages declared: "Would that man prayed all day long,"[15] and again, "For each and every breath that man breathes he is obligated to praise his Creator."[16]

Theoretically, we should be continuously praying to God, praising Him and thanking Him for every moment of our lives. Practically speaking, of course, this would be impossible. To resolve the dilemma, the sages compiled the prayer service. Recited three times daily, with added readings for *Shabbat*, the Festivals, High Holidays, and other special occasions, the prayer service addresses the Jewish calendar of events. At the same time it confronts the ever-present existential condition of man and pays tribute to God for the bounteous blessings that He has conferred upon society. In a sense, obligatory prayer makes spontaneous prayer tenable.

There is another aspect of obligatory prayer of which we must take note: it has a universal quality. By virtue of the fact that many of the prayers in the service are taken from the Bible, and even those that are not, still allude to verses in the Bible and events in Jewish history, obligatory prayer unites Jews the world over in community prayer. A Jew of American descent and a Jew of Spanish descent, an Israeli Jew, and a German Jew can walk into a synagogue anywhere in the world and participate in a service that is familiar to them. Even more, to participate in a service knowing that these very prayers were recited by many of the most profound thinkers of the Jewish people should be most comforting and inspire a true religious experience.

The *Midrash* conveys a beautiful thought: "The angel who is appointed over the prayers gathers all the prayers that were recited in all the synagogues and fashions them into crowns and places them on the head of the Holy One, blessed be He."[17] This teaches us several things. First, that the prayers of man are considered of such importance to God that a special angel is appointed over them. Second, that every prayer is significant to God, for they are not fashioned into a single crown but rather into crowns. Third, that prayers recited with a *minyan* (a quorum of ten men) at the synagogue have special significance to God, for the *Midrash* does not speak of personal prayers. Fourth, that the prayers of man rank most high on God's priority list, so to speak, for they are placed not at His feet but on His Head.

Despite what we have said about the meaningfulness of obligatory prayer, many people find synagogue services to be very uninspiring, and we should spend some time on an approach to resolving this dilemma. The question is posed: How can the unemotional and thus ineffective litany that takes place at the synagogue service be compared to the sincerity and fervor felt by an individual who is moved to turn to God in a spontaneous prayer?

Making Prayer a Meaningful Experience

In truth, prayer that is recited as mere litany falls far short of what Jewish law considers proper prayer. The sages were well aware of the fact that obligatory prayer can become routinized and they warned, "Do not regard your prayer as an appointed routine but as an appeal for mercy and favor before the Omnipresent,"[18] and again, "If a man makes his prayers a fixed task, it is not a genuine supplication."[19] We mentioned earlier that obligatory prayer is concerned with humanity, society at large, and as such cannot be expected to be approached by the average person with the same intensity and sense of urgency as spontaneous prayer. Nonetheless, it can and must be made more than a fixed routine, devoid of emotional involvement. The key to accomplishing this is *kavanah* ("concentration").

Kavanah means concentration on the meaning of the texts and the theme and intent of the prayers in order to attain a directedness toward God. If prayer is to be more than litany, it needs preparation and intelligent participation. Although there is something to be said for those who merely attend the services and recite the prayers without knowing their significance or even the meaning of the words, most of us are capable of much more than this bare minimum. The texts of the prayers should be studied carefully and the themes analyzed intensively so that we understand what we are saying, as well as the significance and the order of the service. Even more. The *Mishnah* records: "The pious men of old used to wait an hour before praying in order that they might concentrate their thoughts upon their Father in heaven."[20] These pious men did not stand idle during this waiting period, to be sure. In fulfillment of the charge of Amos 4:12: "Prepare to meet your God O Israel," they thought deeply about what they were about to do, and prepared themselves physically, mentally, and spiritually for the experience of confronting the Holy One, blessed be He, in prayer.

Our sages taught: "When a man prays, he should direct his heart to heaven."[21] Maimonides adds, "He must vacate his heart of all mundane thoughts in order to fill it with the consciousness of standing in God's presence."[22] Through *kavanah* man feels the needs of his fellow man almost as a pressing personal need, thus approximating at least to some extent what he feels in spontaneous prayer. One needs only to observe a truly righteous person in prayer to be convinced of the power of *kavanah*.

Obligatory prayer must take place in the proper atmosphere if it is to be a true religious experience. Synagogue design is an important contributing factor to this experience. The synagogue should be beautiful but not so beautiful as to be distracting. Its decor should be simple and should reflect man's humility rather than his haughtiness. Ostentatious decor may impress the visitor, but the mood it creates is the antithesis of what prompts one to pray. The *mehitzah*, which separates men and women in the synagogue, is of paramount importance in inducing proper *kavanah*. Togetherness and the family pew is a Christian concept; it is diametrically opposed to the posture of humility and existential loneliness that leads the Jew to approach God in prayer. Also to be considered is the fact that in our society it is very difficult for a man to "let loose" emotionally in mixed company. Finally, the natural distraction that takes place when sitting next to a person of the opposite sex inhibits proper *kavanah* for both men and women.

Music can move mountains; it is extremely potent in setting a mood. Jewish liturgical music must reflect the mood of the prayers, and when it does, it works wonders in enhancing and even in inducing *kavanah*. But like all other forms of music, one must be trained in order to appreciate it. The first step must be to engage a committed and properly trained cantor to lead the service. Ideally, he should be fluent in classical Hebrew, a scholar in Jewish law and tradition, well trained in the liturgy, with a pleasant voice. Talking during the service is indicative of boredom, and boredom is usually the result of ignorance. Classes should be arranged to train the congregants, both men and women, to understand and appreciate the music of the service. In addition, congregational singing can be initiated, simple melodies that the worshipers can learn in one or two sessions.

The role of *kavanah* is so crucial in obligatory prayer that Maimonides ruled that one who is preoccupied with a personal problem should not pray until it passes and he is able to concentrate properly on the matter at hand.[23] The rationale for Maimonides' ruling is explained by Rabbi Eliezer Berkovits as follows: "A man preoccupied with the moment may not be able to embrace in sincerity the basic principle of obligatory prayer, i.e., that at all moments man is equally dependent upon God and that at all times God is indeed near."[24]

Prayer is the medium through which man communes with his Creator. Our sages explained that man stands before God as a humble servant stands before his master. In obligatory prayer man expounds on God's greatness and offers thanks for God's bounteous blessings. He petitions God not merely for himself but for all mankind, and he prays for the restoration of Jerusalem and the kingdom of Israel. Seen from one perspective, man stands humbly before God, but seen from another, the experience of prayer raises man to the greatest heights. The hasidic masters claim that in contemplative obligatory prayer, man ascends from this world to the heavenly realm by divesting himself of all corporeality and uniting with the Holy One, blessed be He. Indeed, obligatory prayer needs no apology. It stands on its own merit.

One of the many precious gifts with which man has been endowed by the Almighty is memory, the ability to recollect awesome events and pleasant experiences. Depressed by the vicissitudes of life, one can recollect the good times of the past and by doing so gain a new hope for the future. This is true not only for the individual in his personal life but of the nation as well. Among other things, the Jewish festivals and holidays are recollections and commemorations of the past history of our people, and we shall devote the next session to this topic and explaining its significance to us as individuals and to Israel as a nation.

Session XI
The Jewish Holidays
and Festivals
as Recollections
and Commemorations

At our last session we mentioned the precious gift of memory, with which man has been endowed by the Almighty. We indicated that the process of recollection and commemoration, which marks the holidays and festivals, plays an important role in Judaism. The past is over, but it dare not be forgotten. From events that transpired centuries ago, we can learn a great deal about God's attributes, and we can perceive His involvement in the historical process. Most important, from the history of the Jewish people, the redemption from Egypt, and the revelation of the Torah at Sinai, we can see that we are of special concern to God. He has granted us eternal life as a nation, in consequence of which we must adopt the lifestyle that He has ordained for us.

The providential hand of God, seen in the events of the past, must serve as a lesson to us in the present and as a guide to us in planning for the future. This is the purpose of recollection and commemoration. By keeping the events of Jewish history and the principles derived therefrom fresh in our minds, we strengthen our commitment to God and to the Torah, and thus ensure a brighter future for ourselves and our children.

There is another purpose to the recollection and commemoration of the holidays and festivals; it is to teach us to sanctify time, the most precious gift granted to us by the Creator. King David wrote: "The days of our years themselves are seventy years, or with vigor eighty years. . . . "[1] Our life span is short; we must try to make every moment meaningful. By occupying ourselves with *mitzvot*, those that pertain to the holidays and festivals in particular, we enrich our lives. While others are plagued by existential boredom, the Jewish people give importance to every day. We anchor our lives in God, Who is Eternal, and in His Torah, which is eternally significant, and we attain peace of mind and a zest for life.

Let us, therefore, briefly outline the themes of the holidays and festivals that we recollect and commemorate annually, beginning with *Shabbat.*

Shabbat

Shabbat is the first and foremost of the Jewish holidays: first historically and foremost ideologically. It is a unique day, commemorated and observed not only by man, but by God as well. For we read in Genesis 2:2:

> The heavens and the earth were finished, and all their array. And on the seventh day God finished the work which He had been doing, and He rested on the seventh day from all the work which He had done. And God blessed the seventh day and declared it holy, because on it God rested from all the work which He had done.

It has been correctly noted that even more than the Jew has kept the *Shabbat*, the *Shabbat* has kept the Jew. How insightful are these words! No wonder the *Shabbat* has been designated by our sages as the most sacred day of the year. The emphasis that has been put on the sacredness of *Shabbat* and the meticulous observance of its laws and customs by both the Torah and the rabbinic authorities through the generations has made the committed Jew a unique entity in society. It is the observance of *Shabbat*, perhaps more than any other facet of Jewish tradition, that has preserved the Jewish people as a nation in exile through centuries of suffering and persecution. Truly, there is not a religion in the world today that can lay claim to a day so distinctive and so sublime.

The Biblical Obligations

In the Torah we find the following:

> Remember the *Shabbat* day and keep it holy. Six days you shall labor and do all your work, but the seventh day is a *Shabbat* of the Lord your God: you shall not do any work. . . . For in six days the Lord made heaven and earth and sea, and all that is in them, and He rested on the seventh day; therefore the Lord blessed the *Shabbat* day and hallowed it. (Exodus 20:11)

> The children of Israel shall keep the *Shabbat*, observing the *Shabbat* throughout the generations as a covenant for all time: it shall be a sign for all time between Me and the people of Israel. For in six days the Lord made heaven and earth, and on the seventh day He rested from work and was refreshed. (Exodus 31:16, 17)

> Observe the *Shabbat* day and keep it holy, as the Lord your God has commanded you. . . . Six days shall you labor and do all your work, but the seventh day is a *Shabbat* of the Lord your God: you shall not do any work. . . . Remember that you were a slave in the land of Egypt and the Lord your God freed you from there with a mighty hand and an outstretched arm; therefore the Lord God has commanded you to observe the *Shabbat* day. (Deuteronomy 5:12–15)

In God's Ways

In Deuteronomy 28:9 there is a *mitzvah* that reads: "The Lord will establish you as His holy people, as He swore to you, if you keep the commandments of the Lord your God and walk in His ways." A Jew is charged with *imitatio Dei*, to walk in God's ways, but what does this mean? How does a human being walk in the ways of God? Our sages answered the question as follows: just as He is kind, so must you be kind; just as He is slow to anger, so must you be slow to anger; just as He is truthful, so must you be truthful. We must study God's ways in the world, how He relates to man in particular, and we must incorporate those facets of Divinity into our personality. Where relevant, we must let them determine how we interact with our fellow man. "On the seventh day He rested from work." If for no other reason than the fulfillment of the *mitzvah* of *imitatio Dei*, it behooves us to desist from creative activity on *Shabbat*. But there is much more.

Six days a week the Jew occupies himself with the mundane, the physical and material concerns of life, but on *Shabbat*, he puts these concerns aside and involves himself with the sacred: the spiritual and intellectual values of life. This engagement refreshes and delights his soul, enabling him to begin the coming week with renewed energy and a positive outlook on life.

Shabbat commemorates two historical events: the creation of the world and the redemption of the Israelites from Egypt. The former is the most important event in the history of humanity; the latter, the most important event in the history of the Jewish people. In light of this, the *Shabbat* has both universal and national significance.

Shabbat *and Creation*

Jewish law prohibits one from engaging in creative activity on *Shabbat* to commemorate the fact that on the seventh day of creation God ceased from such activity. But how does the seventh day differ from the other days of creation? On each of the six days of creation God created something new. On the seventh day nothing new was created. What God did was initiate a system that would continue to bring those things into the world that He had created on the first six days. The meaning of the words "God rested on the seventh day" is that He rested or ceased from creating *new* things on this day. What follows from this notion is that what is popularly referred to as the "law of nature" is no law at all because nature does not operate independently. God must continuously energize the world for it to continue to exist, much like an electric current energizes a machine. This is the meaning of the words we recite in our prayers every morning, "He renews the creation every day continually."[2]

Shabbat also establishes two fundamental principles: first, that God exists; second, that He created the world. But the definition of "creative work" is not simply left to man's discretion; it is clearly defined by the Oral Law. The thirty-nine categories of work that took place in the erection of the Tabernacle, which is the house of worship that the Israelites built in the wilderness, and any kind of creative activity that resembles these categories, are prohibited on *Shabbat.*

Maimonides makes an interesting point. God commanded us to abstain from work on *Shabbat* for two reasons: first, "that we might confirm the true theory, that of creation which at once and clearly leads to the theory of the existence of God;" second, "that we might remember how kind God was in freeing us from the burden of the Egyptians." As such, the *Shabbat* gives us correct notions and promotes the well-being of our bodies as well.[3]

Shabbat *and Redemption*

Nahmanides saw a much more fundamental association between creation and the redemption from Egypt. Creation establishes the omnipotence of God, but should there arise any doubt, the redemption from Egypt, an event replete with miracles that were witnessed by the entire nation of Israel, confirms the matter unequivocally. Seen from this perspective, one must conclude that not only does the *Shabbat* commemorate the redemption from Egypt, but the redemption from Egypt commemorates the *Shabbat.*[4]

Perhaps there is another link between *Shabbat* and the redemption from Egypt. The notion of *Shabbat* is diametrically opposed to the institution of slavery. Shabbat teaches man the sanctity of time and the value of freedom as an opportunity for self-perfection. No one questions the importance of work, and the dedication that a person has to his profession, business, or trade is certainly admirable. But one must allot ample time for family togetherness and Torah study, both of which are the pursuits of man's soul. Slavery sees only man's body; it has no concern or tolerance for the human soul. A slave has no concept of time. Bereft of freedom, his time belongs to his master; it is never his own. But a free man can prioritize his time, accommodating the physical, the material, and the spiritual values of life. On *Shabbat* he can desist from the mundane and engage in the sublime. He can rest his weary body and free his mind from all things that occupy his thoughts during the week. He can engage in the study of Torah and meditate on the meaning of life.

The Pilgrimage Festivals

Exodus 23:14 reads: "Three times [lit., pilgrimages] a year shall you hold a festival for Me." It is a *mitzvah* for every adult Jewish male living in Israel to visit the Temple in Jerusalem on Pesah, Shavuot, and Sukkot, the three pilgrimage festivals. It was on these occasions more than any other time during the year that the individual Jew felt himself to be at one with the entire nation, and it was in the Temple in Jerusalem, the most sacred place in the world, that this wholesome feeling was generated. In Temple times Israel was an agrarian society. For the farmer to leave his home and journey to Jerusalem at the seasons of the year when concern for his crops was uppermost in his mind was a great sacrifice. It meant giving the *mitzvot* of the Torah highest priority. The lesson learned from this experience, however, must have been well worth the effort. Mark the words of Rabbi Samson Raphael Hirsch:

> Inasmuch as when he gets there he learns to look on himself as only a member of a great circle, all bearing a common mission, it is just in these times which normally call him most pressingly to look after his own personal welfare, that the feeling of national unity is awakened in him; and it is this feeling combined with his innate powers of enthusiasm which banishes the curse of selfishness and egotism from the Jewish character.[5]

The importance of this lesson in national unity and national pride under the banner of Torah cannot be overemphasized. It is fundamental to ensuring Jewish survival in both the land of Israel and the Diaspora. It was the pilgrimage festivals that reinforced this lesson from year to year.

Let us now proceed to the individual festivals, each of which had its own historic events and signs of providential concern for Israel, which are recollected and commemorated.

The Festival of Pesah

Although the redemption from Egypt is mentioned in our prayers every day of the year and is, indeed, a recurring theme not only on *Shabbat* but on all of the holidays and festivals, there is no occasion as replete with recollections and commemorations of this awesome event as the festival of Pesah ("Passover"). In Israel, it is celebrated for seven days, from the fifteenth through the twenty-first day of Nisan. Outside of Israel it is celebrated for an additional day. Referred to in our prayers as *z'man herutenu* ("the season of our freedom"), the festival of Pesah commemorates freedom from slavery to free-willed, unqualified self-obligation to God and to the commandments of the Torah. In the calendar year, it is the first of the three pilgrimage festivals. Technically speaking, the name Pesah, by which this festival is most commonly known, applies only to the fourteenth of Nisan, the day on which the *paschal* lamb was brought as a sacrifice. The days that follow are referred to in the Torah as "the festival of unleavened bread." In Exodus 12:17, 18, we read:

> You shall observe the [feast of] unleavened bread for on this day I brought your ranks out of the land of Egypt; you shall observe this day throughout the generations as an institution for all time. In the first month, from the fourteenth day of the month at evening, you shall eat unleavened bread until the twenty-first day of the month at evening.

Pesah is indeed a time for recollections and commemorations. The Torah ordains that the medium through which this should be done is food, primarily, unleavened bread, or *matzah*. The *matzah* that is eaten on Pesah serves two purposes: it recollects the bread of affliction that the Israelites ate as slaves in Egypt, and it commemorates the bread of redemption that they hurriedly baked as they left Egypt, embarking on the journey to Canaan.

The Seder

Our sages ordained that in every generation a Jew must experience the Exodus from Egypt as if he himself had been redeemed. At no time during the festival is this idea brought to bear more poignantly than at the *seder* service performed on the first and second nights of the festival. Let us review the symbolism of the other special foods that are eaten at the *seder* service in commemoration of the redemption from Egyptian slavery. The book from which the *seder* service is read is called the Haggadah ("the telling").

It is customary to drink four cups of wine, symbolizing the four expressions of redemption mentioned in Exodus 6:6, 7. The verse reads:

> Say, therefore, to the Israelite people: I am the Lord, I will *free* you from the burdens of the Egyptians and *deliver* you from their bondage. I will *redeem* you with an outstretched arm and through ordinary chastisement. And I will *take* you to be My people and I will be your God. . . . "

The roasted shankbone—which is the only food on the *seder* plate that is not eaten—commemorates the roasted *paschal* lamb sacrifice that had to be brought by the Israelites before they were redeemed from Egypt. This sacrifice was brought annually in the land of Israel until the Holy Temple in Jerusalem was destroyed. The roasted lamb was to be eaten only in Jerusalem.

The cooked or roasted egg commemorates the special *haggigah* sacrifice that was brought in the days of the Temple on all three festivals: Pesah, Shavuot, and Sukkot. Unlike the *paschal* lamb, the *haggigah* offering did not have to be roasted.

The *karpas* is a vegetable. Potato, celery, or parsley are those most frequently chosen. In early times a vegetable was eaten as an appetizer at the beginning of the meal. Many people do so today as well. On Pesah, however, it has special significance. The Hebrew letters for *karpas*, when reversed, stand for the words "six" and "rigor" and recollect the time when six hundred thousand Israelites were enslaved and worked rigorously in Egypt. It is customary to dip the *karpas* in salt water to recollect the tears that the Israelites shed in their enslavement.

The *maror*, or bitter herb—horseradish or romaine lettuce are most frequently chosen—is also meant to recollect the bitter times in Egypt. It is dipped in *haroset*, (a mixture of apple, cinnamon, ginger, and nuts), which resembles mortar in its appearance and texture, to recollect the mortar used by the Israelite slaves in making the bricks for the fortress cities of Pithom and Raamses.

During the *seder* service, we recite and recollect the ten plagues that were brought by God upon Egypt. As we recite these plagues, it is customary to spill drops of wine from our goblets: ten drops of wine, one for each of the plagues.

Finally, a special cup of wine is placed on the table for the prophet Elijah. According to tradition, Elijah will come in Nisan, the month in which Pesah occurs, to announce the arrival of the Messiah, who will usher in the final redemption and the Messianic Era.

Very much like *Shabbat,* Pesah contrasts enslavement with freedom. Interestingly, the first day of Pesah is referred to in the Torah as a *"Shabbat."*[6] But while *Shabbat* focuses primarily on cessation from creative physical activity in commemoration of the redemption, Pesah focuses on the recognition of God's providential hand in the redemption, His involvement in the process of history on behalf of the people of Israel. Indicative of this emphasis is the opening paragraph of the story of the redemption that we recite at the *seder:*

> We were slaves of Pharaoh in Egypt, but the Lord our God brought us out of there with a mighty hand and with an outstretched arm. Were it not for the fact that the Holy One, blessed be He, had brought our fathers out of Egypt, then, surely, we, our children, and our children's children would still be enslaved by some Pharaoh in Egypt.

Were one merely to peruse the story, one would be impressed with God's concern, the hand of providence. Were it not for Divine intervention, the ancient Hebrews would have remained slaves in Egypt, never to have been formed into the nation of Israel, never to have received the Torah, and never to have been designated a "kingdom of priests and a holy nation."

The Torah tells us that the enslaved Israelites cried out to God for an end to their suffering and bondage. Finally, God took notice of them, and in Exodus 3:7, 8, we read that He addressed Moses with the following words: "I have marked well the plight of My people in Egypt. . . . I am mindful of their suffering. I have come down to rescue them from the Egyptians and to bring them out of that land to a good and spacious land. . . . "

As such, the festival of Pesah is a lesson in faith to every generation. It is put quite succinctly in the words we recite at the *seder*: "For not only one tyrant has risen against us to destroy us, but in every generation the wicked have risen against us to destroy us. But the Holy One, blessed be He, delivers us from their hands."

God did not abandon His people in Egypt; He intervened in the process of history in their behalf when the time was ripe. So has He done time and time again in the past. The State of Israel bears witness to the fact that He has done so in the present, and it is our firm belief that He will continue to do so in the future until the arrival of the Messianic Era, the final redemption of the Jewish people.

The Festival of Shavuot

Shavuot, the second of the three pilgrimage festivals, is also known as Yom HaBikurim ("the day of the first fruits") and Hag HaKatzir ("the feast of harvest"). It is celebrated for two days, on the sixth and seventh day of the Hebrew month Sivan. In the Torah it is spoken of as an agricultural holiday, marking the beginning of the harvest season for fruit and wheat. In the days of the Jewish Commonwealth, the Jews would bring the first fruits of their crops to the priest in the Temple in Jerusalem and, as recorded in Deuteronomy 26:3, say to him: "I acknowledge this day before the Lord your God that I have entered the land which the Lord swore to our fathers to give us." The priest would set the basket down before the altar, after which the donor would say:

> My father was a fugitive Aramean. He went down to Egypt with meager numbers and sojourned there; but there he became a great and very populous nation. The Egyptians dealt harshly with us and oppressed us: they imposed heavy labor upon us. We cried to the Lord the God of our fathers, and the Lord heard our plea and saw our plight, our misery and our oppression. The Lord freed us from Egypt by a mighty hand, by an outstretched arm and awesome power, and by signs and portents. He brought us to this place and gave us this land, a land flowing with milk and honey. Wherefore I now bring the first fruits of the soil which You, O Lord have given me.[7]

The First Fruits

On Pesah, we put the redemption into proper perspective by contrasting it to the enslavement. On Shavuot we do likewise. In addition, the Torah ordains that on Shavuot we bring the first fruits of our crop as a thanksgiving offering. It is important that we understand the significance of an offering of "first fruits."

Psalms 24:1 reads: "The earth is the Lord's and all that it holds, the world and its inhabitants." King David recognized God as the Creator and Master of the universe. By what right do we partake of that which belongs to God? You will recall that Cain's motivation for bringing an offering to God differed from that of his brother Abel. Cain had brought fruit, but he was not selective; Abel, on the other hand, had brought the firstlings of his flock, the best. By bringing the first ripened produce to the Temple on Shavuot, our ancestors made an important statement; they acknowledged that, in truth, their entire crop belongs to God. This acknowledgement gave them the right to partake of the rest of their crop. But it was also an expression of thanksgiving to God for fulfilling His promise to our forefathers that their children would inherit the Promised Land of Canaan.

Counting the Omer

On the second day of Pesah, an *omer* ("measure") of the newly harvested barley was brought to the Temple as an offering. In the evening, Jews began to count the days for a period of seven weeks. On the fiftieth day, Shavuot (lit., "weeks"), two loaves of bread, each made of two-tenths of a measure of choice flour, were brought as an additional first-fruits offering to God. Of course, with the destruction of the Temple, the offerings ceased. In commemoration of the Temple offerings, the sages ruled that the *mitzvah* of counting the days be retained.

Revelation of the Torah

Last, and most important, we recollect and commemorate the revelation of the Torah on Mount Sinai, clearly the greatest manifestation of God's concern for the welfare of Israel and humanity. Revelation was, indeed, the greatest single event in Jewish history. Accordingly, this festival is referred to in our prayers as *z'man matan Toratenu* ("the season of the giving of our Torah"). It was in the third month after the Israelites left Egypt that they encamped in the wilderness of Sinai. Here again the message of unity is introduced. Unlike other encampments that had been marked by friction among the people, this time they were united as one person with one heart in preparation for the revelation of the Torah.[8] This should serve as a lesson to us that only as a united people can we hope to succeed in our Divinely ordained mission. We dare not rest until there is unity among us.

Some Beautiful Customs

On the sixth day of Sivan, the Israelites received the Torah. Some beautiful customs arose in commemoration of this awesome event. In many communities the congregants gather together in the synagogue on the first night of the festival, where they spend the entire night studying the Torah. In the sixteenth century, Rabbis Solomon Alkabetz and Joseph Karo compiled excerpts from the Bible and the Oral Law to be studied on this night. The text, called *Seder Tikkun Lel Shavuot,* has become the basis for the study sessions on this night in congregations the world over.

In the Morning Service, a poem called *Akdamot millin* ("At the beginning of His words") is chanted before the Torah reading. It is a song of praise to God for His having chosen to reveal the Torah to the nation of Israel.

On the second day of Shavuot, it is customary to read the book of Ruth. This inspiring story tells of Ruth, the Moabite, who had married a Jew and had converted to Judaism. It depicts Ruth's devotion to Naomi, her mother-in-law, and her allegiance to the Jewish people. The story begins with calamity: a famine in the land of Israel, the death of Elimelech, Naomi's husband, and the death of Mahlon, the husband of Ruth. Urged by Naomi to return to her people, Ruth refuses, uttering the now famous words: "Do not urge me to leave you, to turn back and not follow you. For wherever you will go, I will go; wherever you will lodge, I will lodge; your people shall be my people and your God my God" (Ruth 1:16). Her words very poignantly express her love for Judaism and her commitment to the Jewish people, which she retained despite the trials and tribulations that marked her life.

The book is read on Shavuot because its heroine is symbolic of the Jewish people. Like Ruth, the Jewish people accepted upon themselves the yoke of the kingdom of heaven. When Moses told them that the Torah was about to be revealed and he needed their promise of commitment, they responded in one voice, "All that the Lord has spoken we will do." When we read the book of Ruth on Shavuot, we recollect and commemorate the life of this extraordinary woman, but we also recollect and commemorate the Jewish experience at Sinai. It serves as a lesson in Jewish responsibility, the obligation to obey and to defend the Torah way of life in every generation.

The Festival of Sukkot

The third and last of the pilgrimage festivals has both an agricultural and a historical theme. In Israel it is celebrated for seven days, from the fifteenth through the twenty-first day of the Hebrew month Tishre. In Exodus 23:16 the festival is referred to as Hag Ha-Asif ("the festival of ingathering"), in celebration of harvest time in Israel in the days of the Temple. In Leviticus 23:34 it is referred to as Hag HaSukkot ("the festival of tabernacles"). According to one opinion in the Talmud, the festival recollects the "temporary huts" in which the Israelites lived in the wilderness to protect them from the scorching rays of the sun; according to another, it recollects the "clouds of glory," a pillar of cloud by day and a pillar of fire by night, that surrounded the Israelites and accompanied them for forty years on their journey to the Promised Land of Canaan.[9]

The Mitzvah of Sukkah

In celebration of this festival, the Torah bids us to leave our permanent homes and take residence in temporary huts for a period of seven days. Designated one of the 613 *mitzvot*, the festival of Sukkot is of great significance for its symbolism, and the lessons it is meant to teach are relevant in every generation. Let us outline them briefly.

In Leviticus 23:42–43 we read: "You shall live in huts seven days: all citizens of Israel shall live in huts. So that your generations may know that I made the Israelite people live in huts when I brought them out of the land of Egypt." The Israelites traveled in the wilderness for forty years. As the Israelites moved from one encampment to the other, their destination always in mind but never in sight, the time must have seemed endless. One cannot help but wonder why it was necessary for them to remain in the wilderness for so long.

The Torah does tell us that the generation that had left Egypt was punished. In rejecting the positive report given by Joshua and Calev on the quality of the land of Canaan, its produce, and their ability to conquer it, the Israelites betrayed a lack of trust in God. By suggesting that they would be better off returning to Egypt, they betrayed their slave mentality. Such a generation was not fit to enter the land, hence the severe Divine decree. Not until everyone who had left Egypt, save Joshua and Calev, had died in the wilderness would the promise made to the Patriarchs, that their children would inherit the land of Canaan, be fulfilled. Only the new generation would be privileged to enter and conquer the land, to sanctify it, and to establish it as the inheritance of the Jewish people for all time.[10] But was this the only reason for the forty years' stay in the wilderness? Perhaps not.

The Lessons of the Sukkah

In Deuteronomy 8:2–6 we read:

> Remember the long way that the Lord your God has made you travel in the wilderness these forty years, that He might test you by hardships to learn what was in your hearts: whether you would keep His commandments or not. He subjected you to the hardships of hunger and then gave you manna to eat . . . in order to teach you that man does not live by bread alone, but that man may live on anything that the Lord decrees. The clothes upon you did not wear out, nor did your feet swell these forty years . . . Therefore keep the commandments of the Lord your God; walk in His ways and revere Him.

Our sages tell us that during those forty years in the wilderness the Israelites were taught an important lesson in life. Our recollection and commemoration of this period brings this lesson to mind. According to Rabbi Samson Raphael Hirsch, it was a lesson in humility. The Israelites spent forty years in the wilderness to teach them not to idolize their skill and ingenuity in obtaining their sustenance. Their survival under those adverse conditions was entirely in God's hands. It was God who provided them with the *manna* for food, the pillar of cloud by day to guide them, and the pillar of fire by night to protect them. Man's intelligence and skill are significant contributing factors to his successes in life, but his survival is to a great extent due to the providential hand of God.

It is my contention that life in the wilderness taught the Israelites another lesson. In the wilderness, the Israelites lived humble lives. Their homes were temporary huts, but all their needs were met. Under God's providential hand, they were able to survive for forty years without deficiency. Faced with the Divine decree to spend the rest of their lives in the wilderness, oblivious to the material things that bear the stamp of man's initiative in the world, the Israelites were compelled to focus on the more important and the more enduring things in life: friendship, marriage, and family, values that are given highest priority in the Torah and are the source of true happiness in life.

We all derive pleasure from material acquisitions, but pleasure is not to be confused with happiness. Happiness is a state of mind that comes mostly from feeling good about oneself, about what one has accomplished in life: the actualization of one's intellectual and spiritual potential and what one has done for one's fellow man. True happiness is never attained by acquiring material things, nor is it in any way dependent upon them. This was a lesson the Israelites had to learn before they entered the land of Canaan, where plentiful crops and the acquisition of wealth might confuse them and distort their sense of priorities in life. Indeed, it was Divinely ordained that this lesson in values and priorities be commemorated in every generation.

From year to year we leave our homes, the luxurious residences that we have acquired through our intellectual prowess and the strength of our hands. We dwell for seven days in fragile temporary huts that pale by comparison, in order to recollect the lives of our ancestors in the wilderness and commemorate the values that they were taught. It is *z'man simhatenu* ("The season of our rejoicing"), and there is no greater way to rejoice than for family and friends to come together for festive meals interspersed with words of Torah, to sing songs of praise to God, and to express their love for each other.

The Four Kinds

Finally, the festival of Sukkot teaches us the importance of unity in the Jewish community. There is nothing more detrimental to the Jewish community than dissension. Much to our dismay, we have suffered from this corrosive force from the earliest times, and today it threatens our very survival as Jews. And so we are told in Leviticus 23:40: "On the first day you shall take the fruit of goodly trees [citron], branches of palm trees, twigs of myrtle and willows of the brook, and you shall rejoice before the Lord your God seven days." Taking the "four kinds" on this festival and rejoicing before the Lord sends another important message.

Our sages have explained that the "four kinds" represent four parts of the human body. The citron represents the human heart; the palm branch, the spine; the twigs of myrtle, the eyes; and the willow, the lips. Individually, each of these parts performs a unique and vital function that in and of itself is of great value to man. From a broader perspective, however, they can be seen as components in a chain of physiological systems that operate harmoniously to preserve life. Seen from this perspective, their functions take on infinitely greater significance. The whole is, indeed, greater than the sum of its parts.

The Jewish community includes a multiplicity of "kinds," men and women with diverse interests, talents, and intellectual abilities. Every Jew is important, both to God and to the Jewish community, and every Jew has something to offer. Our sages teach us, "Despise not any man, and carp not at any thing; for there is not a man that has not his hour, and there is not a thing that has not its place."[11] The "four kinds" that we take on the festival of Sukkot is symbolic of the diversity of "kinds" that exist in the Jewish community. The *Halakhah* that requires us to hold them close to one another as we rejoice before God on this festival teaches us that the Jewish community must be unified and brought to work together harmoniously for the fulfillment of Torah and the Jewish mission.

But let no one accuse the Torah of naivete, of preaching equality in a world where our knowledge of genetics has made it perfectly clear that no two people are equal. Some are wise and others are simple; some intelligent and others ignorant. Some of us are gifted while others are completely devoid of talent. Nonetheless, our humanness, our dependency on each other and on God for survival, must serve to bind us to one another. Our differences are irrelevant in this regard. This is the message of Sukkot.

Hoshana Rabbah

The seventh day of Sukkot is a solemn day. As we shall explain in our discussion of the High Holidays, it is during the month of Tishre that men are judged on their behavior during the past year, and their destinies for the coming year are determined. On this day the final judgment of man is sealed. It is called Hoshana Rabbah in recognition of the many prayers recited on this day that begin with the word *hoshana* ("please help"). The solemnity of this day is reflected in the chanting of parts of the *Shaharit* and *Mussaf* services, which are identical with those of the High Holidays.

Shemini Atseret and Simhat Torah

The following day is called Shemini Atseret ("eighth day of assembly"). Its source is biblical. In Numbers 29:35 we read: "On the eighth day you shall hold a solemn gathering; you shall not work at your occupations." The sages regarded this day as a distinct holiday by itself. Some say it is a plea by God to the people of Israel to tarry with Him for one more day. Two special prayers are recited on this day: *Yizkor*, the memorial prayer for the dead, and *Tefilat Geshem*, the prayer for rain. In Israel, the last section of the weekly Torah portions is read on this day, thus completing the entire Torah. It is a day of great joy and celebration. In the Middle Ages, this day was also given the name Simhat Torah. Outside of Israel, Shemini Atseret and Simhat Torah are on separate days, making the festival a nine-day celebration.

The High Holidays

The first ten days of the month of Tishre, from Rosh Hashanah through Yom Kippur, have been designated by Jewish law as the *aseret y'me teshuvah* ("ten days of penitence"). It is at this season that God takes accounting, as it were, of the deeds of every human being the world over and judges them for health or for sickness, for life or for death. Every Jew takes notice of his life at this season of the year as well. Sincere soul-searching leaves him overwrought, beset by fear and trembling. He knows that he has not actualized the potential for good in his life. Some of us have fallen short of our obligations to family; others have not been considerate enough of their fellow man. Introspection and repentance are the major themes in the recollections and commemorations of Rosh Hashanah and Yom Kippur, the days our sages referred to as *yamim noraim* ("days of awe"). Let us develop this.

Rosh Hashanah

On the first day of the month of Elul, God told Moses to ascend Mount Sinai once again, this time with the new tablets that he had hewn. These tablets were likewise inscribed by God with the Ten Commandments.[12] The *shofar* was sounded in the camp of Israel to indicate where Moses had gone. He was to remain on the mountain for forty days and forty nights. After Yom Kippur, Moses would descend from the mountain, the people of Israel having been granted full atonement for the sin of the golden calf. The sages recognized these forty days as a period of special grace, and they designated it to be commemorated every year as a time for taking accounting of one's life and for repenting for one's sins. To set the tone, it is customary to sound the *shofar* during the entire month of Elul with the exception of the day before Rosh Hashanah. During the week of Rosh Hashanah, it is customary to recite special penitential prayers called *Selihot.*

The name Rosh Hashanah means "Head of the Year." Some are of the opinion that this name signifies that on Rosh Hashanah the world was created. Two of the prayers recited on this day would indicate this. One of them reads, "This day, on which was the beginning of Your work, is the memorial of the first day"; the other, "Today is the birthday of the world." In point of fact, there is a difference of opinion among the sages of the Talmud as to whether the world was created in the month of Nisan or Tishre.[13]

The Day to Remember

Rosh Hashanah is celebrated for two days on the first and second day of the Hebrew month Tishre. It is also known as Yom HaZikaron ("The Day of Remembrance"), for this is a day of recollection for both God and man. God recollects, as it were, the events of the past and present in the life of every human being. Man asks Him to recollect Abraham's willingness to sacrifice his son Isaac, in whose merit he implores Him to temper justice with mercy. Parenthetically, the *shofar* is sounded on this day to recollect and commemorate this event as well. Abraham had sacrificed a ram that he saw caught in the thicket in place of his son Isaac.

Man recollects the fact that God remembered His promise to Noah to multiply his seed like the dust of the earth and saved him from the flood. He also recollects that God remembered the Israelites in Egypt, that He heard their groaning, and that He remembered His promise to Abraham, Isaac, and Jacob to redeem His children from slavery. Finally, he recalls the revelation of the Torah, the awesome event at Sinai, perhaps the greatest manifestation of Divine compassion. Having recalled these events, man appeals to God with the words, "so may Your compassion soften Your anger against us; in Your great goodness may the fierceness of Your wrath turn aside from Your people, Your city and Your inheritance."

The *Mishnah* records, "At four seasons [Divine] judgment is passed on the world: . . . on the New Year all creatures pass before Him [God] like children in single file."[14] Rosh Hashanah is therefore celebrated first and foremost as Yom HaDin ("The Day of Judgment"). We make reference to this theme continually in the prayers of this holiday. Israel is not the only nation that is judged on this day. Note the following words: "Regarding countries, it is said on this day which is destined for the sword and which for peace, which for hunger and which for abundance."[15] The nations of the world are judged on this solemn day as well.

The Shofar

The uniqueness of Rosh Hashanah is perhaps best characterized by the *mitzvah* of the *shofar*. In point of fact, this holiday is also called Yom Teruah ("The Day of Sounding"). The source for the *mitzvah* of *shofar* is Numbers 29:1, which reads, "In the seventh month, on the first day of the month you shall observe a sacred occasion: you shall not work at your occupations; you shall observe it as a day when the *shofar* is sounded." By tradition, a ram's horn is used. Although there is a difference of opinion among the rabbis as to whether the *mitzvah* is to sound the *shofar* or to listen to it, most conclude the latter. Jewish law requires that one hundred blasts be sounded on each of the two days of the holiday. There are three sounds that are produced: *tekiah* is a single unbroken blast; *shevarim* is three short blasts; *teruah* is a staccato of nine notes. Here, too, there is a difference of opinion as to the meaning of *teruah*. To satisfy all opinions, various combinations of the three sounds were instituted at the service.[16]

In Jewish communities in the land of Israel the *shofar* was sounded for a multiplicity of reasons. It announced the decision by the rabbis for a communal fast day in anticipation of an impending danger or trag-edy.[17] It publicized the decision of the rabbinic court to place a person under ban for some wrongdoing.[18] In some communities it was sounded to announce a death summoning the residents to attend the funeral.[19] But it was also sounded on festive occasions: to announce the onset of *Shabbat*,[20] the proclamation of the beginning of the new month,[21] and the arrival of the Jubilee Year.[22]

On Rosh Hashanah, however, the sounding of the *shofar* takes on a new meaning. We already mentioned that it commemorates the sacri-fice of Isaac and the revelation of the Torah at Sinai.[23] But most impor-tant, since the eighth century B.C.E. the *shofar* has become a call to re-pentance. The prophet Joel declared: "Sound a *shofar* in Zion, solemnize a fast, proclaim an assembly! Gather the people, bid the congregation purify themselves. Let the priests . . . weep and say, 'O spare Your people Lord!'"[24] The very tone of the *shofar* sets the mood. For the Talmud speaks of two kinds of weeping sounds: the *teruah*, which is a wailing sound, and the *shevarim*, which is more like groaning.[25] In the Ashkenazic rite the *shofar* is sounded immediately before the *Mussaf* service, again after each of the three sections in the repetition of the *Amidah*, and once more in the *Kaddish* recited after the *Amidah*. In the Sefardic rite, it is also recited in the silent *Amidah*. Finally, the *shofar* symbolizes the Messianic Era, as we read in Isaiah 27:13: "And in that day, a great *shofar* shall be sounded; and the strayed who are in the land of Asseria and the expelled who are in the land of Egypt shall come and worship the Lord on the holy mountain in Jerusalem."

Yom Kippur

Yom Kippur ("Day of Atonement"), which occurs on the tenth day of the Hebrew month of Tishre, has been established as the most solemn and most sacred holiday in the Jewish calendar. Its solemnity is marked by the fact that it is the last of the "Ten Days of Penitence." On this day man's destiny for the coming year is sealed, and he trembles at the thought of what it might hold for him. The sacredness of Yom Kippur is marked by the fact that it is the only day of the year when the High Priest was permitted to enter the Holy of Holies in the Temple in

Jerusalem. It was there that he offered sacrifices on behalf of all Israel in atonement for their sins.

In ancient Israel Yom Kippur was also one of the most joyous holidays. The Talmud points out: "There never were in Israel greater days of joy than the fifteenth of Av and the Day of Atonement."[26] The transformation from solemnity to joy is not at all a strange phenomenon. In point of fact, it follows quite logically from the Yom Kippur experience. Having returned to God in sincere repentance, the Jew is confident that his sins have been forgiven, and this fills him with joy and happiness.[27] In the days of the Temple, the High Priest made a festive party for all his friends to celebrate the fact that he had emerged from the Holy of Holies alive and unscathed. Indeed, the Almighty Himself, the sages tell us, is joyful on this day, for it pleases Him that His children have earned forgiveness in His eyes.[28]

The Biblical Source

Unlike Rosh Hashanah, Yom Kippur is mentioned in the Torah by name. In Leviticus 16:30–31 we read: "In the seventh month, on the tenth day of the month, you shall afflict your souls; and you shall do no manner of work . . . For on this day atonement shall be made for you to cleanse you of all your sins; you shall be clean before the Lord . . . it is a law for all time."

To afflict one's soul is to induce the proper mood for confession and sincere repentance. According to our sages, the prohibited acts included under the rubric "affliction" are as follows: eating, drinking, washing, anointing, wearing leather shoes, and sexual relations.[29]

The Temple Service

Although we are almost completely preoccupied with confession and repentance on Yom Kippur, recollection of the service performed by the High Priest in the Temple on this day is given major consideration in our prayers. Much of the text of the *Mussaf* service is devoted to this theme. We recall the preparations that were made on the night before the High Priest was to enter the Holy of Holies, and we describe the rituals and list the sacrifices he brought on the following day. We also recall the confessionals that he recited on his own behalf and those that were on behalf of all the people of Israel. Whenever he mentioned the Name of God during the service, the High Priest would bow and prostrate himself on the ground as a gesture of homage. When we recall this gesture in the Yom Kippur *Mussaf* service, we commemorate it by bowing and prostrating ourselves three times.

When the High Priest emerged from the Holy of Holies at the conclusion of the Temple service, he uttered a beautiful prayer of petition to the Almighty in which he appealed for successful crops, for atonement for all of Israel, and for a year that would be blessed with health, peace, and tranquility. In commemoration of this gesture, this stunning prayer has been made part of our service. We conclude our recollection of the service performed by the High Priest on this sacred day by bemoaning the fact that the Temple was destroyed, which brought an abrupt end to what must have been an awe-inspiring experience for all who had witnessed it. With sadness in our hearts, we turn to the Almighty with the words

> What shall we say, and how can we clear ourselves? What shall we answer Him from Whom is the utterance of speech? He has bestowed good upon us, but we have rendered evil. What right therefore have we left that we should cry unto the King? Forgive us, our Father, for in the abundance of our folly we have gone astray.

The Book of Jonah

Following the *Minhah* ("Afternoon Service") Torah reading, the book of Jonah is read. Among the shorter books of the Bible, Jonah conveys two important lessons: no one can escape God's judgment, and even the most wicked sinners will be forgiven by God if their repentance is sincere. Would any book be more relevant on this sacred holiday?

The Ne'ilah Service

The concluding service of Yom Kippur is called *Ne'ilah* ("closing"). According to one opinion, the name refers to the closing of the "gates of heaven," so to speak; according to another, the closing of the gates in the Temple in Jerusalem.[30] Since the Temple gates were closed at dusk, it is customary to begin the *Ne'ilah* service while it is still daylight and not terminate it until nightfall.

The final gesture of Yom Kippur is the sounding of the *shofar*, which indicates that the holiday is over. With the possible exception of the *Kol Nidre* service on the previous night, there is probably no time during the holiday when the synagogue is more crowded. A mass of humanity waits in anticipation. A hush comes over the assembly and the *shofar* is sounded. Listening to this single unbroken tone, we recollect once again all that the *shofar* symbolizes and commemorates: the call to repentance, the sacrifice of Isaac, the revelation of the Torah, and the coming of the Messianic Era. Cleansed of sin, we emerge from this sacred and unique day with a new perspective on life. We return to the mundane tasks of living with renewed vitality, spiritually refreshed, somewhat wiser and much more hopeful about the future.

Hanukkah

The festival of Hanukkah recollects two events: the victory of the Judeans in their revolt against the Seleucid Greeks in the year 165 B.C.E., and the miracle of the cruse of oil.[31] Hanukkah means "they encamped on the twenty-fifth," indicating the day of the month on which the victory was won. The festival is also known as "The Feast of Dedication," in commemoration of the former, and as "The Feast of Lights," in commemoration of the latter. It is celebrated for eight days, from the twenty-fifth of the Hebrew month Kislev through the second day of Tevet.

Much to our dismay, there is clear evidence from early historical sources that Antiochus, the Greek ruler over Judea, would never have attempted to convert the Jews to Greek culture were it not for the encouragement he was given by the wealthy Jews and the corrupt Temple priests in Judea at the time. They assured him that they no longer held any allegiance to Judaism, and that the lower classes who still held such an allegiance could easily be persuaded or forced to accept such a conversion. This encouraged Antiochus to take action.[32] Jason, the High Priest at the time, confronted Antiochus with an offer of great sums of money to erect a gymnasium and to grant the Judeans of Jerusalem full citizenship in Antioch. The king was convinced, and he accepted the offer. Jason began immediately to influence the Jews to adopt Hellenic customs. The movement toward Hellenism became very strong among the people; even the priests left the Temple service to participate in the Greek games. "But it was just those people for whose sake they faced the greatest difficulties, whose way of life they strove so eagerly to imitate, and to whom they wanted to become assimilated, it was precisely they who were their enemies, the avengers of their backsliding; for to sin against Divine law is no small matter."[33]

There was one priestly family, however, that remained loyal to Judaism: Mattathias and his five sons of the Hasmonean family. When an altar was placed in the marketplace in the town of Modein and Mattathias was summoned to offer sacrifice to the Greek god, he refused. Under the battle cry "Whoever is for God, follow me," he fled to the mountains. He formed a small army that attempted to free the Judeans from the rule of Antiochus.

The Judeans won many victories under Judah Maccabee, who had assumed the reins of leadership after his father died. When the troops returned from the war, they cleansed the Temple and destroyed the idols put there by the Greeks. They tore down the altar that had been desecrated and built a new one, and they demolished the heathen places of worship. On the twenty-fifth day of the month of Kislev in the year 165 B.C.E. the Temple was rededicated: the morning sacrifice was offered and the menorah was lit. Only a single cruse of pure olive oil that bore the unbroken seal of the High Priest had been found. Untouched by the heathens, it was fit to be used in the Menorah. Unfortunately, there was only enough oil to burn for one day. Undiscouraged, they lit the Menorah and began the process of preparing new oil. Miraculously, the cruse of oil lasted for eight days, enough time for the new oil to have been prepared for use.

The Festival Lights

The Talmud records that in the following year an eight-day festival was declared. It was ruled that these events were to be celebrated annually by the recitation of prayers of praise and thanksgiving to God, music, and song. In commemoration of the miracle of the cruse of oil, the sages ruled that lights be kindled in every Jewish home for eight days. The number of lights to be kindled each day, the order of lighting, the placing of the lights, the order of preference with regard to oils, and the wording of the blessings to be recited, as well as many other rules and regulations pertaining to this festival, are found in the Talmud[34] and in the Code of Jewish Law.[35]

The following are some practical rulings. All oils are permissible to be used in the *menorah*, but the most preferable is olive oil. Candles may be used in the *menorah* as well. On the first night, one light is kindled and an additional light is added each night thereafter, so that on the last night of the festival eight lights are kindled.[36] The candles (or oil cups) are placed in the *menorah* from right to left, but they are lit from left to right, the newest oil, or candle, being lit first. The *menorah* is placed where it can be seen by passersby in fulfillment of the principle of *pirsume nisa*, "publicizing the miracle."

The beautiful glow of the lighted menorah warms our hearts as we recollect the miracles of Hanukkah. Not so much the physical victory of Judah Maccabee and his force over the vast army of the Greeks, for that achieved only a temporary respite—less than two hundred fifty years—but the spiritual victory of Judaism over Hellenism in the minds of the Judeans, is what marks Hanukkah as an occasion for celebration.

Hellenization did not save the Jews; it was Mattathias and his sons who saved them. By remaining true to Judaism and rejecting the Greek culture, he set the example for the rest of the people. Assimilation is never the antidote to persecution. Quite the contrary! Most often, assimilation only serves to exacerbate matters. As Rabbi Samson Raphael Hirsch notes:

> Respect yourself, respect your past, respect your own sanctuary, and you will see that whatever opinion is held of you . . . respect will not be denied you. But if you do not respect yourself, if you look contemptuously at the tombs of your ancestors, if you no longer consider your sanctuary worthy of respect, how can you demand that a stranger shall respect you. . . ."[37]

During Hanukkah, the tiny flickering lights that come from every Jewish home and stand out in the night like precious jewels proclaim a lesson in Divine providence to all passersby. The Jewish people as a nation are indestructible. The providential hand of God will protect them for all time. Confirmed by history, this lesson is never to be forgotten by Jew and Gentile alike. We recall once again the words of encouragement that have fostered Jewish survival through the ages. "Not only one tyrant has risen against us to destroy us, but in every generation the wicked have risen against us to destroy us. But the Holy One, blessed be He, delivers us from their hands."

Purim

Purim occurs on the fourteenth day of the Hebrew month Adar. The *Shabbat* preceding Purim is called *Shabbat Parashat Zakhor*. In addition to the regular Torah reading, it is customary to read Deuteronomy 25:17–19, which reads:

> Remember what [the nation] Amalek did to you on your journey, after you left Egypt—how undeterred by fear of God, he surprised you on the march, when you were famished and weary, and cut down all the stragglers in your rear. Therefore, when the Lord your God grants you safety from all your enemies around you, in the land that the Lord your God is giving you as a hereditary portion, you shall blot out the memory of Amalek from under heaven. Do not forget!

It is a biblical commandment to hear these words as they are read in the synagogue every year at this time. The nation of Amalek was not just an enemy to the Jews, as were the Egyptians and the Greeks. As the text indicates, Amalek was undeterred by the fear of God. Their land was not threatened; they were not provoked. They had no just cause, yet they viciously attacked the people of Israel when they were famished and weary. One would have expected sympathy for this wandering multitude of people, not hostility. One would have expected gestures of peace, not war. As Moses pointed out in his song at the Reed Sea: Philistia feared, Edom was stunned, Moav trembled, and Canaan was dumbfounded by the deeds that God had wrought for Israel. Only Amalek remained unimpressed and had the audacity to attack Israel. What was their motivation? Rabbi Samson Raphael Hirsch put it well: "His attack was . . . urged either by pure joy of massacre or possibly by some inkling of the danger which the principle of pure humanness and obedience to duty which you [Israel] were to introduce into history would begin to threaten his principle of the power of the sword."

Amalek lived by the sword; Israel lived by God's word. Amalek was dedicated to war and the subjugation of the weak; Israel, to peace, Divine ethics, and morality. Amalek worshiped only power; Israel worshiped the One Supreme God of the universe. The philosophy and lifestyle of the nation of Israel is not only incompatible with Amalek, it is diametrically opposed to all that Amalek represents. In point of fact, the Torah tells us that God Himself detests Amalek and his philosophy. Thus, we read in Exodus 17:16: "The Lord will be at war with Amalek throughout the generations." Recollect what Amalek did to you in the wilderness, says the Torah, and dedicate yourselves throughout the generations as individuals and as a nation to blotting out the philosophy of Amalek in the world wherever and whenever it rears its ugly head.

Our sages instructed us, "With the beginning of Av rejoicing is curtailed, with the beginning of Adar rejoicing is increased."[38] Life advances in cycles, and as King Solomon so poignantly put it: "There is a time for weeping and a time for laughing, a time for wailing and a time for dancing."[39] Purim, which occurs on the fourteenth day of the Hebrew month Adar, is indeed a time for great joy. It commemorates the Divine deliverance of the Jews of Persia (Iran today) who, in the fourth century B.C.E., were threatened with extermination by Haman, the wicked court minister. Purim means "lots"; the festival is called by that name to recollect the fact that Haman, a descendant of Agag, the king of Amalek, cast lots to determine on what day the massacre of the Jews should take place. Mordecai, the Jew, and his cousin Esther, who had assumed the throne to become the queen of Persia, were the agents through whom the Divine deliverance was implemented.

An Important Lesson

Perhaps there is also a lesson of a more personal nature that can be learned from Amalek. Let me associate it with the Torah reading on this day and it will serve as a mnemonic. There is some question as how the Hebrew term for "memory" is to be vocalized in the phrase "you shall blot out the memory of Amalek from under heaven." Is it *zekher*, vocalized with a *segol*, or *zaykher*, vocalized with a *tsayre*? The custom is to repeat the phrase and vocalize it both ways. Perhaps this is to teach us that there are two aspects to the *mitzvah*. Amalek lies dormant in each and every one of us. Not only are we required to blot out the memory of the nation of Amalek of ancient times; not only must we crush that philosophy if it manifests itself in contemporary society, but in those instances in which this philosophy finds a haven in our own hearts and manifests itself in greed, unprovoked and unwarranted hatred of a fellow Jew, insensitivity to the feelings of others, or simply in extreme self-centeredness, we must blot it out as well. Remember . . . do not forget!

The Lessons of Purim

The deliverance on Purim teaches us two important lessons, and we must celebrate this festival by recollecting and commemorating them. The first is the lesson of history. Jews have always been regarded as strangers in the lands of their dispersion. Their uniqueness drew attention to them, and their successes aroused the envy of others, leading to anti-Semitism, even persecution. In some countries it even resulted in expulsion. Witness the words of Pharaoh to his people: "Look, the Israelite people are much too numerous for us. Let us, then, deal wisely with them, lest they increase and, in the event of war, join our enemies in fighting against us and gain ascendancy over the country."[40] In the same vein spoke Haman to King Ahasuerus: "There is a certain people, scattered and dispersed among the other peoples . . . whose laws are different from those of any other people and who do not obey the king's laws; and it is not in your majesty's interest to tolerate them."[41]

There is only one way to end oppression and exile. We refer to it time and time again in our prayers. "Bring us in peacefulness from the four corners of the earth, and lead us with upright pride to our land"; and again, "Draw our scattered ones near, from among the nations, and bring in our dispersions from the ends of the earth. Bring us to Zion Your city, in glad song, and to Jerusalem, home of Your sanctuary, in eternal joy." A Jew needs a homeland, and the only homeland for the Jew is the land of Israel.

The second lesson to be learned from the festival of Purim is the lesson of providence. When Esther was ordered by Mordecai to appear before the king to plead for her people, she seemed to hesitate. She informed Mordecai that to appear before the king, one had to be summoned. To do otherwise was to endanger one's life. Then came Mordecai's powerful words, "Do not imagine that you, of all the Jews, will escape with your life by being in the king's palace. On the contrary, if you keep silent in this crisis, relief and deliverance will come to the Jews from another quarter, while you and your father's house will perish. And who knows, perhaps you have attained to royal position for just such a crisis."[42] The destiny of the Jewish people rests in the hand of the Almighty. They may be subjugated and persecuted in the lands of their dispersion, even exiled to other lands, but they will never be totally annihilated. The providential hand of God will intervene in the process of history to protect them as a nation. In the end, relief and deliverance will come to the Jewish people, and, like in the Purim story, the plans of its enemies will be frustrated.

Laws and Customs

As was the custom from the time Moses led the Israelites against Amalek, the Jews fasted and turned to God in petition for mercy before going to battle against their enemies. In commemoration of this event, in the eighth century the sages declared a public fast day to be observed by Jews throughout the generations on the thirteenth day of Adar, the day before Purim. It was called *Taanit Esther* ("the Fast of Esther") to remind them that just as God came to the aid of Esther in her time of need in response to her fasting and sincere repentance, so does He come to the aid of all Jews who fast and return to Him in sincere repentance.[43] There are some who fast for three days after Purim: Monday, Thursday, and again on the following Monday to commemorate Esther's three-day fast before she went to see the king.[44]

Mordecai recorded the events of Purim and he sent messages to all the Jews of the land, instructing them to observe the fourteenth and fifteenth of Adar, the days on which the Jews enjoyed relief from their enemies, as days of feasting and merrymaking and as an occasion for sending gifts to each other and giving presents to the poor.[45] The Jews accordingly assumed as an obligation that which Mordecai prescribed for them, and it has been held through the generations. In fulfillment of the *mitzvah* of *pirsume nisa*, publicizing the miracle, the story of Purim is read in synagogues throughout the world from a handwritten scroll called a *Megillah*, on the eve of the fourteenth of *Adar* and again on the following morning.

Joy reaches its maximum potential when it is an experience shared with others. Perhaps this is the rationale for the feast that is held on Purim day with family and close friends. To extend the joy to others, we send gifts of food and drink: a minimum of two items to each. Equally important, and certainly not to be forgotten, are the poor to whom there is no greater joy than to receive a gift from a fellow Jew.

The Three Weeks

The destruction of the First Temple in the year 586 B.C.E. and the Second Temple in 70 C.E. are among the most profound national disasters experienced by the Jewish people. Commemorated for a three-week period, it begins with the seventeenth day of the Hebrew month Tammuz and ends with the ninth day of Av, both of which have been declared fast days. The seventeenth day of Tammuz commemorates five other tragedies: the Tablets of the Law that were broken when Moses descended from Mount Sinai; the *Tamid* sacrifice brought twice daily during the First Temple period, which had to be abolished; the invasion of the city of Jerusalem; and the burning of the Torah by Apostomus the wicked[46] and his placing of an idol in the Temple. The ninth of Av commemorates the destruction of both Temples.[47]

In the Jewish tradition, tragedy is commemorated by mourning. The first to introduce laws of mourning for the loss of the Temple was Rabbi Yohanan ben Zakkai, in the first century C.E. As soon as he heard that the Temple in Jerusalem was destroyed, he rent his clothes and wept.[48] The sages divide the laws of mourning for the Temple into three progressive levels of severity: the three weeks, the week in which the ninth day of Av occurs [which Ashkenazic custom has extended to all the nine days of Av], and Tishah B'Av, the ninth day of Av itself.[49]

Two other days associated with the destruction of the Temple are also observed as fast days. In 2 Kings 25:1 we read: "Zedekiah rebelled against the kings of Babylon. And in the ninth year of his reign, on the tenth day of the tenth month [Tevet], Nebuchadnezzar [king of Babylon] moved against Jerusalem with his whole army. He besieged it; and they built towers against it all around." This was the beginning of the destruction of the Judean community and the exile of the people to Babylon. The king did not exile all the people, however. He left a remnant in Judea, which consisted, for the most part, of the poor. He appointed Gedaliah, son of Ahikam, in charge of the towns of Judea. The book of Jeremiah 41:1, 2, records the following:

> In the seventh month, Ishmael son of Nethaniah son of Elishama, who was of royal descent and one of the king's commanders, came with ten men to Gedaliah . . . at Mizpah. Then Ishmael . . . and the ten men who were with him arose and struck down Gedaliah . . . and killed him because the king of Babylon had put him in charge of the land.

In commemoration of the besiegement of Jerusalem, which led to the destruction of the First Temple, and the murder of Gedaliah, son of Ahikam, which spelled out the end of what was hoped to be the reconstruction of the Judean community, the sages declared fast days: the tenth of Tevet and the third of Tishre for the latter.

Tishah B'Av

Tishah B'Av is the day of maximum mourning. All the laws of mourning that we enumerated when we discussed Yom Kippur apply to Tishah B'Av. A glaring exception is the last meal eaten before the fast. On Yom Kippur, it is a *mitzvah* to eat heartily. On Tishah B'Av the meal is limited to a single cooked dish, usually a hard-boiled egg, the symbol of mourning.

Unlike the three other fast days that commemorate the siege of Jerusalem and the destruction of the Temple, the fast on Tishah B'Av begins at night. Following the evening service, the book of *Eikhah* ("Lamentations") is read in the synagogue. Written by the prophet Jeremiah, the book bewails the loss of the First Temple, and attributes the destruction of Jerusalem and the exile of the Judeans to Babylon to their iniquity. "Let us search and examine our ways," says Jeremiah, "and return to the Lord" (3:40). The only way to regain favor in God's eyes is to return to Him in sincere repentance. Several laments taken from a collection called *Kinot* are also read at night, the rest are read on the following morning.

Interestingly, a variety of reasons are given by the sages of the Talmud for the destruction of the Second Temple:[50] the neglect of the education of schoolchildren; the neglect of the recitation of the *Shema* morning and evening; the desecration of *Shabbat*; the lack of shame among the people and the failure to rebuke the sinners; and finally, the sin of hatred without cause.[51] Because of its potential to destroy the Jewish people from within, hatred without cause or, as we referred to it earlier, *Sin'at Hinom*, is one of the most dangerous of all sins.

The mourning period that prevails for three weeks is ushered out on the *Shabbat* that follows Tishah B'Av with words of comfort chanted in the *Haftarah* taken from the book of Isaiah, *Nahamu nahamu ami* ("comfort, O comfort My people"). Jerusalem has received of the Lord's hand double for all her sins. A period of rebirth is on the horizon, says the prophet, Israel's deliverance from exile is at hand, and with it the promise for the restoration of Jerusalem. There is a time to weep, but there is also a time to laugh.[52]

In our brief outline of the themes of the Jewish holidays and festivals, we have demonstrated the process of recollection and commemoration. Its role in Jewish tradition is to initiate a time continuum, linking the past to the present and the present to the future. Through the process of continually recalling the major events of Jewish history and the lessons we learn from them about God and His involvement in history, the past becomes relevant to both the present and the future. Every time we celebrate a Jewish holiday or festival, we are reinspired with faith in God and commitment to our sacred mission as a kingdom of priests and a holy nation. We have explained the importance of recollecting Jewish history as a means to linking the generations and reinforcing Jewish faith. We must now turn to the present, day-to-day living.

In our next session we will learn how signs and symbols, rituals and ceremonies relieve the boredom of life and contribute to make living in the present more cheerful, more interesting, and more meaningful.

Session XII
Symbols and
Ceremonies in the
Cycle of Jewish Life

As we indicated at the close of our last meeting, we will devote this session to a discussion of the cycle of Jewish life. We will follow the Jew from birth to death, and we will introduce the special ceremonies that take place in his life consecutively. As with the holidays and festivals, we will not go into full detail regarding the laws and customs of the various ceremonies. To do so would be beyond the scope of this work. Instead, we will focus on the symbolism and philosophy of these events, and the ideas they are meant to imbue within the heart and mind of the Jew.

Circumcision

A male Jew is initiated into the fold when he is eight days old, in a ritual that dates back to the time of Abraham. Abraham was ninety-nine years old when the word of God came to him, saying:

> Such shall be the covenant which you shall keep, between Me and you
> and your offspring to follow: every male among you shall be circum-
> cised. . . . At the age of eight days, every male among you throughout
> the generations shall be circumcised. . . . Thus shall My covenant be

marked in your flesh as an everlasting pact. . . . An uncircumcised male who does not circumcise the flesh of his foreskin—such a person shall be cut off from his kin; he has broken My covenant.[1]

On the very day that the word of God came to him, Abraham circumcised himself and his thirteen-year-old son Ishmael. But it was Abraham's son Isaac who was the first Jew to be circumcised on the eighth day after birth, in accordance with the biblical prescription.[2] Is there a rationale for the rite of circumcision?

To be sure! God does not burden His creations with purposeless obligations. In point of fact, were one to research the matter one would find much speculation of interest in religious as well as secular literature on the meaning and purpose of circumcision. But speculation is an activity of the human mind, an exercise in what man defines as reason. It is limited in its scope and its depth and subject to human frailties. While the possibility does exist that one may discover the true reason for a *mitzvah*, unless and until such reasons are verified by the Almighty Himself they remain in the realm of speculation.

An Eternal Covenant

Circumcision is a Divine command, and it has been designated by Jewish law as one of the 613 commandments. That fact alone establishes both its validity and its binding authority. *Mitzvot* need no human confirmation from man to establish their validity. Having said that, let us ponder the rationale offered by Rabbi Samson Raphael Hirsch for circumcision simply as an exercise in reason. As is true of most of Hirsch's explanations of the *mitzvot*, it is both interesting and timeless.[3]

The *Brit Milah* ("covenant of circumcision") was made between God and Abraham, but it was to be transmitted to the Jewish people and kept by them as an eternal covenant. How interesting it is that the name of God that appears in the biblical text is *Sha-dai* ("the Sufficing One"). It is the God Who limited the development of the world Who appears to Abraham, the Creator Who said to the world, "Enough!" Were it not for this limiting gesture, says Rabbi Hirsch, the world would have kept on evolving to this day.

"I am *E-l Sha-dai*," says God, " conduct yourself before My Presence and be perfect." I have set limits for all My creations, says God; they have no choice but to comply. Man is the only exception; having been endowed with free will, he must make the conscious choice to comply. He can and must set his own boundaries. Consequently, says God to Abraham, "Be perfect!" To be perfect, says Rabbi Hirsch, man must with free will obligate himself to the boundaries that God has set for him. It means "to take full advantage, to the full extent in every direction, of the limits which God has indicated," but never to overstep them. In essence, this is the fundamental nature of Jewish lawfulness.

> Within the elbow room which God has given us, everything, the life of our senses, too, is holy and good. In itself, nothing in man is absolutely good and nothing bad. No prohibition demands the complete killing of any tendency of our lives but only directs it to be kept within the given permitted limits.[4]

The Rationale

Judaism is not addressed merely to man's soul; it is concerned with his body as well. "The uncircumcised body does not bear the sign of submission. With cutting away the foreskin, the whole body receives the stamp of submission to the spirit carrying out the Divine law of morality," says Rabbi Hirsch. Circumcision is the symbolic expression of the *mitzvah* to be *perfect*, with which every Jew has been charged.[5] It is the obligation to limit both his body and his soul to the parameters that have been set for him by God, as revealed in the Written and the Oral Law. With the act of circumcision on the eighth day after birth, every Jewish father stamps his son with the sign of submission to God and to the laws of the Torah. He begins a program that, if carried through properly and sincerely, will in all likelihood win the commitment of his son to honor this principle of submission to God, and to the Torah as well.

Just as the Jew is different from the Gentile spiritually, so must he be different physically, says God. The sexual organ was chosen to bear the stamp of Judaism because it is the organ of procreation, the implication being that the uniqueness of the Jew must be made apparent in every generation. Now one might ask, "If the foreskin symbolizes imperfection, at least for the Jew, why was he not created without it?" Perhaps, says Rabbi Hirsch, it is to establish and firmly implant within man's mind the fundamental principle in life that no human being is born perfect. To a great extent, we are all self-made. Perfection is a goal the attainment of which is an ongoing process that begins in the cradle and ends only in the grave. God does His part, but man must contribute as well.[6]

The Obligation

The *mitzvah* of circumcision rests primarily on the father of the child.[7] If he is incapable of performing this *mitzvah*, he may appoint a *mohel* (lit., "circumciser") to perform the *mitzvah* for him. Nowadays, this is usually the case. If the child is not well, the circumcision must be postponed until he recovers and a qualified physician gives his permission to proceed with the *mitzvah*. Circumcision on schedule, however, must be performed on the eighth day even if that day is *Shabbat* or Yom Kippur. A qualified rabbinic authority must be consulted on precisely how to proceed with the arrangements. If the father fails to fulfill his obligation to circumcise his son, the burden of responsibility reverts to the son himself when he comes of age. A prospective convert to Judaism who has already been routinely circumcised by a physician need only undergo a symbolic circumcision, which consists merely in the drawing of a drop of blood.

In medieval times there was a beautiful custom practiced by Ashkenazic Jews. After the circumcision, the child was visited by ten men of the community. They would place a Bible near him and say, "May this one fulfill what is written herein."[8]

Redemption of the Firstborn

The thirty-first day is a turning point in the life of a newborn child because with the passing of thirty days, it attains viability.[9] If the child is a firstborn male to its mother, an interesting ritual is performed. It is called *Pidyon HaBen* ("redemption of the son"), and it is usually performed on the thirty-first day after birth. To understand the significance of this ritual we must turn to the Torah and recall the story of the redemption of the Israelites from Egypt.

The last of the ten plagues brought upon the Egyptians was the death of the firstborn son. To avoid this plague, the Israelites were instructed to bring a *paschal* lamb sacrifice and sprinkle some of its blood on their doorposts. Those who did so were spared. In commemoration of this manifestation of Divine mercy, the *paschal* lamb sacrifice was designated to be kept as an institution for all time. [Understandably, with the destruction of the Temple in Jerusalem, the *paschal* lamb sacrifice was terminated.] At the time, Moses was further instructed as follows:

> Consecrate to Me every firstborn; man and beast, the first issue of every womb among the Israelites is Mine. . . . You shall set apart for the Lord every first issue of the womb: every male firstling that your cattle shall drop shall be the Lord's. But every firstling ass you shall redeem with a sheep; if you do not redeem it, you must break its neck. And every firstborn male among your children you shall redeem. And when, in time to come, you son asks you, saying, "What does this mean?" you shall say to him, "It was with a mighty hand that the Lord brought us out from Egypt, the house of bondage. When Pharaoh stubbornly refused to let us go, the Lord slew every firstborn in the land of Egypt, the firstborn of both man and beast. Therefore I sacrifice to the Lord every first male issue of the womb, but redeem every firstborn among my sons."[10]

The Rationale

Rabbi Samson Raphael Hirsch offers an interesting rationale for the consecration of the firstborn son.[11] When God declared the firstborn sons of every Jewish family to belong to Him, He endowed them with special status and a special calling. They are to be God's representatives in the Jewish family. Their calling is to awaken in their family an awareness of the sacred mission with which the Jewish people were entrusted: to love God, to fulfill His commandments, and to set the example of Divine ethics and morality.

By definition, the firstborn male child spoken of here is a *peter rehem* ("one who opened the womb"), the first child carried by and born to the mother. What is implied by this commandment? "Inasmuch as this first child is born, not only for the home and family, but . . . equally for God, this makes the woman's womb, declared as being dedicated to God," says Rabbi Hirsch. "This makes all the following children, all that pass through this womb, all births, all the houses and families that are being built up in Israel, as belonging to God." What seems to be implied here is that the mother's womb itself is being consecrated. The purpose of the redemption from Egypt, therefore, is to call the entire nation of Israel into service to God.[12]

Originally, the firstborn sons were to serve Aaron, the *kohen* ("priest"), in performing sacred duties in the Tabernacle. After the sin of the golden calf, however, they were replaced by the tribe of Levi. As it is written: "I [God] hereby take the Levites from among the Israelites in place of all the firstborn, the first issue of the womb among the Israelites: the Levites shall be Mine."[13] Having lost the privilege to serve in the Tabernacle, the firstborn sons of all future generations had to be redeemed from such service by the *kohen*.[14]

The Ritual

It is the duty of a father to redeem his firstborn male child on the thirty-first day after his birth. If the thirty-first day falls on a *Shabbat*, a festival, or a holiday, the ritual is postponed till the next day. Technically, any *kohen* can be selected to perform the redemption ritual, but families tend to seek out a *kohen* who is pious and learned. The ritual is as follows:

The father presents his son to the *kohen*. He declares that the child is his firstborn. He then places five silver dollars before the *kohen*. The *kohen* asks him whether he wishes to give up his son or redeem him. The father replies that he wishes to redeem him, and he gives the money to the *kohen*. The *kohen* then returns the child to the father, who recites two blessings. The *kohen* holds the money over the child's head and affirms the exchange. He concludes the ritual with two biblical blessings.

The term "firstborn" is taken quite literally. It must be the first child, it must be male, and it must have been born to its mother through a normal birth. A firstborn male child born through Caesarean section is exempt from *Pidyon HaBen*. Firstborn sons of priests and Levites, or of daughters of priests and Levites, are likewise exempt.

Bar Mitzvah

To be a traditional Jew is to accept upon oneself the belief in God—
what is referred to as *kabbalat ol malkhut shamayim* ("the acceptance of
the yoke of the kingdom of heaven"). To commit oneself to observing
the *mitzvot* as they have been interpreted by the Oral Law and applied to their times by the sages of subsequent generations is termed
kabbalat ol mitzvot ("the acceptance of the yoke of the commandments").
Despite the all-encompassing nature of this undertaking, the Jew
never looked upon it as a burden or a hardship. Quite the contrary.
To have been worthy to receive the Torah and to have been given
the responsibility to observe it is deemed an honor and a privilege.
In light of this wholesome attitude, coming of age to the Jew is a
momentous occasion. A child is introduced to Judaism at a very young
age, but the responsibility to fulfill *mitzvot* does not begin for a male
child until he reaches the age of thirteen. A female acquires that responsibility at the age of twelve.[15] A male who has come of age is called
Bar Mitzvah; a female, Bat Mitzvah. The terms simply mean "to come
under the obligation to follow the commands."

In past generations, there was no formal ceremony or celebration
that marked the coming of age for females. Bat Mitzvah celebrations
are of recent vintage in the traditional Jewish community, and the practice has been rather slow in gaining acceptance. To date, there is no
standard ceremony that has been established to mark the coming of age
of a female, and communities differ in their preferences. Be that as it
may, it is of the utmost importance that what is done to mark this important occasion in a girl's life be in full accordance with both Jewish
law and the dignity of the synagogue.

The Ceremony

Bar Mitzvah, as a ceremony in which a male child at the age of thirteen
is called to the Torah for an *aliyah* ("Torah honor"), is already noted in
the thirteenth century. In most families, the celebration takes place at
the morning service on *Shabbat*, but it can also take place on a Monday
or Thursday morning or any day on which the Torah is read at services. The Torah blessings are most appropriate for a Bar Mitzvah.
They express thanks and appreciation to God for having been chosen

from among the nations of the world to receive the Torah, and they declare the Torah to be a document of absolute truth, which grants its adherents eternal life. There are other functions that a boy marking his Bar Mitzvah may perform during the service, but these depend upon his knowledge and educational background, as well as his ability to master the liturgical chants.

The *Mitzvah* of *Tefillen*

When a Jewish boy reaches the age of thirteen, he begins to don *tefillen*. The *tefillen* are two cube-shaped containers made from the hides of kosher animals to which leather straps are attached so that they can be worn like a crown on the head and bound on the arm. They hold parchments upon which verses from Exodus 13:1–10, 11–16, Deuteronomy 6:4–9, and 11:13–21 are written. *Tefillen* are worn during the weekday morning services. In the *tefillah* that is worn on the arm, all four excerpts are written on one parchment, which is placed in its single compartment. In the *tefillah* worn on the head, however, all four excerpts are written on separate pieces of parchment and placed in its four compartments. The source for the *mitzvah* of *tefillen* is Deuteronomy 6:5–8, which reads:

> You must love the Lord your God with all your heart and with all your soul and with all your might. Take to heart these words with which I charge you this day. Impress them upon your children. Recite them when you stay at home and when you are away, when you lie down and when you get up. Bind them as a sign on your hand and let them serve as a symbol in the center of your head. . . .

In Exodus 13:9 the following reason is given for this *mitzvah*. "And this shall serve you as a sign on your hand and as a reminder in the center of your head—in order that the teachings of the Lord may be in your mouth—that with a mighty hand the Lord freed you from Egypt." The *mitzvah* of *tefillen* is rich in symbolism, and it behooves us to discuss some of these ideas. We have already mentioned that the redemption from Egypt is one of the greatest miracles that happened to the Jewish people as a nation. It is not enough that we recollect and commemorate the redemption once a year on the festival of Pesah. The

Torah charges us " . . . so that you may remember the day of your departure from the land of Egypt all the days of your life." The sages interpreted this to mean: the days as well as the nights, in this world and in the Messianic Era.[16] How then do we fulfill this obligation?

The *tefillen* serve as a daily reminder of the redemption.[17] They are placed on the arm, which represents man's physical power, and on the head, which represents his intellectual abilities. This is to remind man that his entire being should be dedicated to God, to heeding His word as expressed in the Torah through the 613 commandments. Finally, the *tefillen* are meant to help resolve the ongoing conflict between the body and the soul. The body demands gratification, and the soul attempts to temper these demands. The *tefillen* remind us of our responsibility to obey God's commandments in appreciation for His concern and unbounding mercy. As such, they support the efforts of the soul.[18]

The *tefillen* are one of the Jew's most cherished possessions; they are a sign of the eternal bond between God and Israel. The Talmud adds something more. In Deuteronomy 28:10 we read: "And all the people of the earth shall see that the Lord's name is proclaimed over you, and they shall stand in fear of you." Rabbi Eliezer the Great says, "This refers to the *tefillah* of the head."[19] In past generations, Jews wore *tefillen* all day long, removing them only at night. They became the emblem of the Jew. In later times, wearing *tefillen* all day became problematic, and the rabbinic authorities ruled that one fulfills his obligation by wearing the *tefillen* during morning services.

The Power of Responsibility

There is no question that in our society a boy at the age of thirteen and a girl at the age of twelve are still children, far from ready to assume adult responsibilities. They want the independence that comes with adulthood, but are not yet ready to handle it. Regrettably, in the American culture teenagers are given a great deal of freedom but very little responsibility. Society has paid a heavy price for this indulgence. Be that as it may, Judaism tells teenagers who are Bar and Bat Mitzvah that they are now responsible Jews, no less obligated to fulfill the *mitzvot* than their parents. At this tender age, such an obligation does wonders for their ego. Most Jewish teenagers who are raised in observant homes and have been given a good Jewish education take this responsibility very seriously. They become meticulously observant of Jewish law for two reasons: first, because well-educated and well-mannered young people are idealistic almost by definition; second, because commitment to an ideal makes them feel grown up. If the obligations to Judaism that begin with Bar and Bat Mitzvah are taken seriously, they can have a considerable effect in easing the tension between parents and children in the turbulent transitional years between childhood and adulthood. Society at large would do well to learn from this example of true Jewish power.

Marriage

Human beings are gregarious creatures; they need others with whom to communicate and with whom to share their experiences in life. In the company of others, they flourish; alone, the routines of life, even life's adventures, tend to become depressing and boring. A good marriage meets the need for companionship, and fulfills the desire of most people for that measure of immortality that can be attained through children. It enhances life's moments of happiness and eases the pain when tragedy strikes. It helps to overcome the blight of boredom and prevents the onset of loneliness. A bad marriage, on the other hand, is a living horror for all who are involved. It wrecks the lives of husband, wife, and children. It even leaves its mark on in-laws and grandparents, though they are only peripherally involved. All too often, the painful scars that are incurred during the period of conflict persist and cause anguish and aggravation even after the legal bond that held the family together has been severed through divorce. Suffice it to say that marriage is clearly the most important step one takes in life. It demands very careful consideration.

The Marriage Ceremony

We have already discussed the significance of a Jewish marriage at a previous session. We will limit today's discussion to the marriage ceremony, its laws, and its symbolism.[20]

Originally, a Jewish marriage was a two-step process that consisted of *erusin* ("betrothal") and *nesuin* ("marriage"). Jewish betrothal resembles what in today's society is called "engagement," in that it is an understanding between the parties and their immediate families that a marriage will take place on a mutually agreed-upon date. But it differs categorically from engagement, in terms of the status of the potential bride and groom once the betrothal has been finalized.

Erusin is completed when the man puts the marriage ring on the woman's finger, declares her to be his bride, and she accepts. (This ritual is also called *kiddushin* ["sanctification"].) With this gesture he assumes the status of a married man and she that of a married woman. It is important to note that notwithstanding the fact that as individuals they have at this point assumed marital status, they are not yet married to *each other*, which means that they are not permitted to live together as husband and wife.[21] It should also be noted that should they want to break the betrothal, a *get* ("Jewish divorce") must be issued.

Nesuin, the second step in the process of marriage, is consummated either through sexual relations, or what is termed *hupah*, which for all intents and purposes means "acting in a way that demonstrates unequivocally that the couple are husband and wife."[22] In about the fifteenth century it became generally accepted that the two-step process of *erusin* and *nesuin* be combined into a single wedding ceremony.[23]

The wedding day is a solemn occasion; it should not be marked by frivolity. As a gesture of repentance, it is customary for the bride and groom to fast on this day and to pray that they may be spared any serious problems in their marriage.[24] Our sages tell us that God in turn also makes a gesture, so to speak. In light of the fact that the bride and groom are sincere in their repentance and are beginning a new life, He forgives all their sins. In the *Amidah* of *Minhah*, the afternoon service that the bride and groom recite, they insert *Anenu* ("Answer us"), the special prayer of petition said on fast days, and they append the Yom Kippur confessional.

It is of the utmost importance that the bride and groom be fully aware of the legal procedures that take place before and during the marriage ceremony so that with free will they take upon themselves all the obligations that come with marriage. This is another reason why the bride and groom fast until after the wedding ceremony: it keeps them from inadvertently becoming intoxicated.

The Ketubah

A very important legal procedure takes place before the wedding ceremony—the writing and witnessing of the *ketubah* ("marriage contract"). As a legal document, the *ketubah* must be dated correctly, worded properly, and all names and places must be spelled correctly. In this document the groom declares that he will support his wife and meet all the obligations Jewish law requires of him as a husband. He must be fully aware of what is in the contract, and he must indicate his awareness before two proper witnesses who subsequently sign the document. In some communities it is customary for the groom to sign the *ketubah* as well. At the conclusion of the wedding ceremony, the groom will give the *ketubah* to his wife, who will retain it throughout the marriage. Without the *ketubah* the couple may not live together.

The Veiling Ceremony

Before the wedding processional, a little ceremony takes place in the presence of the assembly. Accompanied by his father and the father of the bride as well as other guests, to the sound of joyous music, singing, and dancing, the groom is led from the reception room to the main hall where the bride is seated. Upon arrival, he veils her face. Among several explanations given for this gesture, one suggests that this is done to indicate that it is the bride's spiritual qualities rather than her physical beauty that is the groom's primary interest.

After the veiling ceremony, it is customary for the bride to be blessed with the words in Genesis 24:60 spoken to Rebecca, the second matriarch of the Jewish people: "Our sister, may you grow into thousands of myriads."

Wearing White

In early times, it was customary for both the bride and the groom to wear white on their wedding day. All their sins having been forgiven, it symbolizes spiritual purity. Nowadays, the bride still wears white, but the groom dons a white robe called a *kittel* for the wedding ceremony, which he wears over his suit. The *kittel* is also a shroud. It reminds the groom of his mortality, a sobering experience that should keep him from sin. Lastly, white is also known as the color of royalty. It is most appropriate for the bride and groom, for on this day they are regarded as royalty. As they march down the aisle, all the guests rise in respect before them.

Hupah

The bride and groom are led to the *hupah* ("canopy"), under which they stand for the wedding ceremony. In its simplest form, the *hupah* is a piece of cloth held up by four poles. It is symbolic of the home in which they will be united.[25] Our sages found many other beautiful ideas symbolized by the *hupah*. It is reminiscent of the marriage of Adam and Eve in the Garden of Eden, for God had created ten canopies for them.[26] At Sinai, a symbolic marriage was initiated between God and the people of Israel. The *hupah* is reminiscent of the mountain that God held over them at the time. Last, the *hupah* represents the "clouds of glory" that covered the Israelites in their journey through the wilderness. As the clouds symbolized God's protection of the Israelites, the *hupah* symbolizes His protection of the newly married couple.

The groom is the first to be led to the *hupah*; the bride follows. When the bride reaches the *hupah*, she encircles the groom seven times. Many explanations are given for this custom. A most interesting one is offered by the late Rabbi Aryeh Kaplan, who writes:

> The seven circuits represent the seven revolutions that the earth made during the seven days of creation. The earth is represented by the woman ("mother earth"). Since every marriage is a re-enactment of the creative process, she walks around the groom to indicate that these seven cycles are now being repeated.[27]

The Ring

As we already mentioned, the process of *erusin* is completed when the groom gives the bride a ring. This act is introduced with the blessing recited over wine, thanking God for creating the fruit of the vine, followed by *Birkhat Erusin* ("Prenuptial Blessing"), which states the fundamental difference between betrothal and marriage: the former is when marital relations are prohibited, the latter is when they are permissible.

After both the bride and the groom have tasted the wine, the *kiddushin* ("sanctification") takes place.

The giving of the ring must be appropriately witnessed. This means that the witnesses must be Jewish males who are observant of Jewish law and above the age of thirteen, who are not in any way related to each other, to the bride, or to the groom. They should be officially designated for this purpose to the exclusion of everyone else present. Having indicated that the ring belongs to him, the groom places it on the index finger of the bride's right hand and recites the words, "With this ring you are wedded unto me in accordance with the law of Moses and Israel." The *ketubah* is then read aloud, after which the groom gives it to the bride, to whom it now belongs, for safekeeping.

The Seven Blessings

Over a second cup of wine, the *Birkhot Nesuin*, the seven "marriage blessings," are now recited. Although it is permissible for one person to recite all seven blessings, it is customary to distribute the honor among several people. The first blessing is the one recited over wine; the second affirms that all things were created for God's glory. The third blessing thanks God for the creation of man; the fourth, for creating human beings in the image of God and for creating "woman," through which the species can be propagated. The fifth blessing is for Jerusalem, who rejoices in her children; the sixth invokes God to bring joy to the new couple as He had done for Adam and Eve in the garden of old. The seventh blessing acknowledges God as the creator of joy and gladness, mirth and exultation, pleasure and delight, love, brotherhood, peace, and fellowship. Turning again to Jerusalem, it beseeches God to infuse the cities of Judah and the streets of Jerusalem with the sound of the rejoicing of brides and grooms.

Following the seven blessings, husband and wife drink from the cup of wine. They are now legally married. It is the happiest moment of their lives, the height of joy, and it is at that point that the groom breaks a glass. Different reasons are given for this age-old custom. Some say it is to remind those assembled of the destruction of the Temple in Jerusalem;[28] others, the broken Tablets of the Law.[29] Perhaps it symbolizes human mortality, for like the shattered glass, every life will one day be shattered.[30] Whatever the symbolism, the effect is the same. Our joy is tempered with a little sadness, a measure of reality. We pause . . . a brief moment of silence to reflect on life.

The marriage ceremony is over. To the shouts of *mazal tov*, and the accompaniment of joyous music, singing, and dancing, husband and wife leave the *hupah* and proceed to a special room for *yihud*, a few moments of privacy. How fitting a conclusion to a sacred ceremony!

Death and Mourning

There are four fundamental principles that are of major consideration in the Jewish laws of mourning: two of them apply to the deceased, the other two to the mourner. The first principle is that the human body is sacred. As it must be treated with dignity in life, so must it be treated in death, and as we shall see, the laws of burial amply demonstrate this principle. The second principle is to honor the departed soul and perpetuate his or her memory. This commences with the eulogy given at the funeral and is complemented by the laws of *yahrzeit* and *Yizkor*. The third principle is to provide a setting that will allow the mourner to freely vent his feelings while offering him consolation to ease his pain. This need is met by the laws of *shivah*, the first stage in the mourning process. The last principle is to set limitations on the obligatory grief of the mourner, gradually leading him back to a normal life. This is brought about by the laws of *sheloshim* ("thirty-day period"), and for those who mourn parents, an additional eleven-month period.

Before the Burial

In other than extenuating circumstances, Jewish law mandates that the body of the deceased be interred on the day of death. To delay interment is to degrade the human body and to contaminate the environment. Until the interment, the body must never be alone. A special person called a *shomer* ("watchman") is appointed to the task of being with the body of the deceased. Engaged in the performance of a *mitzvah*, the *shomer* is exempt from all *mitzvot* until he is relieved from his obligation. In recognition of the fact that the deceased was once alive, a creature created in the image of God and endowed with a soul, he must be treated with the utmost respect.[31] Consequently, the ritual of preparation for interment called *taharah* ("purification") must be done with the highest regard for the laws of modesty. The law mandates that the body be washed, and the procedure must be done in a designated sequence. The body must be kept covered exposing only those parts that are being washed. At different points in the *taharah*, chapters from the book of Psalms are read. When the *taharah* is concluded, the body is clothed with special linen shrouds. This, too, must follow a designated sequence. Where the deceased is male, he is enwrapped in a *tallit*, which is placed over the shroud. Finally, the body is placed in the coffin, and the coffin is closed. It must never again be opened.

The Laws of Mourning

Some of the laws of mourning are based on customs that date back to biblical times. In Genesis 23:2 we read that Abraham mourned for Sarah and eulogized her. In Genesis 37:34 we read that Jacob rent his clothes, and in the following verse we read that his sons and daughters came to comfort him. In Genesis 50:10 we read that Joseph observed a seven-day mourning period for his father Jacob, and in Deuteronomy 34:8 we read that the children of Israel mourned Moses for thirty days. The Prophets and the Writings mention other customs. From 2 Samuel we learn that mourners wore special garments, and from Ezekiel 24:17 that they removed their shoes and were offered a meal of condolence.

Aninut: *The First Stage*

As we have already indicated, the mourning process consists of several stages: *aninut* marks the initial period. It begins when the mourner first becomes aware of the death of his kin,[32] and it ends with interment. In order to enable him to concentrate on his responsibilities, that is, the preparation of the body for interment and the funeral arrangements, the mourner, who is called an *onan* at this stage, is exempt from many but not all positive *mitzvot*.[33] For example, he is forbidden to partake of a festive meal, eat meat, or drink wine. On *Shabbat*, however, these laws are canceled. He may not bathe for pleasure, shave, or take a haircut. He may not conduct business or even study Torah. On Sukkot, he is not obligated to sit in the *sukkah*. On the first night of Pesah, however, he should observe all the *mitzvot* of the *seder*, and on Purim, he must hear the reading of the *Megillah*.

Even in a situation where the mourner is not directly involved in arranging the funeral—the preparation of the body is done by a specially trained group of men or women and everything else that need be done is taken care of by another member of the family—the laws of *aninut* apply. As long as the mourner can potentially become involved at some point, he is considered an *onan* until the interment takes place.

Keriah ("rending of the garment") is an expression of anguish, and an opportunity for the mourner to vent his feelings of pain and anger. It may be performed by the mourner either at the moment he hears of the death, at the chapel prior to the service, or at the cemetery before the interment. Where the deceased is a parent, *keriah* is done on the left side of the garment; for other relatives, it is done on the right side. How insightful were the sages, who ordained that the mourner recite the following blessing before performing the act: "You are blessed, O Lord, our God, King of the universe, the true Judge."

There is no finality like the finality of death, and there is no goal pursued with greater vigor and no triumph more sought after than the conquest of death. Accordingly, there is no shock more traumatic than the moment one hears of the loss of a parent, a spouse, a sibling, or a child. Upon impact, the experience shatters a person's peace of mind, often plummeting him into the depths of despair. He weeps and cries out in pain: "How could this have happened?" Despair breeds anger, and anger generates the ungodly notion that there is no justice in the world, and there is no Judge. At that moment the *Halakhah* steps in and mandates that the mourner proclaim before all but, most important, to himself that there is a Judge and there is justice in the world. Despite his pain and perhaps because of it, he turns to God with the words: "You are blessed, O Lord, our God, King of the universe, the true Judge."

Shivah: *The Second Stage*

The second stage of mourning is called *shivah* ("seven"). It is a seven-day period commencing with the interment of the deceased. It is customary that when the mourner returns from the cemetery that his first meal, the "condolence meal," be provided by friends. The meal consists of bread and hard-boiled eggs. The round shape of the egg represents the recurring cycle of nature and alludes to the resurrection of the dead sometime in the future, which is a fundamental principle in Jewish tradition. For the mourner, to be reminded of this principle in his bereavement helps to ease his pain.

Shivah is divided into two parts. The first three days are designated in the Talmud as the "three days of weeping."[34] The shock and the pain still lingering, the wound still fresh, Jewish law mandates that communication with the mourner be kept to a minimum. He does not respond to greetings nor does he engage in the normal amenities of life such as bathing, shaving, grooming, wearing leather shoes, or donning freshly laundered garments. Consolation visits by friends and relatives are discouraged during the first three days. Seated on a low stool that reflects his depressed state, clothed in his rent garment, the mourner is left to himself to meditate and to lament his loss.

On the fourth day, the process of healing is initiated, and the mourner is encouraged to begin to interact with society. Consolation visits that allow him to reminisce somewhat about the life of the deceased and to express his feelings among friends and relatives are an important first step in the gradual process of healing and the effort to bring him back into the normal routine of day to day living.

Sheloshim: *The Third Stage*

The third stage of mourning is called *sheloshim* ("thirty") and indicates a thirty-day period from the day of interment. The laws of *sheloshim* begin after *shivah*. With the exception of the prohibition against participating in pleasurable events such as weddings, parties, and taking a haircut, the restrictions upon the mourner are lifted, and he is encouraged to get back into his daily routine.

For those who mourn parents, the prohibition against participating in pleasurable events is extended for the balance of the year. This extension is not a matter of mourning; it is a gesture of honor and respect.

Kaddish

For the entire mourning period it is obligatory for the mourner to recite the *Kaddish* at services. If he is capable of leading the service, he should do so as well. During the *shivah* period a quorum, or *minyan*, is usually arranged in the mourner's home, but after *shivah* he should attend the synagogue services daily to fulfill these obligations. The *Kaddish* is not a memorial prayer; it is a litany in praise of God. Originally composed to separate parts of the service, the *Kaddish* is recited responsively by the cantor and the congregation. Given its meaning and function, one might justifiably ask, "What relevance does the *Kaddish* have to the mourner?"

As we have already pointed out, the death of a dear one is the ultimate tragedy to the one who mourns. He is despondent and tends to conjure up thoughts of life as being a hopeless struggle in a meaningless universe. It is precisely at such times that he must reaffirm in his mind that God exists, that He is good, and that His ways, though often imponderable, are ultimately just. As such, the *Kaddish* serves a purpose similar to the blessing recited before *keriah*.

Yahrzeit

Time usually heals all wounds, but the lives of our dearly departed loved ones must never be forgotten. Jewish law mandates that the memory of the deceased be honored on the *yahrzeit* ("anniversary") of his death. The mourner does so by leading the services in the synagogue on that day if he is capable of doing so, reciting the *Kaddish*, and, if it falls on a day when the Torah is read, being called up for a Torah honor. Some have a custom of fasting on that day. It is also customary to give charity in honor of the departed soul and to light a candle for him at home, in recognition of Proverbs 20:27, which reads, "The soul of man is the lamp of the Lord."

Yizkor

Among Ashkenazic Jews a special memorial prayer for the dead called *Yizkor* ("may He remember") is recited on the last day of the pilgrimage festivals (Pesah, Shavuot, Sukkot) and on Yom Kippur. The prayer was introduced into the Ashkenazic rite in the latter half of the sixteenth century.[35] It is a plea to God that He remember the departed souls who have passed to their eternal home and in whose memory the family pledges charity. We pray that their souls be bound in the bond of life together with the souls of the righteous.

What are the notions that inspired this prayer? First and foremost, we recall the souls of our departed parents and relatives with the hope that their virtues will earn them peace in the hereafter. If they have sinned, we pray that in merit of our charity God will forgive them and grant them peace. For in Proverbs 10:2 King Solomon wrote: "Charity will deliver from death." According to the Talmud, charity saves the soul from punishment in Hell.[36] At the same time we harbor the hope that the virtues of the departed may work in our behalf, so that in their merit God will favor us and grant us long life and contentment.

The laws of mourning betray the profound insight our sages had into the workings of the human personality, for they understood where man's vulnerability lies and how to keep him from succumbing to despair.

With the laws of death and mourning, we have completed our survey of the cycle of Jewish life. It is obvious that we have merely touched the surface on these matters, but as you will recall, our purpose was merely to present and explain the rationale behind the various customs and ceremonies with the hope that doing so would engender a sincere appreciation of their value and whet the appetite for further study. It is my sincere conviction that to do so will prove not only intellectually rewarding but spiritually satisfying as well.

At our next session we will discuss what is perhaps the most difficult topic of all—the theodicy, in other words, why God is often silent to the suffering of the righteous and the good fortune of the wicked.

Session XIII
The Theodicy:
Where Was God?

I have waited until now to approach the topic of the theodicy—that is, why God is silent and allows evil to exist in the world—not because it is a very sensitive one and extremely difficult to handle, though it is, nor because the problem defies a definitive answer, though it does. I waited until now because I wanted you first to acquire some knowledge of the fundamentals of Judaism. I wanted you to appreciate the Jewish approach to God and the proofs of God's existence, and I wanted you to concur with me on the credibility of Jewish tradition. I wanted to enlighten you as to the role of ethics and morality in the Jewish weltanschauung, and to introduce you to the sophisticated system of Jewish law. I wanted you to understand the meaning of the chosenness of the Jewish people, and the way Jewish law treats the Gentile.

I had hoped that the knowledge you would gain through these sessions would dispel some of the arrogance and anger I heard in your voice the first time we met, and I had faith that the sessions we spent together would engender within your heart and mind a sincere respect for the ideas and the ideals of Torah-true Judaism. Most important, I wanted you to begin to understand where man stands in the Divine scheme of things, for, as we shall see, it is not God but man who is the central figure in the theodicy.

The Silence of God

Let us begin with the prophet Jeremiah, who complained to God with the following words:

> You will win, O Lord, if I make claim against you, yet I shall present charges against You: Why does the way of the wicked prosper? Why are the workers of treachery at ease? You have planted them, and they have taken root, they spread, they even bear fruit. . . . You are present in their mouths, but far from their thoughts.[1]

Jeremiah speaks from experience, and his words do not surprise us. Every human being is confronted with the dilemma of the theodicy at some junction in his life, whether it is from personal experience or from contemplation of the realities of existence. It is a dilemma that staggers the mind. In our hearts we believe with perfect faith in a beneficent God Who rewards the righteous and punishes the wicked, but life experience teaches us that all too often the wicked prosper and the righteous suffer. From earliest times man has struggled with this dilemma, and it remains unresolved until today.

When Adam and Eve witnessed the lifeless body of their son Abel lying in the field, were they not consumed by this dilemma? Was it not Abraham who turned to God with the words, "Far be it from You to do such a thing, to bring death upon the innocent as well as the guilty, so that the innocent and the guilty fare alike . . . Shall not the Judge of all the earth deal justly?"[2]

Where was God in the eleventh and twelfth centuries during the Crusades, when thousands of innocent Jews were murdered by Christians marching through Europe on their way to Jerusalem? Where was God during the blood libels, when Jews were falsely accused of using Christian blood in their Passover rituals? Where was God during the inquisitions against the Jews of Spain, Portugal, Netherlands, and Italy? Where was God during the pogroms against the Jews of Europe? And finally, where was God during the Holocaust of European Jewry, when six million innocent men, women, and children were herded into cattle cars and brought to concentration camps and forced to live in conditions unfit for animals until they were finally sent to the gas chambers where they were brutally murdered? The horrors suffered by innocent

Jews through the centuries seem to be interminable. Indeed, why would a beneficent God allow these things to happen?

For those who fault God for the existence of evil yet insist on maintaining the belief in Divine beneficence, an acceptable rationale is still forthcoming. Through the centuries, thinkers of all persuasions have offered theories, but the fruits of reason have proved disappointing. Shall we conclude from this that the matter must remain in the realm of the imponderable? Perhaps! Nonetheless, we will offer some food for thought.

Approaches in the Book of Job

The Book of Job is included among the "Writings" of the Bible. Job, the main character of the book, might well have been considered "the man who has everything." Blessed with health, wealth, a devoted wife, and a family of seven sons and three daughters, Job, a righteous man, lived a contented life. Suddenly, he loses everything. His wealth is taken away, his children are killed, and he is afflicted with a terrible disease. Only his wife remains to comfort him. The trauma of his destiny overwhelms him, and he sits on the ground among the ashes, mourning for his children and lamenting his life. He is embittered, and he curses the day on which he was born. Three friends come from afar to console him. They sit with him among the ashes. For seven days and seven nights they sit in silence. Eventually, each of Job's friends offers a rationale for the tragedy that has befallen him. Thus, the author presents us with three theories on the matter of why the righteous suffer.

The Argument of Eliphaz

The first speaker is Eliphaz. His experience has taught him that no man suffers unless he has sinned. "As I have seen, those who plow evil and sow mischief will reap them,"[3] says Eliphaz. For the most part, God rewards the righteous and punishes the wicked. But in those instances when a truly righteous person suffers, it is to punish him for the few sins that he has committed in this world, for no man is so perfect that he has never sinned. He is punished in this world so that he may enter the hereafter in perfect righteousness. Man is not determined by God. Limited, yes, but he does have some freedom of choice. Be that as it may, Divine retribution is confined to that which is in man's control, says Eliphaz.

The Argument of Bildad

Bildad, the second speaker, reiterates the position of Eliphaz that God is just and man is free. His point of departure concerns the suffering of the righteous. There are times when the righteous suffer, says Bildad, but rather than it being to their detriment it is to their benefit. For in this way God can reward them in the hereafter in measure far above that which they have earned for their righteousness. This is implied in Bildad's statement in Job 8:6–7: "If you are blameless and upright He will protect you, and grant well-being to your righteous home. Though your beginning be small, in the end you will grow very great." In the Talmud this notion is referred to as "chastisement of love."

> If a man sees that painful suffering comes upon him, let him examine his conduct. . . . If he examines and finds nothing [objectionable], let him attribute it to the neglect of the study of Torah. . . . If he did attribute it [thus], and still did not find [this to be the cause], let him be sure that this is chastisement of love.[4]

Divine retribution comes upon man for one of two reasons, says the Talmud: either his conduct toward God and toward man is objectionable or he has neglected the *mitzvah* of Torah study. If neither of these failings apply to him, he should consider his suffering to be "chastisement of love." Rashi explains the notion as follows: "The Holy One, blessed be He, afflicts him with suffering in this world though he has committed no sin, in order to compensate him in the next world over and above his merits."

The Argument of Zophar

The third theory comes from Zophar. He focuses on perception, and differentiates between that which is perceived by God and that which is perceived by man. Zophar's theory is implied in the words, "But would that God might speak, and talk to you Himself. He would tell you the secrets of wisdom, for there are many sides to sagacity. . . . "[5] There is objective reality and subjective reality, says Zophar. God alone knows things objectively, that is, as they really are. Man's perception of reality, his judgment of his fellow man in particular, is highly subjective. Man never knows things as they really are. He cannot possibly know for a certainty who is so wicked that he deserves severe punishment and who is so righteous that he deserves only reward.[6] Besides, man's understanding of things is continually being modified as he discovers more and more about the nature of man and the parameters of human freedom of will. His understanding of himself is limited and continually being revised in his mind, all the more so his understanding of his fellow man.

Zophar makes another significant point. In order to determine whether an individual is righteous and worthy of reward or a sinner deserving punishment, his accomplishments must be carefully weighed against his potential. This is humanly impossible. Can any human being know his own potential definitively, let alone the potential of another human being? Only God knows the potential of every human being, and He alone is privy to man's innermost thoughts and deeds. God is the only true Judge of righteousness and wickedness; only He can mete out proper reward or punishment.

The Argument of Elihu

The fourth speaker is Elihu.[7] Focusing on man rather than God in his approach to the theodicy, Elihu posits that God is the Master of the universe Who is in complete control of all that exists, and he insists that for all intents and purposes man is master of his own destiny. Man has been given the intellectual ability and the free will to create a good and amiable society. He has been charged by God to subdue the earth and have dominion over all its inhabitants. This means that when he witnesses man's inhumanity to man, he must take definitive action; it is his responsibility to uproot wickedness and stem the tide of evil wherever and whenever it manifests itself. If he does not meet his responsibility, the consequences he suffers are due to his own negligence. For man's righteousness and his wickedness affect only himself and his fellow man; they have no effect on God. Mark Elihu's words in Job 36:6–7: "If you sin, what do you do to Him? If you are righteous, what do you give Him; what does He receive from your hand? Your wickedness affects men like yourself; your righteousness, mortals." Elihu "pulls no punches." His argument makes good sense, and though it does not resolve all the difficulties posed by the theodicy, it is well worth pondering.

A Proper Perspective

I believe that the blame for the evil that exists in the world has been misdirected. It was not God Who killed Abel; it was Cain. It was not God Who caused Sodom and Gemorrah to be destroyed; it was the people, the wicked and those who stood by and tolerated their wickedness. It was not God Who led the Crusaders or Who concocted the libelous blood accusations during the Middle Ages; it was the work of evil men. It is not God Who is to blame for the Holocaust of European Jewry, but the Nazi murderers and the German people who cooperated with them, as well as those who were silent witnesses to the corruption and evil in their midst. Man's perennial question, "Where was God?" should really be "Where was man?"

The Torah teaches that man has been endowed with a spark of the Divine. In Genesis 1:27 we read: "And God created man in His image, in the image of God He created him. . . ." Our sages teach us that the image of God refers to man's ability to reason and his freedom of will.[8] It was on this basis that man was charged to subdue the earth and have dominion over all its creatures. Man is, indeed, God's representative on earth. He must live up to his responsibilities or suffer the consequences.

In Deuteronomy 11:26 and 30:19–20, the people of Israel were given an additional charge.

> See this day I set before you blessing and curse: the blessing if you obey the commandments of the Lord your God which I enjoin upon you this day; and the curse, if you do not obey the commandments of the Lord your God but turn away from the path which I enjoin upon you this day. . . .
>
> I call heaven and earth to witness against you this day: I have put before you life and death, blessing and curse. Choose life—if you and your offspring would live—by loving the Lord your God, heeding His commands and holding fast to Him.

For our purposes, the key words here are "choose life." We have already pointed out that the Torah way of "life" is meant to bring man to intellectual and moral perfection, to maintain harmony in the family, and to promote peace among the nations. God could have programmed man to do only good, to be ethical and moral and create the most perfect of all worlds. However, this was not the Divine Will. God wanted man to *choose* the ethical and moral way of life so he endowed him with a spark of the Divine, a measure of free will. But free will, by definition, means the ability to choose *either* good *or* evil. Both paths must be open to man. The promise is that the choice of good would bring on "the blessing," that is, Divine reward; the choice of evil would bring on "the curse," that is, Divine punishment, but the choice is left to man. This would all be fine and proper were it not for the fact that all too often experience belies the promise: the righteous are not always rewarded and the wicked are not always punished. Why must this be?

Evil must be a viable option if freedom of choice is to have any meaning. If evil offered no benefits to man, there would be no temptation and, consequently, no choice. Everyone would follow the word of God. In point of fact, the terms *good* and *evil* only have meaning when they can be contrasted to each other. In a world where there is no choice but to do God's bidding, the terms *good* and *evil* are meaningless. History clearly testifies to the fact that evil has always been a viable option for man. Were this not the case, man would never have been charged by God to "choose" life.

The propensity to submit to the temptations of evil differs from individual to individual, from society to society, and from generation to generation. It is to a great extent subject to psychological and sociological factors. But if precedent and experience are to any extent reliable on this matter, it is safe to say that in a given generation there will always be some who choose the path of evil. Consequently, unless there is a fundamental change in society affecting the way people think and behave, there will always be "man-induced" evil in the world.

Why the Wicked Prosper

Let us now turn to the matter of the prosperity of the wicked. King David wrote: "How long shall the wicked, O Lord, how long shall the wicked exult? They bluster, they speak arrogantly; all the evildoers act boastfully . . . You fools, when will you understand? He who sets the ear, will He not hear . . . He who punishes the wicked, will He not punish you?"[9] And again: "When the lawless spring up as the grass where all the abusers of might flourish it is so that they may be destroyed forever."[10]

Addressing the wicked leaders of society, termed here the "abusers of might," King David predicts their future. Evil breeds evil and will eventually result in self-inflicted punishment to the wicked. By using their power for selfish gain, the wicked leaders of the world set the example for the rest of society, who follow suit. As Rabbi S. R. Hirsch explains:

> If the leaders of human society demonstrate by their own evil example how power can be used for selfish gain, and that the motive which guides the acts of men is not the standard of moral worth but the measure of the possibility of success, the result will be the spread of contempt for everything that is morally good. . . . even the mightiest man will perish . . . for as a result of the demoralization which he himself will have spread among his fellows, he will eventually find no man whom he himself can really trust.[11]

This is equally true of corrupt societies: they produce wicked leaders who persecute the masses from whom they are chosen. Seen from this perspective, there is no need for direct Divine intervention because wickedness will eventually expunge itself.[12]

We have already explained that so long as man is free, there will always be individuals who choose the way of evil. The human heart cries out that in order to save the innocent the evildoers should be punished instantly, but logic insists that in order to maintain human freedom, the wicked must be allowed to act on their choice. Consequently, there have always been and perhaps always will be innocent people who suffer. There have always been those who are plundered by thieves, rapists, and murderers, and there have always been wars that bring casualties suffered by innocent men, women, and children. Such is the nature of society.

Nevertheless, history has taught us that there are times when God intervenes with human freedom, and He prevents man from actualizing his plans. The Torah tells us that God hardened the heart of Pharaoh, preventing him from releasing the Israelites from bondage, so that he would receive punishment appropriate to his crimes.[13] God withheld freedom of choice from Balaam, preventing him from cursing the Israelites, by changing his curses to blessings.[14] But these are rare occasions. Man is not privy to the Divine plan for the world. The where and when of Divine intervention is beyond human understanding.

Be that as it may, for the most part God does not interfere with man's freedom. The creation of the good society is man's responsibility. He is duty-bound to elect and maintain honest government officials who will uproot corruption and see to it that the wicked are punished. The world rests on man's shoulders, and just as man must be praised for the good he engenders in the world, so must he be faulted for the evil.

All this notwithstanding, it is eminently clear that some human suffering in this world is not the result of evil perpetrated by man against his fellow man, and we must define and address evil of this sort as well. Earthquakes, tornados, tidal waves, and volcanos that destroy property and leave the dead and the maimed in their wake are clearly not the result of man's inhumanity to man. Surely, man cannot be faulted for such tragedies as the birth of handicapped children. Would not the question "Where was God?" be appropriate in these instances?

Of course, there are those who would declare these matters imponderable and designate them as subjects that are beyond human comprehension, recalling the words of Isaiah 55:8: "For My thoughts are not your thoughts, neither are My ways your ways, declares the Lord." This approach does not resolve the issue, but who is to say that the pursuit of a rationale for such clearly unverifiable matters is worthwhile? Who knows whether God's "reasoning" on these matters is even comprehensible to man, that is, whether it is within the scope of man's limited intelligence? For that matter, who is to say that God's "thinking" must in any way conform to the principles of human reason? Consequently, those who take the position of silence on these matters are certainly not to be faulted. Nevertheless, I would be remiss if I did not bring to your attention the thinking of Rabbi Dr. Eliezer Berkovits, the philosopher par excellence whom we have quoted many times in our discussions, for his ideas on this matter are well worth pondering.[15]

The Suffering of the Innocent

God created an awesome and very beautiful world, in many ways a
Garden of Eden on the planet Earth. A human lifetime is much too
short, indeed, to partake of all the beauties of nature. At the same time
we must recognize that there are aspects of the natural world that
are not at all considerate of man, or for that matter any other living
creature. We already mentioned earthquakes, tornados, and tidal
waves that wreak havoc with the world and seem to be governed by
principles that are irrelevant to man. We must see these things as im-
perfections in nature, says Berkovits, and if we equate imperfection
with evil, the imperfection of nature is a clear manifestation of evil in
the world (at least from man's perspective.)[16]

Now, this poses a serious question. Can we posit that God created an
imperfect world? Would not such a contention contradict our definition
of God as the omnipotent Supreme Being? Not at all, says Berkovits. We
might say that man would not create an imperfect world if he were God,
but that would be man's decision. What bearing does this have upon the
decisions that God makes?

> It would be the worst form of anthropomorphism to suggest that an
> omnipotent and omniscient God would only be responsible for an im-
> maculate universe. . . . We know of God from the encounter; from the
> same encounter we also know Him as the Creator; and we know also of
> the imperfections of the creation by experience. It is, therefore an im-
> perfect world that the perfect God decided to create.[17]

In point of fact, since God created the universe as an entity outside Himself, it must by definition be imperfect. "The world is apart
from God; it is, therefore, of necessity imperfect. . . . A perfect creation
would have extinguished itself by tumbling back into God."[18] Jewish
mysticism teaches that the universe was created through the process
of *tsimtsum,* Divine "self-limitation." Additionally, says Berkovits, if
the universe is to exist outside God, as a non-god, so to speak, it must
forever remain imperfect. Taking all of this to its ultimate conclusion, Berkovits writes, "Since, however, imperfection is essentially attached to creation, it must itself be willed by the Creator."[19]

Now we can understand the words of God found in Isaiah 45:7: "I
am the Lord, there is none else, I form the light, and create darkness; I

make peace and create evil." How can God refer to Himself as the creator of evil? Since God created the universe as an entity that exists outside Himself, it is by definition imperfect. Imperfection by its very nature includes elements of evil. We must conclude, therefore, that only in this sense does Isaiah speak of God as the creator of evil.

Imperfection applies not merely to nature but, in its broadest sense, to society in general and every individual in particular. It goes hand in hand with human freedom. "A perfect being in a perfect world would forever live and act in accordance with its inherent law, from which no deviation of any kind would be conceivable."[20] Perfect beings in a perfect world would not be human; they would be robots programmed to Divine design.

In a sense, God took a risk with the world by delegating the responsibility for its preservation and its perfection to man. Left to his own devices, man could destroy the world. There is no better example of the significance of the risk that God has taken with the world than our own generation. Would anyone deny the gravity of the threat to both society and the natural world posed by nuclear and biological warfare?

Assuming that it is God's will that the world endure, there must be safeguards to protect society from the threat of total annihilation. Jewish tradition teaches us that God has not withdrawn from the world but is actively involved in the process of history, and experience has taught us that there have been instances when God has intervened in Jewish history to maintain His plan for the world. The miracles recorded in the Torah are one example; the preservation of the Jewish people throughout the generations is another. There are those who contend that the establishment of the State of Israel is further evidence of the way in which God safeguards His people and the world.

To summarize: Evil has existed in the world since creation, and in all likelihood it will exist in the world so long as man and nature retain their present state. There are two kinds of evil: that which is brought about by man's inhumanity to man and that which is inherent in nature. The former being man's doing, the responsibility to uproot it falls upon man. If he is negligent, he must suffer the consequences. It is not God Who should be faulted for man's inhumanity to man; it is man. The evil in nature is beyond man's control; it is due to imperfection in the universe, and so long as the universe exists outside God, Who alone is the Perfect Supreme Being, it will remain imperfect.

On the brighter side, imperfection engenders challenge, and challenge is the source of human dignity. The monumental advances that man has made in science and technology are due to the fact that he has been challenged by an imperfect universe. How unfortunate for society that despite his progress in the physical sciences, man has advanced little beyond the primitive stage in the realm of ethics and morality. History has recorded where man's lust for power has taken him in the past. We are all witnesses to the present, and we know that for all intents and purposes human nature has not changed. Is there any hope for the future? Will the time come when man sickens of the ravages of war? Will he finally grow weary of the pain and suffering brought upon innocent men, women, and children as a result of his lust for power? Will he at long last commit himself to his Divinely ordained responsibility to create a better society? The world is being threatened with nuclear war the likes of which has never been experienced by man. A catastrophe of monumental proportions, there would be no victors in such a war, only victims. If there was ever an appropriate time for man to say "Enough!" it is now. For if not now . . . when?

> He has told you, O man, what is good, and what the Lord requires of you: only to do justice and to love goodness, and to walk humbly with your God.[21]

Postscript

If nothing more, the thirteen sessions that Moshe and I spent together resulted in a change in his attitude, perhaps even a change of heart. The bold, self-assured man of science who had considered Judaism irrelevant in today's society had accepted my challenge. As a result, his notion that Judaism should be tossed into the trash heap of discarded relics from the past was undermined, he was now able to see things more objectively, and he had the desire to study more intensively. Witness our conversation at the last session.

"Well, Moshe, you have been given a taste of Torah and the method of Jewish law. I hope that I haven't wasted your time?"

"Not at all, Rabbi. I now realize that my attitude toward Judaism was based on misinformation and prejudice, and I'm not proud of that. But the truth of the matter is that I am only partially to blame. My Jewish education is severely limited, and at home I was never exposed to Jewish laws and customs nor was I encouraged to observe even the little that I had learned in religious school. What I have retained through the years are the Bible stories, a few Hebrew expressions, and some of the laws of the holidays. As a child, I found the biblical narratives fascinating, but when I matured, I regarded them as mere myths, no more credible than the myths of other nations. To practice the customs and ceremonies of Judaism or to be at all concerned with them was simply a waste of time, unbecoming a sophisticated, scientifically oriented, and technologically advanced society such as ours."

"And now that you have been exposed to some of the principles of Judaism, where do you stand Moshe?"

"I'm not quite sure, Rabbi. No! That's not exactly accurate. I certainly realize now that Judaism is not merely a relic of the past. Your arguments for the existence of God certainly have merit. You have clearly demonstrated the rationality of Jewish law. Having seen how Jewish law works, I know now that legal decisions are not made by whim; they are based on precedent and logic. I found your definition of Jewish 'chosenness' to be impressive, and your explanation of the Jewish attitude toward Gentiles was quite different from the way I had understood it to be. I was quite surprised to learn about the important role ethics plays in Jewish tradition, and I find that I must agree with you that any ethical system devised by man is highly subjective and can easily be subverted. I was intrigued by the notion that the Jewish holidays and festivals are recollections and commemorations of important events in history that testify to Divine providence. It makes these celebrations relevant to all Jews in every generation.

"At this point I feel very much 'in limbo.' I have a taste of Torah knowledge—not enough to inspire a commitment to the practice of *mitzvot*, but enough to know that I can no longer be oblivious to the great Jewish heritage into which I have been born. Tell me, Rabbi, where do I go from here?"

"It may surprise you, Moshe, but I'm neither angry nor even disappointed that at this point in time you feel that you cannot make a commitment to traditional Judaism. To me, your attitude betrays your strengths, not your weaknesses. You are a man of science and an intellectual. As a physician, you have been trained not to accept things too hastily, and as an intellectual you crave more knowledge. To sincerely commit yourself to Torah-true Judaism would mean a fundamental change in your life. You feel that you are not quite ready for such a drastic change, and I agree with you. So hear me out.

"Judaism encourages the pursuit of knowledge. Jewish education has always been among the highest priorities in the Jewish weltanschauung. I would recommend that you set aside a portion of each day to be spent exclusively on the study of the Torah, Jewish law, and Jewish philosophy. If it can't be more than an hour or two, so be it. But don't let anything take precedence over Torah study during that period. Don't concern yourself at this point in time with commitment; it will come gradually in its own time."

"I believe you're right, Rabbi. I 'll take your advice. I must tell you that I thoroughly enjoyed these sessions we spent together. It has been an honor and a true intellectual experience. I'm only sorry that I didn't meet you when I was still a teenager. If I'm not imposing, I would really appreciate direction in setting up my home study. Perhaps you can give me a reading list."

"Certainly, Moshe, but I hope that this doesn't mean that we will no longer see each other. I am prepared to meet with you on a monthly basis to discuss ideas and monitor your progress if you choose to do so. Think it over. In the meantime I'll work out a reading list. Give me a call in a day or so."

"I was hoping that you would make such a suggestion, Rabbi. Meeting with you once a month would be perfect."

Moshe turned and began to walk to the door. Suddenly, he stopped and turned back to me.

"Before I go, Rabbi, I must ask you something that I've been wondering about since the first day we met. Why did you insist on knowing my Hebrew name and calling me by that name whenever we studied together?"

"Well, Moshe, I wanted to know whether you connected at all with your people. I felt that if you were concerned enough to have remembered your Hebrew name, there was some hope that you and I might also connect. I insisted on calling you by that name to give you a sense of belonging, of being no less a member of the Jewish people than some of the great sages of whom we spoke."

Moshe took my advice. We met once a month and studied together. It was almost a year later that he informed me that he was then ready to make a full commitment to Torah-true Judaism. He became fascinated with Jewish law and philosophy and began attending classes in the evenings in a neighborhood yeshivah. It has been five years since I first met Moshe. Presently, he and his family live in strict accord with Jewish tradition.

Notes

Session I

    1. Philo, Judaeus, *De Specialibus Legibus* I, 6 (Cambridge; Loeb Classics Library, 1950), Vol. 7, p. 119.

    2. Cf. P. Davis, *God and the New Physics* (New York: Simon and Schuster, 1983), p. 183, who writes: "The delicate fine tuning in the value of the constants, necessary so that the various different branches of physics can dovetail so felicitously, might be attributed to God. It is hard to resist the impression that the present structure of the universe, apparently so sensitive to minor alterations in the numbers, has been rather carefully thought out . . . the seemingly miraculous concurrence of numerical values that nature has assigned to her fundamental constants must remain the most compelling evidence for an element of cosmic design."

    3. Cf. M. Wertheim, "God Is Also a Cosmologist," *New York Times*, June 8, 1997, p. 16.

    4. Cf. N. Aviezer, *In the Beginning* (New Jersey: Ktav Publishing House, 1990), and G. Schroeder, *Genesis and the Big Bang* (New York: Bantam Books, 1990).

5. E. Berkovits, *God, Man and History* (New York: Jonathan David, 1959), p. 101.

6. Ibid., chapter 3.

7. Ibid., p. 20.

8. Ibid., p. 27.

9. I. Epstein, *The Faith of Judaism* (London: The Soncino Press, 1954), p. 122.

10. Cf. *Tosefta: Shavuot* 3:6.

11. N. Berdyaev, *Freedom and the Spirit*, trans. Oliver F. Clarke (London: G. Bles, 1948), p. 217.

12. E. Berkovits, op. cit., pp. 70–72.

13. Genesis 20:11.

14. S. R. Hirsch, *Torah Commentary to Genesis* 20:11.

15. Cf. *Bava Metzia* 58b.

16. *Ethics of the Fathers*, Chap. 2, 1.

Session II

1. Jerusalem Talmud: *Peah*, Chap. 3.

2. Zevi Hirsch Chayes, *The Student's Guide through the Talmud*, trans. J. Schachter (New York: Feldheim Publishers, 1952), p. 4.

3. *Ibid.*, p. 13.

4. This is derived from Leviticus 18:5, which reads: "You shall keep My laws and My norms by the pursuit of which man shall live: I am the Lord." Cf. *Sifra* 144:13.

5. There are three exceptions: murder, idolatry, and incest. One is forbidden to commit any of these acts even at the cost of one's life.

6. Meir Leibush Malbim, Torah commentary to Leviticus 19:14.

7. *Avodah Zarah* 6b.

8. Cf. Session VII, for a full listing of the seven Noahide laws.

9. Cf. *Magen Avraham, Shulhan Arukh: Orah Hayyim* 347:1, who opines that the rabbinic ruling that prohibits a Jew from being an accessory when the individual can get the forbidden food himself would not apply to giving a Gentile that which is forbidden to him.

10. *Shulhan Arukh: Orah Hayyim* 163:2. Of course, we are speaking here of ritual washing. One whose hands are dirty would be forbidden to feed another person for many other reasons.

11. Cf. *Magen Avraham*, commentary ad loc. An important qualification of this law is made by the *Peri Miggadim* commentary. In a situation where being an accessory is only rabbinically prohibited, namely, where one can transgress the law without the help of an accessory if one chooses to do so, where the transgression is biblical, the sages took a stringent position and forbade it. Where it is only rabbinically prohibited, however, they allowed it because one does not institute a preventative measure in order to prevent the violation of another preventative measure.

12. M. Maimonides, *The Guide of the Perplexed*, trans. M. Friedlander (New York: Hebrew Publishing Company), Part 3, Chap. 48, p. 253.

13. M. Maimonides, op. cit., pp. 253–254.

14. Eliezer, the servant of Abraham, was sent to the city of Nahor to find the proper wife for Isaac. As he approached the city, he uttered the following prayer: "O Lord, God of my master Abraham, grant me good fortune this day, and deal graciously with my master Abraham: and as I stand here by the spring and the daughters of the townsmen come out to draw water, let the maiden to whom I say, 'Please lower your pitcher that I may drink,' and who replies, 'Drink and I will also water your camels'—let her be the one whom you have decreed for your servant Isaac'" (Genesis 24:12–14). In his commentary to Genesis 24:14, Rabbi Samson Raphael Hirsch writes: "The sign by which Eliezer wanted to know the girl who was the destined wife of Isaac was one which belongs to the special traits of character which still today, are the most characteristic signs of the descendants of Isaac and Rebecca, and which we summarize under the heading *gemilut hassadim* (acts of benevolence)."

15. M. Maimonides, op. cit., Chap. 17, pp. 77–78.

16. See note 1.

17. Y. Weinberg, *Seride Esh* (Jerusalem: Mossad Harav Kook, 1977), Vol. 1, No. 7.

18. J. D. Bleich, *Judaism and Healing* (New York: Ktav, 1981), p. 125.

19. *Midrash, Sifre Zuta* to Numbers 19:11.

20. Cf. *Niddah* 70b.

21. *Bava Metzia* 114a.

22. Cf. Ibid., in the *Tosafot*, commentary, s.v. *Amar*.

23. Cf. J. Reicher, *Shevut Yaakov*, Vol. 3, No. 75.

24. *Kiddushin* 31a.

25. *Shabbat* 118b.

26. M. Maimonides, op. cit., Part 3, Chap. 52, p. 294.

27. M. Maimonides, *Mishneh Torah: Laws of Ethics* 5:6.

28. J. M. Epstein, *Arukh HaShulhan: Orah Hayyim* 2:10.

29. David HaLevi, *Ture Zahav, Shulhan Arukh: Orah Hayyim* 8:2.

30. Cf. M. Feinstein, *Iggrot Moshe* (New York, 1959), Vol. 1, No. 1, where we read: "Nowadays, since this is prohibited as a custom of the Gentiles, it applies when seated [as well] and even when walking less than four cubits."

31. Ibid.

32. Cf. *Shulhan Arukh: Orah Hayyim* 91:3.

Session III

1. A. Steinsaltz, "Where Do Torah and Science Clash?" *The Torah U'Madda Journal* (New York: Yeshiva University, 1944), p. 160.

2. *Bava Batra* 14b.

3. Ibid. An interesting point is made by Don Isaac Abravanel in his introduction to Deuteronomy. Most of this book consists of Moses' own words spoken to the people of Israel, says Abravanel. How did Moses' words become part of the Torah? The Almighty repeated them to him. In that way Moses received his own words from the Almighty, in the same manner that he had received the other four books of the Torah. Thus, the book of Deuteronomy took on the same sanctity as the rest of the Torah.

4. M. Maimonides, *Mishneh Torah: Laws of Repentance* 3:8.

5. D. Z. Hoffmann, *Sefer Vayikrah* (Jerusalem: Mossad Harav Kook, 1942).

6. *Soferim* 6:4.

7. *Moed Katan* 3:4.

8. Cf. S. R. Hirsch, *The Hirsch Siddur* (New York: The Samson Raphael Hirsch Society, 1972), p. 38, where this principle is explained as follows: "When God through Moses caused that law to be written down which He had already made known orally in full detail, He caused this holy Writ to be composed in accordance with thirteen basic rules which made it possible to present the Written Word in such a pregnant and compact form that the detailed intention of the lawgiver could be in-

vestigated from the written words by means of the application of these rules which were handed down simultaneously with the Written Law."

9. Cf. D. Hoffmann, op. cit., p. 4.

10. Ibid., p. 6.

11. Cf. Y. Kaufman, *The Religion of Israel* (Chicago: Chicago University Press, 1960), Chap. 5, pp. 154–155.

12. Ibid., p. 203.

13. The Torah begins with the most general principle of creation, i.e., "In the beginning God created the heavens and the earth." The Torah then specifies what was created each day. It lists genealogical tables of the generations, but tells us little if anything about these people until Abraham is born, and we are given details of his life. Abraham has two sons: Ishmael and Isaac. We are told little of Ishmael, but we are given details of the life of Isaac. We are told almost nothing of Esau, Isaac's son, but Jacob's life is detailed. The purpose seems to be to briefly trace the generations, emphasizing only the lives of those people who are relevant, indeed, crucial to the development of the nation of Israel.

14. *Shabbat* 88a.

15. J. B. Soloveitchik, "The Lonely Man of Faith," *Tradition* (Summer, 1965): 10.

16. Ibid., p. 16.

17. Ibid., p. 24.

18. Cf. S. Rypins, *The Book of Thirty Centuries* (New York: The Macmillan Company, 1951), p. 260.

19. S. Izhaki, (Rashi) Commentary to Genesis 1:1.

20. U. Cassuto, *The Documentary Hypothesis* (Jerusalem: Magnum Press, 1953), Chap. 2, pp. 19–38.

21. Cf. *Da'at Zekanim* commentary to Exodus 5:4. Moses advised Pharaoh that if the Israelites were given a day of rest, they would work harder and accomplish more during the other six days of the week. Pharaoh acquiesced, and the Israelites chose *Shabbat*. In the wilderness Moses said to the Israelites: "Mark that the Lord has given you the *Shabbat* . . . " reminding them that the *Shabbat* as a day of rest had already been given to them in Egypt.

22. U. Cassuto, op. cit., p. 32.

23. S. R. Hirsch, *The Nineteen Letters of Ben Uziel* (New York: Bloch Publishing Company, 1942), p. 13.

Session IV

1. *Shabbat* 31a.
2. Cf. Ibid., *Maharsha* commentary.
3. S. R. Hirsch, Torah Commentary to Leviticus 19:18.
4. Cf. Aaron HaLevi, *Sefer HaHinukh, Mitzvah* 243.
5. *Shulhan Arukh: Orah Hayyim* 46:1, in the *Magen Avraham* commentary.
6. S. R. Hirsch, op. cit., 4:15.
7. *Yoma* 9b.
8. Cf. M. Maimonides, *Mishneh Torah: Laws of Ethics* 6:7.
9. *Betzah* 30a. Cf. *Yevamot* 65b.
10. The *Magen Avraham* commentary to *Shulhan Arukh: Orah Hayyim* 608:3 states: "One who occupies a rabbinic position and has been appointed to supervise town affairs, instruct them in the way of life, rebuke and admonish them, and maintain the faith as much as possible shall not spare himself. His heart and eyes shall be committed at all times only to the honor of heaven. . . . However, every situation must be judged individually by the Rabbi, depending on whether they will accept his words."
11. Cf. *Sifra* to Leviticus 19:14.
12. Ibid., in the Rashi commentary.
13. As was mentioned in Session II, n. 3, whether the prohibition is biblical or rabbinic depends on whether the one who is about to commit the act can do it alone or needs an accessory. In the former the prohibition is rabbinic; in the latter it is biblical. Cf. *Avodah Zarah* 6b and *Shulhan Arukh: Orah Hayyim* 347:1 and *Magen Avraham commentary*, ad loc.
14. Cf. *Bava Kamma* 83b and *Shulhan Arukh: Hoshen Mishpat: Laws of Monetary Damages* 420:3.
15. *Ethics of the Fathers* 2:17.
16. *Shulhan Arukh: Hoshen Mishpat* 359:5.
17. S. R. Hirsch, op. cit., Leviticus 19:11.
18. Cf. *Bava Metziah* 110a–112a, for a detailed discussion of this matter.
19. Cf. Rema, *Shulhan Arukh: Hoshen Mishpat* 37, and Yehiel Michel Epstein, *Arukh HaShulhan: Hoshen Mishpat* 9.

20. S. R. Hirsch, op. cit., Leviticus 19:15.

21. *Ethics of the Fathers* 2:5.

22. Ibid., 1:6.

23. *Sanhedrin 73a* and Rashi commentary, ad loc.

24. Cf. M. Maimonides, *Sefer HaMitzvot*, Negative Command #297. One's first obligation is to preserve one's own life. One has no right to forfeit one's own life to save the life of another human being. The Talmud, in *Bava Metziah* 62a, gives the following example: "If two are traveling on a journey (far from civilization) and only one has a flask of water. If both drink, both will die. But if one drinks, he can reach civilization. Ben Patura taught: it is better that both should drink and die rather than one should behold his companion's death. Until Rabbi Akiva came and taught: ' . . . that your brother may live with you' (Leviticus 25:36). Your life takes preference over his life." Of course, this is a situation where the flask belongs to one of the travelers exclusively. Where it belongs to both of them, there is no choice other than that they both drink and die.

25. For an example of foolish piety, see *Sotah* 21b.

26. Deuteronomy 8:12–18.

27. Cf. *Ketuvot* 67b.

28. *Bava Metziah* 71a.

29. J. B. Soloveitchik, "Confrontation," *Tradition* 6 (Spring–Summer 1964): 17.

30. It should be noted that some rabbinic authorities contend that the Jewish people can make the greatest inroads for the welfare of society in the spiritual realm, and even in this realm their influence should not manifest itself by taking an active role but rather by setting an example.

31. *Kohelet Rabbah* 7:28.

32. Deuteronomy 20:19–20.

33. Cf. M. Maimonides, *Mishneh Torah: Laws of Kings* 6:8, 10.

34. *Bava Batra* 24b–25a.

35. Cf. M. Maimonides, op. cit., *Laws of Neighbors* 11:1, 5.

36. Ibid., *Laws of Kings* 6:10.

37. *Ethics of the Fathers* 3:2.

38. *Gittin* 10b.

39. Cf. *Ethics of the Fathers*, op. cit., in the gloss of *Rabbenu Yona*.

Session V

1. Genesis 20:17.
2. Genesis 25:21.
3. Cf. *Onkelos* and Rashi, ad loc.
4. *Bava Kamma* 85a.
5. Ibid., in the commentary of *Tosafot*, s.v. *reshut*. The definitive statement is found in *Shulhan Arukh: Yore De'ah: Laws of a Physician* 336:1, where we read: "The Torah gave permission for the physician to heal. It is a positive commandment in the category of saving a life. One who refuses to do so is considered a blood shedder even if there is another physician present who can do so, for a patient is not necessarily healed by every physician. However, one should not practice medicine unless he has mastered it, and one should not treat if there is a greater one than he present, for that, too, would be considered bloodshed." It is interesting to note that while it is clearly obligatory for the physician to heal, the term "permission" is used here. The meaning is as follows: True healing is the result of a petition to God for mercy, for God heals, not man. Man is not worthy of this method, however. He must resort to the aid of a physician, in consequence of which God has given the physician permission to heal. Cf. *Ture Zahav*, commentary ad loc.

6. Cf. *Yevamot* 69b; *Mishnah, Niddah* 5:3; also, *Shulhan Arukh: Yore De'ah* 374:8; and Rashi, commentary to Exodus 21:12.

7. *Mishnah, Oholot* 7:6.

8. Ibid.

9. Cf. *Tiferet Yisrael*, commentary ad loc.

10. *Mishneh Torah: Laws of Murderers* 1:9. It seems that Maimonides did not accept the position of Rashi and others that the fetus is simply not viable when it is in the womb. According to Rabbi Hayyim Soloveitchik in his commentary, Maimonides felt that although the fetus does not have full status when the birth process has begun, it has *near* full status. Consequently, the law of saving a life applies to the fetus and the mother equally. The only reason the mother is saved is because the fetus is considered a *rodef*. Cf. *Shulhan Arukh: Hoshen Mishpat* 425:1, 2.

11. *Shulhan Arukh: Yore De'ah: Laws of Visiting the Sick* 338:2.

12. *Avodah Zarah* 18a.

13. Judah ben Samuel, *Sefer Hassidim* (Warsaw, 1901), No. 5323.

14. F. Rosner and M. Tendler, *Practical Medical Halakhah* (New York: Feldheim Publishers, 1980), p. 56.

15. Cf. M. Maimonides, op. cit., *Laws of Wounding and Harming* 5:1.

16. Cf. M. Klein, *Mishneh Halakhot* 4, Nos. 246, 247.

17. Cf. *Ketuvot* 72b, 74b.

18. M. Klein, op. cit.

19. Cf. Y. Breish, *Helkat Ya'akov*, 3, No. 11.

20. *Sanhedrin* 46b.

21. M. Maimonides, op. cit., *Sanhedrin* 15:8.

22. S. Israeli, in an article in *Noam* (Jerusalem, 1963).

23. M. Tendler, op. cit., p. 59.

24. F. Rosner, *Modern Medicine and Jewish Ethics* (New Jersey: Ktav Publishing house, 1991), pp. 265–266.

25. Cf. M. Maimonides, op. cit., *Laws of Shabbat* 2:19. The ruling of Maimonides is brought in the *Shulhan Arukh: Orah Hayyim* 329:4.

26. Cf. I. Y. Unterman, "Points of Halakhah in Heart Transplantation," *Noam* (1970), 8, No. 19. See also E. Waldenberg, *Tzitz Eliezer*, Vol. 9, No. 46, and Vol. 10, No. 25:4.

27. M. Feinstein, *Iggrot Moshe: Yoreh De'ah*, Part 3, No. 132.

28. M. Maimonides, op. cit., *Laws of the Ritual Impurity of the Dead* 1:15.

29. Cf. F. Rosner, op. cit., p. 271.

30. Cf. E. J. Veith, J. M. Fein, M. D. Tendler, "Brain Death: I. A Status Report of Medical and Ethical Considerations," *Journal of the American Medical Association* 238 (1977): 1661–1665.

31. Cf. J. D. Bleich, *Contemporary Halakhic Problems* (New York: Ktav Publishing House, 1977), pp. 372–393; also, A. Soloveitchik, "Jewish Law and Time of Death," *Journal of the American Medical Association* 240 (1978): 109.

32. Cf. Y. Unterman, *Shevet MiYehudah* (Jerusalem, 1955), pp. 313–322. See also M. Tendler, *Practical Medical Halakhah*, op. cit., p. 71.

33. Cf. F. Rosner, op. cit., p. 286.

34. Cf. J. J. Weiss, *Minhat Yitzhak*, Part 6, No. 103:2. See also O. Yosef, "The Laws of Kidney Transplantation," *Halakhah U'Refuah* 3 (1983): 61–63.

35. M. Tendler, op. cit., p. 58.

36. Ibid., p. 73.

37. Cf. *Hagigah* 14b, where Ben Zoma opines that a woman may conceive by bathing in a tub of water in which semen was discharged. See also I. D. Eisenstein, "Alpha Beta de ben Sira," *Otzar Midrashim* (New York, 1928), p. 43. The legend relates that Ben Sira was conceived through that method.

38. Cf. S. Nathanson, *Shoel U'meshiv*, 2nd Ed., Part 3, No. 133.

39. Cf. E. Y. Waldenberg, op. cit., Vol. 9, 51:4.

40. Cf. M. Feinstein, op. cit., Part 2, No. 16; also O. Yosef, *Yabe'a Omer*, Part 2, No. 1.

41. *Yevamot* 65b.

42. *Mishnah Yevamot*, 6:6, and *Shulhan Arukh: Even HaEzer: Laws of Procreation* 1:5.

43. Cf. *Rema, Shulhan Arukh: Even HaEzer* 23:5.

44. *Yevamot* 12b.

45. Cf. I. Jakobovits, *Jewish Medical Ethics* (New York: Bloch Publishing Company, 1962), p. 169.

46. F. Rosner and M. Tendler, op. cit., p. 27.

47. Cf. *Niddah* 70b and *Keneset HaGedolah*, commentary on *Shulhan Arukh: Even HaEzer* 17:2.

48. Cf. 1 Kings 17:21 and *Bava Metzia* 114a–114b, in the commentary of *Tosafot*, s.v. *Amar*.

49. J. Reicher, *Shevut Ya'akov*, Part 3, No. 75.

50. This *mitzvah* is derived from Deuteronomy 28:9, which reads: "The Lord will establish you as a holy people, as He swore to you, if you keep the commandments of the Lord your God and walk in His ways." See M. Maimonides, op. cit., *Hilkhot De'ot* 1:5, 6.

51. Cf. *Bava Metzia* 32b.

52. Cf. Rema, *Shulhan Arukh: Even HaEzer* 5:14.

53. Cf. M. Maimonides, *Guide of the Perplexed* (New York: Hebrew Publishing Company), Part 3, Chap. 17. Addressing the law of kindness to animals, he writes: "that we should not assume cruel habits, and that we should not uselessly cause pain to others, that on the contrary, we should be prepared to show mercy to all living creatures, except when necessity demands the contrary. [This last point refers to the desire to eat meat.] We should not kill animals for the purpose of practicing cruelty or for the purpose of play."

54. Cf. J. D. Bleich, "Judaism and Animal Experimentation," *Tradition* 22:1 (Spring, 1986): note # 17, for the scientific sources for this contention.

55. Cf. M. Maimonides, op. cit.

Session VI

1. *Betzah* 25b.

2. Cf. I. Epstein, *The Faith of Judaism* (London: Soncino Press, 1954), p. 285.

3. Cf. M. Maimonides, *Guide of the Perplexed* (New York: Hebrew Publishing Company), Part 1, Chap. 2, pp. 35–36.

4. E. Berkovits, *Crises and Faith* (New York: Sanhedrin Press, 1976), pp. 46–47.

5. Cf. S. R. Hirsch, Torah Commentary to Genesis 3:19–23.

6. D. Z. Hoffmann, Torah Commentary to Genesis 2:15–17.

7. Cf. S. R. Hirsch, op. cit., Genesis 2:16, 17. The Noahide commands are hinted to in the previous verses. They are as follows: (1) the establishment of courts of justice, (2) the recognition of God, (3) the prohibition against idolatry, (4) the prohibition against murder, (5) the prohibition against illicit sexual relations, (6) the prohibition against robbery, and (7) the prohibition against eating a limb from a living animal.

8. Cf. D. Z. Hoffmann, op. cit., Genesis 4:3–5. There are two opinions concerning the quality of Cain's offering: one opinion says that he brought the worst of his crop, the other that he was indiscriminate in his choice and brought the first fruits that came to hand. In either case, the offering was not of the highest quality.

9. Cf. S. R. Hirsch, op. cit., Genesis 5:4–28, for a full development of this idea.

10. Genesis 13:14–17.

11. Leviticus 18:3, 26–28.

12. S. R. Hirsch, *Nineteen Letters of Ben Uziel* (New York: Bloch Publishing Company, 1942), p. 73.

13. Ibid., pp. 75–76.

14. *Perush HaTorah L'Rebbi Avraham ben HaRambam*, ed. A. Weisenberg (London, 1959); Exodus 19:6.

15. Genesis 6:11–13, see Rashi commentary, ad loc.
16. I. Epstein, op. cit., pp. 286–287.
17. S. R. Hirsch, op. cit., p. 77.
18. I. Epstein, op. cit., p. 287.
19. Ibid., p. 288.
20. S. R. Hirsch, op. cit., Deuteronomy 32:15.
21. *Shemot Rabbah* 26.
22. *Tosefta Sanhedrin* 13.

Session VII

1. Cf. D. Kimhi, *Sefer HaShorashim* (Jerusalem, 1966), on the word *goy*.
2. Meiri Commentary on *Bava Kamma* 37b and *Avodah Zara* 26a.
3. Cf. *Sanhedrin* 59b. For the details on how the seven Noahide laws are traced to Genesis 2:16, 17, see the commentary of S. R. Hirsch on these verses.
4. Cf. *Tanna D'be Menasseh* on *Sanhedrin* 56b.
5. *Sanhedrin* 59b.
6. M. Maimonides, *Mishneh Torah: Laws of Kings* 5:11.
7. *Ethics of the Fathers* 1:12.
8. J. H. Hertz, *Sayings of the Fathers* (New York: Behrman House, 1945), p. 23.
9. Cf. G. Blidstein, "Tikun Olam," *Tradition* 29:2 (New York: Rabbinical Council of America, 1995), where he discusses whether Israel best fulfills its responsibility for the welfare of society by being the example of Divine ethics in practice or by taking an active role in humanitarian concerns.
10. *Tosefta Gittin*, Chap. 3.
11. Cf. *Bava Metziah* 12b.
12. *Shulhan Arukh: Yore De'ah* 148:6.
13. Ibid., 148:7. It should be understood that those prohibitions had originally been instituted in order to avoid the appearance that Jews are in any way involved in the customs of idolaters.
14. Ibid., 148:12, in the gloss of Rema, end of para. 291.
15. Cf. *Meiri* on *Bava Kamma* 37b.

16. M. Maimonides, op. cit., *Laws of Kings* 10:10.

17. *Kol Sifre Maharitz Chayot* (Jerusalem, 1958), Vol. 1, p. 490.

18. J. Henkin, *Hadarom* (New York: Rabbinical Council of America, 1959), Vol. 10, p. 8.

19. *Shulhan Arukh: Hoshen Mishpat* 348:2 and J. M. Epstein, *Arukh HaShulhan: Orah Hayyim* 256:3.

20. *Kol Torah Nisan* (Jerusalem, 5728).

21. Cf. M. Maimonides, op. cit., *Laws of Murderers* 1:14.

22. Cf. *Tosafot* to *Sanhedrin* 28b, s.v. lo.

23. Cf. *Yoma* 85a.

24. Cf. *Meiri* on *Yoma* 84b, and *Pit'he Teshuvah* on *Shulhan Arukh: Yore De'ah* 154:2, where it has been established that the prohibition against violating the *Shabbat* to save the life of a Gentile applied only to uncivilized heathens who had neither regard for God nor for man.

25. *Shulhan Arukh: Orah Hayyim* 334:26, in the gloss of Rema.

26. S. R. Hirsch, Commentary on the Torah to Deuteronomy 33:4.

27. *Sanhedrin* 59a.

28. Cf. J. Emden, Commentary to *Hagigah* 13a.

29. *Meiri*, Commentary to *Sanhedrin* 59a.

30. Cf. Z. H. Chayot, Commentary to *Sotah* 35b.

31. *Hagigah* 13a.

32. Cf. *Mekhilta* on Exodus 12:48 and *Sifra* on Numbers 9:14.

33. *Yevamot* 22a.

34. Ibid.

35. *Kiddushin* 17b.

36. Cf. *Tur Shulhan Arukh: Yore De'ah* 269:4 and *Shulhan Arukh: Hoshen Mishpat*, end of section 33 in the *Ture Zahav* commentary.

37. Cf. *Tur Shulhan Arukh: Yore De'ah* 374:8.

38. Ibid., 269:9. See *Pit'he Teshuvah* and *Dagul Mirvavah*, ad loc. If both are converts and the woman has reached menopause, the three-month waiting period is waived.

39. Cf. *Tur Shulhan Arukh: Even HaEzer* 1:7.

40. Cf. Ibid., *Yoreh De'ah* 268:2.

41. Ibid., 268:8.

42. *Shulhan Arukh: Hoshen Mishpat* 348:5, in the *B'er HaGolah* commentary.

43. *Tiferet Yisrael*, Mishnah, *Bava Kamma* 4:4.

Session VIII

1. *Taanit* 7A.
2. S. R. Hirsch, *The Wisdom of Mishle* (New York: Feldheim, 1976), p. 183.
3. Ibid., p. 184.
4. *Ethics of the Fathers* 4:23.
5. D. Runes, *Dictionary of Philosophy* (New York: Philosophical Library), p. 122.
6. E. Berkovits, *Crisis and Faith* (New York, Sanhedrin Press, 1976), p. 48.
7. *Berakhot* 70b.
8. Rashi, Torah Commentary to Genesis 2:7: "He made him of both, of earthly and of heavenly matter: the body of the earthly and the soul of the heavenly."
9. Cf. Rashi on Genesis 1:26.
10. Cf. *Kohelet Rabbah* 4:15.
11. *Bereshit Rabbah* 9:9.
12. *Kiddushin* 30b.
13. Cf. M. Nahmanides, *Iggeret HaKodesh* (New York: M. P. Press), p. 55a.
14. Cf. J. Mecklenburg, *HaKetav V'HaKabbalah* (New York: Ohm Publishing Company, 1946); Genesis 4:1.
15. Cf. E. Berkovits, op. cit., p. 57, who writes: "There is reason to assume that in the animal kingdom sex is indeed utterly impersonal. It is not what an animal does but something cosmic that enacts itself through the animal. . . . In the human experience, the most impersonal of all instincts demands its satisfaction in the most personal of all interhuman relationships, therefore, what is biologically given loses its natural innocence and moral neutrality. In the context of the most intimately personal, the impersonality of the sexual impulse becomes, due to its incomparable energy and driving power, the most self regarding and the most anti-social of impulses which man has to personalize."
16. *Ethics of the Fathers* 4:1.
17. E. Berkovits, op. cit., p. 73.
18. *Mishnah: Yadayim* 3:5.
19. Genesis 2:18–24.
20. Cf. S. R. Hirsch, Torah Commentary to Genesis 2:18.

21. *Yevamot* 62b.
22. J. Reicher, *Iyun Ya'akov* on *Yevamot* 62b.
23. *Yevamot*, ibid.
24. Cf. *Bereshit Rabbah* 68:4.
25. *Sotah* 2a.
26. Ibid.
27. *Sanhedrin* 22b.
28. Ibid.
29. Ibid.

Session IX

1. *Mishnah, Keritut* 28:1 and *Tur Shulhan Arukh: Yore De'ah* 240.
2. *Kiddushin* 31a.
3. *Kiddushin* 30b.
4. Genesis 4:1.
5. M. Maimonides, *Mishneh Torah: Foundations of the Torah* 2:2.
6. S. R. Hirsch, Torah Commentary to Deuteronomy 22:7; also *Midrash HaGadol to Exodus* 20:12.
7. *Mishnah, Sotah* 1:7.
8. *Shulhan Arukh: Yore De'ah* 240:42.
9. Nahmanides' Torah Commentary to Numbers 33:53.
10. M. Maimonides, op. cit., *Laws of Kings* 5:9.
11. *Kiddushin* 31b.
12. Cf. S. Israeli, *Shanah BeShanah* (Jerusalem; Heichal Shelomo, 5725).
13. A. Danzig, *Sefer Sha'are Zedek: Mishpete HaAretz* 11:5.
14. S. R. Hirsch, op. cit., Exodus 20:12.
15. S. R. Hirsch, *The Wisdom of Mishle* (New York: Feldheim Publishers, 1976), p. 121.
16. S. Azubiv, *Tokhehot Mussar* (Livorno, 1871); Proverbs 10:1.
17. *Sanhedrin* 105b.
18. William Wordsworth, in the poem "My heart leaps up when I behold."
19. Cf. M. L. Malbim, Commentary to Proverbs 20:1.
20. S. R. Hirsch, op. cit., p. 128.
21. *Bava Metziah* 85a.

22. Cf. *Mezudot David* and Rashi on Malachi 3:24.

23. *Taanit* 5b.

Session X

1. *Berakhot* 26b.

2. Cf. M. Maimonides, *Mishneh Torah: Laws of Prayer* 1:1.

3. *Berakhot* 32a.

4. E. Berkovits, *Prayer* (New York: Yeshiva University Press, 1962), p. 44.

5. Cf. Rashi, Torah Commentary to Deuteronomy 3:23.

6. Cf. *Midrash Tehillim* (Jerusalem, 1967), Chap. 31.

7. Cf. D. Z. Hoffmann, Torah Commentary (Bnai Brak: Nezach, 1969), Leviticus, pp. 54–55.

8. Cf. *Shabbat* 118b, also D. Abudraham, *Abudraham HaShalem* (Jerusalem: Usha, 1963), p. 62.

9. *Berakhot* 32a.

10. Cf. *Tur Shulhan Arukh: Orah Hayyim* 93.

11. J. Albo, *Sefer HaIkkarim*, Part 4, Chap. 18.

12. Ibid. The thought is likewise found in the writings of H. Crescas, *Or HaShem*, Part 2, Chap. 1.

13. E. Berkovits, op. cit., p. 74.

14. *Avodah Zarah* 8a.

15. *Berakhot* 21a.

16. *Bereshit Rabbah* 14:11.

17. *Shemot Rabbah* 21.

18. *Ethics of the Fathers* 2:18.

19. *Mishnah, Berakhot* 4:4.

20. Ibid., 5:1.

21. *Berakhot* 31a.

22. M. Maimonides, op. cit., *Laws of Prayer* 4:16.

23. Ibid., 4:15.

Session XI

1. Psalms 90:10.

2. Cf. *Haggadah shel Pesach MiBet HaLevi* (Jerusalem: Orayso, 1983), pp. 96–99.

3. Cf. M. Maimonides, *The Guide of the Perplexed* (New York: Hebrew Publishing Company), Part 3, p. 160.

4. Cf. M. Nahmanides, Torah Commentary to Deuteronomy 5:12.

5. S. R. Hirsch, Torah Commentary to Exodus 23:14.

6. Leviticus 23:15 reads: "From the day after the *Shabbat*, the day that you bring the sheaf of wave offering, you shall keep count until seven full weeks have elapsed: you shall count fifty days until the day after the seventh week; then you shall bring an offering of new grain to the Lord."

7. Deuteronomy 26:5–10.

8. Cf. Rashi, Torah Commentary to Exodus 19:2.

9. Cf. *Sukkah* 11b. The former opinion is that of R. Eliezer; the latter, of R. Akiva.

10. Cf. Numbers 14:29–34. "In this very wilderness your carcasses shall drop . . . not one shall enter the land in which I swore to settle you—save Calev son of Yefuneh and Joshua son of Nun. Your children who, you said, would be carried off—these will I allow to enter; they shall know the land that you have rejected. . . . You shall bear your punishment for forty years, corresponding to the number of days—forty days—that you scouted the land: a year for each day. Thus you shall know what it means to thwart Me." Only Joshua and Calev, the two spies who returned from surveying the land with a good report, would be privileged to enter it.

11. *Ethics of the Fathers* 4:3.

12. Cf. *Pirke D'Rebbi Eliezer*, Chap. 46.

13. Cf. *Rosh Hashanah* 27a.

14. *Rosh Hashanah* 16a, in the *Mishnah.*

15. Cf. *Mussaf* Service for Rosh Hashanah in the prayer *Ata Zokher.*

16. Cf. M. Maimonides, *Mishneh Torah: Laws of the Shofar* 3:3.

17. Cf. *Taanit* 19a.

18. Cf. *Moed Katan* 16a.

19. Ibid., 27b.

20. Cf. *Shabbat* 35b.

21. Cf. *Niddah* 38a, in the commentary of Rashi, s.v. *shapira.*

22. The source for the law of the Jubilee Year is Leviticus 25:9, which reads: "Then you shall sound the *shofar* loud; in the seventh month on the tenth day of the month—the Day of Atonement—you shall have the *shofar* sounded throughout your land." Among many other laws that apply to the Jubilee Year, all property had to be returned to its origi-

nal owner. In determining the value of a property, the number of years that remained until the Jubilee Year was taken into consideration.

23. The source is Exodus 19:16, 19, which reads: "On the third day as the morning dawned, there was thunder and lightning and a dense cloud upon the mountain and a very loud blast of the *shofar* . . . the blare of the *shofar* grew louder and louder."

24. Joel 2:15.

25. Cf. *Rosh Hashanah* 34a.

26. *Mishnah, Taanit* 26b, in the name of R. Simon ben Gamliel.

27. Ibid., 30b.

28. Cf. *Seder Eliyahu Rabbah* 1.

29. Cf. *Yoma* 73b–77a. Although the Torah does not mention fasting as an affliction of the soul, in Psalms 35:13 we find "But as for me, my clothing was sackcloth; I afflicted my soul with fasting . . . "

30. Cf. Jerusalem Talmud, *Berakhot* 4.

31. Cf. *Shabbat* 21b, which reads: "What is [the reason of] Hanukkah? For our Rabbis taught: On the twenty-fifth of Kislev [commence] the days of Hanukkah, which are eight, on which a lamentation for the dead and fasting are forbidden. For when the Greeks entered the Temple, they defiled all the oils therein, and when the Hasmonean dynasty prevailed against and defeated them, they made search and found only one cruse of oil which lay with the seal of the High Priest, but contained sufficient oil for one day's lighting only; yet a miracle was wrought therein and they lit the lamp for eight days. The following year these [days] were appointed a festival with [the recital of] *Hallel* and thanksgiving."

32. Cf. S. R. Hirsch, *Judaism Eternal* (London: The Soncino Press, 1956), Vol. 1, p. 25.

33. Cf. Maccabees 2, Chap. 4.

34. Cf. *Shabbat* 21a–23b.

35. Cf. *Shulhan Arukh: Orah Hayyim* 670–685.

36. Cf. *Tur Shulhan Arukh: Orah Hayyim* 673. The candles of the Hanukkah *menorah* are not to be used for any other purpose but to publicize the miracle of the lights. For fear that one might inadvertently read by this light, a special candle is added to the *menorah* solely for the purpose of giving light. It is called the *shamash*, literally, "the steward," for it serves a special purpose. Later, a "lighting candle" was added as well. Eventually, one candle served both functions. To dis-

tinguish the *shamash* from the other candles, it is placed higher or to the side of the other candles.

37. S. R. Hirsch, op. cit.
38. *Taanit* 29a.
39. Ecclesiastes 3:4.
40. Exodus 1:8–10.
41. Esther 3:8.
42. Esther 4:13, 14.
43. A. Danzig, *Haye Adam* 155:3.
44. *Shulhan Arukh: Orah Hayyim* 686:3.
45. Cf. *Mishnah, Megillah* 5a, and *Mishnah, Berurah; Shulhan Arukh: Orah Hayyim* 688:1. It was ordained that in the city of Shushan the *megillah* was to be read on the fifteenth of Adar, for the Jews had been given the thirteenth and fourteenth days of that month to defend themselves against their enemies. They did not celebrate until the fifteenth of Adar. Shushan was a walled city. In honor of Shushan, it would have been proper to rule that all cities that are surrounded by walls celebrate the festival on the fifteenth. But Jerusalem, which had once been a walled city, lay in ruins. Had such been the ruling, Shushan would have been given greater recognition than Jerusalem. To prevent this, the sages extended the rule to all cities that had been walled since the time of Joshua, even though they were not walled at the time of the Purim event. In this way Jerusalem was included. Even though Shushan was not a walled city in the time of Joshua, an exception was made because it was the city in which the miracle took place.
46. The identity of Apostomus is unclear. Some identify him with Antiochus, the Greek king who ruled over Judea in the second century B.C.E. and who was known to have had an idol placed in the Temple.
47. The Talmud mentions other tragedies that occurred on this day. In *Rosh Hashanah* 18b we read: "On the ninth day of Av the Temple was destroyed both the first and the second time, and Bethar was captured [in the war of Bar Kochba], and the city [Jerusalem] was ploughed."
48. Cf. *Avot D'Rebbi Natan* 4.
49. It is beyond the scope of this work to delineate the differences among these three levels. The reader is referred to *Mishnah, Berurah; Shulhan Arukh: Orah Hayyim* 551, 554, for the laws of mourning that pertain to this period.

50. Cf. *Shabbat* 119b.

51. *Yoma* 9b.

52. Ecclesiastes 3:4.

Session XII

1. Genesis 17:10–11, 13, 14.

2. Genesis 21:4. Flavius Josephus, in his *Antiquities of the Jews*, Book 1, Chap. 12, 2, writes: "And they circumcised him [Isaac] upon the eighth day, and from that time the Jews continue the custom of circumcising their sons within the numbers of days. But as for the Arabians, they circumcise after the thirteenth year because Ishmael, the founder of their nation . . . was circumcised at that age."

3. Cf. S. R. Hirsch, Commentary to Genesis 17:1–13.

4. Ibid.

5. It is interesting that R. Saadya Gaon, the renowned talmudic scholar of the tenth century, understood circumcision as an injunction to Abraham to attain perfection. In his book, *Beliefs and Opinions*, trans. by S. Rosenblatt (New Haven: Yale University Press, 1955), p. 177, he writes: "One might wonder . . . how it could be that so long as a man's body is in its complete natural state he is not perfect, whereas when something is cut off from it, he becomes perfect. What I have reference to is [the rite] of circumcision. Let me explain then, that the perfect thing is one that suffers from neither superfluity nor deficiency. Now the Creator created this part of the body with a redundancy, with the result that, when it is cut off, the redundancy is removed and what is left is the state of perfection."

6. Cf. Aharon HaLevi, *Sefer HaHinukh, Mitzvah* 2.

7. Cf. *Kiddushin* 29a. Interestingly, in Exodus 4:24–25 we read, "At a night encampment on the way, the Lord encountered him and sought to kill him. So Zipporah took a flint and cut off her son's foreskin, and touched his legs with it saying, 'You are truly a bridegroom of blood to me.'"

8. Cf. *Mahzor Vitry* (Jerusalem, Alef Publishing Company, 1963), p. 628.

9. Where it is certain that the birth was full term, i.e., after nine full months to the day, the newborn attains viability at birth; otherwise, it

is not viable until the thirty first day after birth. Viability entitles the newborn to all the rights and privileges of a Jew, such as the right of inheritance.

10. Cf. Exodus 13:2, 12–15, and Numbers 18:15–16, also *Shabbat* 135b, where it is explained that the redemption ritual is not performed until the child has attained viability.

11. Cf. S. R. Hirsch, Commentary to Exodus 13:2, 13.

12. Ibid.

13. Numbers 3:12.

14. Cf. Samuel b. Meir (*Rashbam*), Commentary to Exodus 13:13.

15. *Yoma* 82a.

16. *Mishnah, Berakhot* 1:5.

17. Cf. N. Berlin, *Ha'amek Davar*, Commentary to Exodus 13:9.

18. Cf. M. Nahmanides, Commentary to Exodus 13:9.

19. *Menahot* 35b.

20. For a complete and fully annotated analysis of the wedding ceremony, the reader is referred to A. Kaplan, *Made in Heaven* (New York, Moznaim Publishing Company, 1983).

21. Cf. *Shulhan Arukh: Even HaEzer* 55:1.

22. Cf. *Shulhan Arukh: Even HaEzer* 55:1, in the *Bet Shmuel* commentary. There are three opinions on the meaning of *hupah* here. One is *yihud*, which means that the bride and groom stay together in a room by themselves for a brief period. The second is that the husband fulfills one of his three obligations he must take upon himself in marriage, i.e., providing food, clothing, and conjugal rights. The third is setting up house together. See A. Kaplan, op. cit., for an explanation of what is practiced today.

23. Cf. *Tur Shulhan Arukh: Even HaEzer* 62.

24. Rema, *Shulhan Arukh: Even HaEzer* 61:1.

25. Cf. Y. M. Epstein, *Arukh HaShulhan: Even HaEzer* 55:18.

26. Cf. *Bereshit Rabbah* 18.

27. A. Kaplan, op. cit., p. 160.

28. *Rema, Shulhan Arukh: Orah Hayyim* 560:2.

29. Cf. *Peri Miggadim, Shulhan Arukh: Orah Hayyim* 560:4.

30. Cf. *Maharsha, Berakhot* 31a.

31. Cf. Deuteronomy 21:23.

32. The laws of *aninut* and mourning apply to the loss of: father, mother, brother, sister, son, daughter, and spouse.

33. *Moed Katan* 23b.

34. Ibid., 27b.

35. Cf. Rema, *Shulhan Arukh: Orah Hayyim* 621:3.

36. In *Bava Batra* 10a we read: R. Hiyya B. Abba said: R. Johanan pointed out that it is written, "Riches profit not the day of wrath, but charity [righteousness] delivers from death" (Proverbs 11:4) and it is also written, "Treasures of wickedness profit nothing, but righteousness delivers from death" (Proverbs 10:2). Why this double mention of righteousness? One that delivers him from unnatural death and one that delivers him from Hell.

Session XIII

1. Jeremiah 12:1, 2.

2. Genesis 18:25.

3. Job 4:8.

4. *Berakhot* 5:8.

5. Job 11:5, 6.

6. This interpretation of Zophar's position is delineated by Malbim in his commentary on Job.

7. Only three friends came to visit Job. According to some commentators, a crowd had gathered to listen to the debate. Elihu was one of the crowd. Unable to contain himself, he offered his opinion on this important matter.

8. Cf. Rashi and Malbim on Genesis 1:26, 27.

9. Psalms 94:3–7.

10. Psalms 92:8.

11. S. R. Hirsch, *The Psalms* (New York: Philip Feldheim, 1966); Psalms 92:10.

12. Ibid.

13. Cf. Exodus 10:12, where we read: "But the Lord hardened the heart of Pharaoh and he would not let the Israelites go."

14. Cf. Numbers, Chap. 24.

15. Cf. E. Berkovits, *God, Man and History* (New York: Jonathan David, 1959), Chap. 9.

16. Ibid., pp. 75–76.

17. Ibid.
18. Ibid., p. 76.
19. Ibid.
20. E. Berkovits, op. cit., p. 79.
21. Micah 6:8.

Index

Kaddish, 206
Kadosh, 56
Kant, Immanuel, 11
Kaplan, Aryeh, 231
Karo, Joseph, 198
Kashrut, laws of, 26, 29
Kaufmann, Yehezkel, 45
Kavanah, 184, 185–186
Kedushah, 105
Kedushat Hashem, 173
Keriah, 235, 237
Kiddushin, 229, 232
Kings, Books of, 33, 34, 216
Kinot, 217
Kipah, 35–37
Kittel, 230–231
Kohen, 224
Kol Nidre service, 209

Lamentations, 217
Law, Jewish
  laws and customs of Purim,
    215–216
  the Oral and Written Law,
    23–24
  vivisection in, 29–32
Law, Jewish, attitude toward
    Gentiles, 109
  all too popular
    misconceptions, 117
  converts to Judaism, 122–125
  equality before God, 111–112
  the laws, 114–116
  name terminology, 109–110
  Noahide laws, 111
  the Shahak Affair, 117–119
  the shameful record of history,
    112–114

teaching Torah to Gentiles,
    119–122
Leviathan (Hobbes), 40
Levites, 224
Leviticus, Book of
  ethical principles in, 55, 56,
    58, 59, 60, 62, 63, 65
  honoring an revering parents,
    155
  Jewish holidays, 199, 201–202,
    207
  Jews and Gentiles, 117
  "P" document, 41
  rabbinic reasoning and, 26, 27
  slaughter of animals in, 30
Love, between parent and child,
    152–153
Love thy neighbor, 56–57

Maariv, 178
Maimonides
  on covering one's head, 35–36
  on dilemma of Adam and Eve,
    94
  existence of God, 9–10, 14, 17
  on living in the land of Israel,
    155–156
  on love of God, 153
  on medical ethics, 76, 80, 82,
    83
  on Mosaic authorship of the
    Torah, 44
  on prayer, 171, 185–186
  saving a life, 65
  Shabbat, 191
  on slaughter of animals, 30–31
  treatment of Gentiles, 111,
    116

About the Author

Dr. Walter Orenstein is a graduate of Yeshiva University, from which institution he earned his B.R.E., M.A., and D.H.L. degrees. He is also an ordained rabbi. He has been actively involved in Jewish studies at Yeshiva University for thirteen years, teaching in the James Striar school, Stern College, and the Teachers Institute for Women, where he also served as chairman of the faculty. In 1974 he was listed in "Outstanding Educators of America" and in 1983 he received the coveted "Senior Professor Award" from the students of Stern College. Dr. Orenstein has lectured widely in adult education programs in some of the foremost synagogues in New York. A prolific writer, he is the author of several scholarly articles on Judaism and the following books: *Torah As Our Guide, Torah and Tradition, Etched in Stone, The Cantor's Manual of Jewish Law,* and *Letters to My Daughter.*